A NATION OF SHOPKEEPERS

A NATION OF SHOPKEEPERS

Five Centuries of British Retailing

Edited by
JOHN BENSON AND LAURA UGOLINI

I.B. TAURIS
LONDON · NEW YORK

Published in 2003 by I.B.Tauris & Co Ltd
6 Salem Road, London W2 4BU
175 Fifth Avenue, New York NY 10010
www.ibtauris.com

In the United States of America and in Canada distributed by
Palgrave Macmillan, a division of St Martin's Press
175 Fifth Avenue, New York NY 10010

ISBN 1 86064 709 X (hardback); 1 86064 708 1 (paperback)

A full CIP record for this book is available from the British Library
A full CIP record for this book is available from the Library of Congress

Library of Congress catalog card: available

Printed and bound in Great Britain by MPG Books, Bodmin
from camera-ready copy edited and supplied by the author

CONTENTS

CONTRIBUTORS

Andrew Alexander is Senior Lecturer in Retail Management at the School of Management, University of Surrey. His recent work on retail history has been published in numerous journals including *Business History, Environment and Planning A* and *The International Review of Retail, Distribution and Consumer Research*. His research interests include the evolution of retail systems, retail strategy, and the marketing and management of urban centres.

John Benson is Emeritus Professor of History at the University of Wolverhampton. His books include *The Working Class in Britain, 1850–1939* (Longman, London, 1989), *The Rise of Consumer Society in Britain, 1880–1980* (Longman, London, 1994) and *Prime Time: A History of the Middle Aged in Twentieth-Century Britain* (Longman, London, 1997). He is currently working on a social history of Britain in the twentieth century.

Helle B. Bertramsen received her MA from Odense University, Denmark andher PhD from Lancaster University, supervised by Michael Winstanley. The chapter in this book is drawn from her dissertation on the department store and the construction of commercial space. She is also the author of *The Social Construction of Space: Escapism at the Turn-of-the-Century Brighton?* (Angles, Copenhagen University, 1999); and *What was a Department Store? Defining Victorian Commercial Space* (PEO, Odense University, 1999). She is currently teaching at Copenhagen University.

Richard Coopey is a Lecturer in History at the University of Wales Aberystwyth. His work on retail history includes *The History of Mail*

Order in Britain (with Dilwyn Porter and Sean O'Connell, forthcoming, Oxford, 2003). Related research interests include the history of technology and retail banking, and the history of popular collecting.

Nancy Cox is an Honorary Research Fellow at the University of Wolverhampton. Recent publications include *The Complete Tradesman: A Study in Retailing, 1550–1820* (Ashgate, Aldershot, 2000); *Living and Working in Seventeenth-Century England: Descriptions and Drawings from Randle Holme's Academy of Armory*, (British Library, London, 2000, with N. W. Alcock); and 'Probate, 1500-1800: a system in transition', in T. Arkell, N. Evans and N. Goose (eds), *When Death Do Us Part: Understanding and Interpreting the Probate Records of Early Modern England* (Leopards Head Press, Oxford, 2000, with J. Cox). Current work includes further research into early modern retailing and editing the forthcoming (2005) Dictionary of Traded Goods and Commodities 1550–1800.

Sheryllynne Haggerty received her PhD from the University of Liverpool in 2002. She is particularly interested in the concept of a wider trading community encompassing both men and women, and eighteenth-century mercantile networks. She has recently published 'Trade and the trans-shipment of knowledge in the late eighteenth century', in Y. Kaukiainen (ed.), special issue on information, communications and knowledge, *International Journal of Maritime History* (2002). She is presently researching the business and social networks of eighteenth-century Jamaican merchants at Brunel University.

Deborah Hodson, former Research Fellow at Manchester Metropolitan University, is currently employed as part-time Research Assistant at Lancaster University. She is working with Michael Winstanley on British Academy-funded research into retail provision in late Victorian and Edwardian Britain. Recent publications include collaborations with Andrew Alexander, John Benson and Gareth Shaw for *The Local Historian* (1999) and *Environment and Planning A* (2000).

Dilwyn Porter is Reader in History at University College Worcester and a Visiting Research Fellow at the Business History Unit, London School of Economics. He has made recent contributions to *The International Review of Retailing, Distribution and Consumer Research*, *Media History*, *Business Archives* and Contemporary *British History* and has co-edited a collection of essays on *Amateurs and Professionals in British Sport Since 1945* (Frank Cass, 2000).

Gareth Shaw is Professor of Human Geography at the University of Exeter. He has published numerous papers on retail history and is series editor of History of Retailing and Consumption (Ashgate) and of Tourism, Retailing and Consumption (I.B. Tauris). He is currently researching large-scale retail developments and working on the arrival of the supermarket in Britain.

Jon Stobart is Senior Lecturer in Historical Geography at Coventry University. His research on regional and urban development in Britain from the eighteenth to the early twentieth centuries covers a wide variety of topics, from proto-industrialisation to urban renaissance. Articles on retail development have been published in *Urban History* and *The International Review of Retail, Distribution and Consumer Research*. He is currently working on the spatial and behavioural inter-relationships between retailing and leisure in the eighteenth century.

Laura Ugolini is Research Fellow in History at the University of Wolverhampton, where she is also the director of the Committee for the History of Retailing and Distribution (CHORD). Her publications include articles on late Victorian and Edwardian male supporters of women's suffrage, and an edited collection (with C. Eustance and J. Ryan), *A Suffrage Reader: Charting Directions in British Suffrage History* (Cassell, London, 2000). Her current research focuses on men's experiences of buying and selling clothes in Britain, *circa* 1880-1939, and she has recently published an article on 'Clothes and the modern man in 1930s Oxford', *Fashion Theory* 4/4 (2000).

Claire Walsh is Leverhulme Research Fellow at the University of Warwick, working on the Art and Industry Project under the direction of Maxine Berg. She has published on the subjects of shop design, retailing and advertising in the early modern period, including 'The newness of the department store: a view from the eighteenth century', in Geoffrey Crossick and Serge Jaumain (eds), *Cathedrals of Consumption: The European Department Store 1850–1939* (Ashgate, Aldershot, 1999). Forthcoming publications, arising from the Art and Industry Project, examine tourist shopping in Paris, and compare retail advertising in London and Paris in the early modern period. She is currently writing a book on the skills and social relations of shopping in early modern London.

Michael Winstanley is Senior Lecturer in History at Lancaster University. He has a long-standing interest in retail history and his publications include *The Shopkeeper's World, 1830–1914* (Manchester

University Press, Manchester, 1983), 'Concentration and competition in the retail sector, *c.* 1800–1990', in M. B. Rose and M. W. Kirby (eds), *Business Enterprise in Modern Britain from the Eighteenth to the Twentieth Century* (Routledge, London, 1994); and 'Temples of commerce: revolutions in shopping and banking', in P. Waller (ed.), *The English Urban Landscape* (Oxford University Press, Oxford, 2000). He has a particular interest in North-west England.

INTRODUCTION
HISTORIANS AND THE NATION OF SHOPKEEPERS
John Benson and Laura Ugolini

Recent interest in the history of consumption, the so-called consumer revolution and consumerism in Britain has begun to encourage new interest in the history of retailing.[1] Nevertheless, consumption historians concerned with the history of retailing have tended to concentrate their attention, perhaps understandably, on urban, 'innovative' and often large-scale enterprises, which they believe played a pivotal role in shaping society and culture during the eighteenth, nineteenth and twentieth centuries (and possibly even earlier). Perhaps the clearest example of such an approach can be found in studies that focus on the department store. Indeed, as Geoffrey Crossick and Serge Jaumain have pointed out, 'One is tempted to conclude that the department store has in recent years been explored less as an object of study in itself, and more for what it reveals about other matters of interest to the historian.'[2] Thus consumption historians have devoted a great deal of attention to department stores both as icons of 'modernity' and as gendered spaces, providing new opportunities for women's consumption, sociability and pleasure within the city, particularly in the period between the last quarter of the nineteenth century and the outbreak of the First World War.[3]

It is more surprising that even scholars with a specialist interest in the history of retailing, *qua* retailing, have tended to focus on a relatively narrow range of issues. The pioneering work of James Jefferys remains highly influential. He suggested as early as 1954 that British retailing institutions and practices remained relatively unchanged between the late Middle Ages and the mid-nineteenth century, particularly outside London.[4] So it is that scholars interested in early modern retailing have been particularly keen to uncover

1

evidence of 'modern' retailing predating the mid-nineteenth century. It is an approach that has been important in demonstrating how sophisticated, countrywide networks of wholesaling and distribution were able, even before the end of the sixteenth century, to cater for a significant and growing demand for consumer goods.[5]

Historians of early modern retailing have also challenged the ways in which certain enterprises, notably department stores and chain stores, have often been considered without reference to their pre-Victorian antecedents. They have rejected notions of a sharp distinction between supposedly 'modern' and supposedly 'primitive' undertakings, an approach that can both lead to the identification of late nineteenth and early twentieth-century innovation where none exists, and mask the fact that early modern retailing was 'a dynamic and flexible system well adapted to serve a growing body of consumers'.[6] Claire Walsh suggests, for example, that developments such as fixed-price cash sales, 'window shopping, browsing, the use of seductive display and interior design to enhance the appearance of goods, and shopping as a social activity', usually associated with the late nineteenth-century department store, were already well in evidence a century and more earlier.[7] However, these attempts to stress the innovative nature of early modern retailing have had the unwonted – and unfortunate – effect of concentrating attention on the minority of urban, often London-based, innovative, 'modern' shopkeepers at the expense of the majority of retailers, particularly 'traditional' craftsmen-retailers such as shoemakers, tailors, saddlers, bakers, or cabinetmakers, about whom we still know all too little.[8]

Late modern historians have been even keener to concentrate on successful, large-scale undertakings such as co-operative stores,[9] department stores[10] and multiple stores,[11] all of which from the mid-nineteenth century onwards catered, in their different ways, for a rapidly expanding market for consumer goods. It is not difficult to see why historians should focus on organizations that assumed an increasingly dominant position in the twentieth-century marketplace, and about which sources of information are more readily available than for small and/or unsuccessful undertakings. Nonetheless, not all large-scale enterprises have received the same amount of attention. Indeed, it is curious that historians have displayed relatively little interest in the work of retail geographers or management studies scholars on mail order,[12] supermarkets[13] and superstores,[14] even when such work has been placed in a historical context. In this collection, however, Richard Coopey and Dilwyn Porter examine the development of twentieth-century mail order companies, shedding valuable light on their distinctive marketing strategies and operating methods.

The literature is unbalanced in other ways too. While the political, social and ideological impulses behind the establishment of co-operative selling have received attention,[15] the same cannot be said about multiples, department stores and other forms of large-scale retailing. Narratives of the founding of these outlets still depend to a surprising extent on notions of an 'exceptional man with an exceptional idea'. According to this type of approach, success was achieved by individuals such as Thomas Lipton or Gordon Selfridge through exceptional – and invariably male – qualities of character, drive and business acumen. Failure is seen, conversely, as the inevitable outcome of a slackening of attention to the business, if not on the part of the founder himself, then on that of his successors, in a way that has recently been described as a 'genetic lottery'.[16]

Indeed, recent research into the relationship between business ideology and masculine identities confirms that such images should be understood not as 'facts', but as the outcome of a more or less conscious effort by the proprietors and managers of successful concerns (including those operating at a local level) to build a collective identity based on notions of entrepreneurial manliness, and couched in Smilesian terms of individual effort and hard work.[17] In the case of Thomas Lipton's autobiography, for example, this took the shape of emphasizing the long hours of work he had put in at his first shop: 'I was manager, shopman, buyer, cashier and message-boy all in one ... no watching the clock for the hour to leave off ... I got it into my head that a man could attain almost anything he liked, if only he had the mind.'[18]

Nonetheless, even the most successful entrepreneur had to beware any slackening of effort. As Gordon Selfridge wrote in 1918, in response to those 'foolish enough' to consider trade 'undignified and mean', commerce was in fact 'the great bedrock of strength upon which a nation is built'. The great men of commerce (as distinct from 'petty and insignificant' small shopkeepers) were the representatives of all that was most progressive and intelligent in a country, although they too had to beware 'the seductive but effeminating love of ease' that could 'turn them from the goal of success'.[19]

At the same time, greater attention needs to be devoted to other factors behind the growth of large-scale (or indeed successful small-scale) enterprises. Of greatest relevance seems to be the availability of capital and credit, both formally (through banks and other financial institutions) and informally (through networks of family, religion, political affiliation and so on). Much remains to be discovered. Beverley Lemire, for example, has found intriguing evidence of networks of support among members of the eighteenth-century Anglo-Jewish community, with individual traders working out of co-religionists' dwellings or shops, presumably to defray high rental costs.[20] The growing importance of formal networks of credit, alongside more informal support, would also seem of importance in helping to explain women's absence, by the nineteenth century, from any but the lower rungs of the retailing world.[21]

***

If it is easy to present a rather one-dimensional picture of 'modern' large-scale enterprises, it appears easier still to overlook the continued importance of small-scale retailing. The hawker and peddler, the Saturday-night market, the corner shop and even the specialist grocer, clothes shop and off-licence can all too easily be relegated to a sepia-tinted, Christmas-card version of the world we have lost. As a correspondent asked (rhetorically) in 1999 in a local Wolverhampton newspaper: 'wouldn't it be lovely to do away with that wire supermarket trolley, and go back to the corner-cum-village shop when shopping involved human contact?'[22] Indeed, it is often the case that when historians do consider small-scale retailing, they do so in order to understand not the successes or failures of the distribution system, but the rise and increasing self-confidence of the so-called middling ranks[23] or the cultural, social, political and economic lives of that uneasy stratum, the petite bourgeoisie.[24]

In fact, it can scarcely be overemphasized that small-scale retailing, including hawking, peddling and market selling, deserves study in its own right. Margaret Spufford has shown the importance of petty chapmen in a distribution system that during the seventeenth century brought non-perishable goods such as drapery, haberdashery and ready-made clothing to consumers throughout the country.[25] Indeed, fixed and non-fixed shop forms of retailing interacted in complex ways during the early modern period. It has recently been suggested, for example, that to sell through the 'open-window' facing the marketplace not only gave the shopkeeper access to market customers, but also endowed him or her with an enhanced reputation for selling goods in the open market, 'with all the protection to the customers that this was supposed to afford'.[26]

Non-fixed shop retailing continued to play a vital role in the late modern economy. Janet Blackman suggested almost 40 years ago that nineteenth-century markets and shops performed complementary, rather than competitive, functions; the former providing working-class consumers with perishable foods like fruit, meat and vegetables, the latter supplying them with manufactured and processed foods such as tea, sugar and dairy products.[27] Much more recently, Deborah Hodson's study of Lancashire markets has shown the 'resilience and adaptability' of this form of retailing, not only in the nineteenth century, but also well into the twentieth, with local authorities performing 'a crucial role in transforming markets into ... efficient amenities capable of responding to and capitalizing on a more intense form of demand'.[28]

Small – sometimes very small – shopkeepers also retained a vitality and importance that can easily be overlooked. It is notoriously difficult to trace very small ventures, particularly those active in the 'informal' economy, beyond official control and regulation, whose 'survival .. depended on a judicious cobbling together of opportunities, taking advantage of the commercial niches in the urban landscape'.[29] However, during the last 20 years, the resilience and significance of such small-scale shopkeeping (and of other 'traditional' forms of retailing) have begun to attract a certain amount of scholarly attention.[30] What then were the strategies that allowed small shopkeepers to co-exist alongside large-scale forms of distribution? Christopher Hosgood has studied those whom he calls the 'pigmies of commerce', arguing that 'their commitment to the working-class community, and their stake in their customers' economic and cultural world' helps to account for the survival of this branch of the trade.[31] The emergence of small 'back-street' shops in eighteenth-century England has been explained in similar terms: the role these sometimes tiny ventures played in providing goods and services to the labouring community.[32] No matter how one accounts for the resilience of such 'traditional' forms of distribution, it should be remembered that as late as 1980–81, small independent stores still accounted for more than 30 per cent of all British retail trade.[33]

Historians have also begun to investigate the social and cultural world of small enterprises, an environment that seems to have been characterized most powerfully by status uncertainty and ambiguity. In this collection, for example, Nancy Cox shows that in the early modern period, attitudes towards commerce, trade and retailing were overwhelmingly hostile, the negative characterizations of retailers being fuelled by wider concerns about the balance of trade and about the apparently ubiquitous desire for luxuries. By the second half of the nineteenth century, the contribution of trade to the nation's wealth may no longer have been generally questioned. However, as Gordon Selfridge (among others) clearly realized, the status of individuals involved in trade – with the partial exception of overseas trade – remained highly uncertain.[34] Soames Forsyte put it like this to his French wife in the second volume of John Galsworthy's *Forsyte Saga*, first published in 1920:

> Our professional and leisured classes still think themselves a cut above our business classes, except of course the very rich ... It isn't advisable

in England to let people know you ran a restaurant or kept a shop or were in any kind of trade. It may have been extremely creditable, but it puts a sort of label on you; you don't have such a good time, or meet such nice people.[35]

It was not only in terms of social status that retailers' position was uncertain. During the nineteenth and twentieth centuries at least, trade and shopkeeping seem to have been generally associated with notions of greed, pettiness and narrow-mindedness. The Cambridge geneticist William Bateson, for example, was using a well-established and well-understood language when he complained of 'sordid shopkeeper utility' to express his dislike of contemporary late-Victorian society.[36]

It is true that in working-class communities, small shopkeepers often enjoyed some prestige, particularly as the holders (or withholders) of credit. Evoking his childhood in a Lincolnshire village at the end of the nineteenth century, for example, Fred Gresswell mentioned that the Browns, a family of 'semitradespeople', were 'one of the three main families in the village', and the tailoring shop of one of the brothers, in particular, acted as an important social centre. Tellingly, however, another brother, who worked as an agent for a firm of coal merchants, was denied 'the full status of tradesman because he had to help unload coal from the railway wagons'.[37] Indeed, the dominant characteristic of the retailer, both large and small, seems to have been status uncertainty, which was played out most poignantly in the complex and often stormy relationships that existed between the shopkeeper and his/her customers. The most common complaint (apart from the eternal difficulties of obtaining payment) was about lack of respect, particularly from customers of higher social status. In the 1750s and 1760s, for example, the shopkeeper Thomas Turner 'mixed freely with farmers, clergy and local people of middling ranks',[38] and yet in 1756 he could be found complaining that after having informed a wealthy customer that the livery lace she had ordered had not yet arrived, she 'treated me with as much imperious and scornful usage as if she had been ... more of a Turk and Infidel, than a Christian, and I an abject slave'.[39]

Despite – or more likely because of – street selling's role as a means of survival among the poor, its image was unambiguously negative. Hawkers, peddlers, costermongers and the like always enjoyed an unsavoury reputation among the 'respectable'. Margaret Spufford, for example, has shown that the distinction in the seventeenth century between reputable chapmen and disreputable 'rogues' was not always perceived as clear-cut.[40] Gerry Rubin and Margot Finn have demonstrated that during the nineteenth and twentieth centuries, notions of ethnicity and gender intersected to create an image of

Scotch drapers as canny Scots seducing English women into buying more items than they (or their husbands) could afford.[41]

However, if retailers' claims to respectable status were open to debate throughout the period covered by this collection, their gender identities were even more hotly contested by the nineteenth century. Male shop assistants found, for example, that their working conditions (particularly the living-in system) and their relationship with their employers tended to undermine their claims both to adulthood and to manliness.[42] More generally, male retailers' claims to manliness were rendered increasingly dubious as the craft elements of shopkeeping declined, as the employment of women in the retail sector increased, and as small shopkeepers' assertions of 'independence' were undermined by their dependence on larger ventures. Matthew Hilton, for instance, has shown how tobacconists negotiated the loss of skill and specialist knowledge on which their claim to a manly identity depended. Ultimately, he argues, 'despite the economic survival of specialist retailers ... their cultural role, or their ability to direct patterns of consumption, was greatly reduced by the mid-twentieth century.'[43]

Although male shop workers' manliness was open to doubt, the idea that retail employment was regarded as straightforwardly 'suitable' work for women is far too simple. In a recent study, Margaret Hunt has suggested that a mixture of legal constraints and cultural/social conventions served to set limits to women's role in eighteenth-century trade. Indeed, she suggests that, to some extent, the very notion of 'profit' was gendered, limiting both the viability of women's business ventures and their access to credit: 'Women's profits were complexly hedged and constrained by prior claims ... In contrast, men's profits moved relatively freely within a laissez-faire and possessive individualist universe of economic decision making.'[44]

In this collection, however, Sheryllynne Haggerty shows that despite such handicaps, women were heavily involved in the retail trades of eighteenth-century Liverpool, and played a central role in making new consumer goods available to a rapidly growing urban market. Women's involvement in retailing continued and expanded in the modern period. Significantly, however, most women found employment opportunities as shop assistants, rather than as shop owners or shop managers. In 1861, 19 per cent of shop assistants were recorded as being women, a figure which 50 years later had grown to 31 per cent – and it continued to grow thereafter. The scale and speed of the 'feminization' of shop work in the nineteenth and twentieth centuries, as well as its cultural, social and economic implications, remain greatly in need of further, serious investigation.[45]

✻✻✻

Retailers themselves, both individually and collectively, were producers of cultural meanings and identities, expressed, for example, through their political sympathies and affiliations. However, in Britain at least it has generally been social and political historians, rather than retailing historians, who have examined retailers' involvement in wider political movements, such as their participation in late eighteenth- and early nineteenth-century radical politics.[46] Nevertheless, retailers' politics *per se* have also begun to attract attention. In particular, independent traders' attachment to rigid notions of self-help, and their rejection of all state intervention, has recently been subjected to some debate. Their organizations and political activities – at both local and national levels – have begun to be investigated. In his study of trade associations in Victorian and Edwardian Leicester, for example, Christopher Hosgood observes a new readiness on the part of organizations of independent traders to lobby both local and national government by the end of the nineteenth century: 'The citizen shopkeepers of the mid-Victorian decades were replaced by a new breed of trader who expected associations to represent their particular interests on both the national and the local political stage.'[47]

In this collection, Claire Walsh and Laura Ugolini approach retailers' cultural/commercial world from a different perspective, considering the strategies they employed in order to attract customers. In her chapter, focusing on early modern London's 'shopping galleries', Claire Walsh shows how developers and retailers worked together to create a spectacular shopping environment, centred on notions of luxury, elegance and exclusivity. In her contribution, Laura Ugolini explores the ways in which late-Victorian and Edwardian menswear retailers' advertisements exploited widely shared understandings of desirable masculine lifestyles in order to attract male customers. Although focusing on different periods and different retailing forms, both contributors show how retailers made use of accepted understandings of consumers' desires, and created spaces and discourses whose ultimate aim was to influence consumers' behaviour.[48]

As a number of historians have shown, it was when retailers came into conflict with one another that self-identities were most clearly articulated, often in the form of complaints against the competition, on the one hand, of co-operatives, multiples and department stores, and on the other of unregulated small shops and hawkers. However, this should not lead one to over-emphasize the scale or significance of intra-trade hostility. In the early modern period, even in unincorporated towns or where the power of the guilds had declined, it seems to have been common for local tradesmen to socialize and co-operate with one another. Writing in 1726, Daniel Defoe considered that 'the tradesmen's meetings are like the merchants' exchanges, where they manage, negociate, and ... beget business with one another.' Indeed, he stressed the importance of establishing within a locality 'a settled little society of trading people'.[49] Adam Smith's opinion of such 'little societies' was a good deal more negative, but also suggested that they were commonplace: 'People of the same trade seldom meet together, even for merriment and diversion, but the conversation ends in a conspiracy against the public, or in some contrivance to raise prices.'[50]

Indeed, as the anonymous author of *Reminiscences of an Old Draper* pointed out in his discussion of the early nineteenth-century trade, it could be profitable to foster friendly relations even with one's competitors. One of his previous employers, a draper in Chatham, Kent, had stocked a good deal of ready-made sailors' clothing. When demand exceeded the stock available, more was obtained from a neighbouring pawnbroker and clothes dealer, with whom he made an agreement to share equally any profit.[51] Apart from such *ad hoc* arrangements, evidence of widespread structural interdependence among retailers is not difficult to find. For example, although co-operatives and private retailers were ideologically situated in opposite camps (and the hostility between them is difficult to overestimate[52]), their relationship was closer than is generally supposed when it came to the supply of goods. In the absence of alternative sources of supplies there developed, in mid-Victorian North-east England at least, 'a multitude of working contacts between co-operative retailers and private wholesalers and manufacturers'.[53]

***

The survival, adaptability (and sometimes success) of small-scale forms of retailing throws into question some of the assumptions that are commonly made about the determinants of retail development. It seems to be generally accepted that the way in which retailing has developed in advanced industrializing societies can be explained primarily by changes in consumer demand: the growth and urbanization of the population, improved transport facilities and a marked rise in real incomes.[54]

There is no denying that changes in consumer demand constituted a major determinant of retail change. However, the demand-led model can sometimes be accepted almost unthinkingly, a tendency that might lead to the acceptance of an equilibrium model of retailing whereby every innovation meets a need, every need is met and the inefficient are squeezed out. The eventual displacement of bespoke tailoring in favour of factory-made, ready-to-wear clothing in the menswear trade, for example, is generally explained in terms of the growing demand for cheap clothing of reasonably good quality, as incomes rose among wider sections of the population.[55]

But historians of retailing need to consider supply as well as demand. This does not mean, of course, that they should ignore issues such as changes in income or in cultural/social aspirations on the part of consumers, and adopt some technologically deterministic model whereby innovations in production lead inevitably and seamlessly to advances in distribution and retailing. It means rather that they should look to the broader economic, political and social environment within which retailers (and potential retailers), customers (and potential customers) found themselves. In particular, they need to consider the economic cycle, the nature of local economic/demographic structures, and the impact of legislative and regulatory activity.

The economic cycle, whether national or local, periodic or seasonal, was of more importance than is generally recognized. It was not just that economic growth fuelled consumer demand, but also that economic depression fuelled supplier availability. There is much evidence to suggest that one of the strategies used by members of the working class and the lower middle class to supplement and/or replace other sources of income was to turn to hawking, peddling and small shopkeeping. In 1708, for example, after his drapery and grocery business had failed, William Godsalve left his home in Lancaster to work for a draper in Richmond, Yorkshire, 'where he continued some years, and left his ... [family] destitute of any substance, and left to the charity of ... friends'. A (temporary) solution to his wife's financial problems was reached in 1711, when the Lancaster tradesman, William Stout, aware that she was 'capable of business ... tooke [sic] a shop for her ... and put her in it about ten pounds value of grocery goods and other small ware at the first cost, to pay me when she could well.'[56]

In mid-nineteenth-century London, the street trades provided a refuge for the seasonally unemployed. According to Henry Mayhew, the presence on the streets of the capital of so many Irish sellers of oranges and nuts during the winter months was explained by the fact that 'the Irish, as labourers, can seldom obtain work all the year through, and thus the ranks of the Irish street-sellers are recruited every winter by the slackness of certain periodic trades in which they are largely employed – such as hodmen, dock-work, excavating, and the like.'[57] In early twentieth-century Wolverhampton, it was small shopkeeping that seemed to promise an escape from the deprivations of both cyclical and structural unemployment. In a 1934 article entitled 'Adventurers of the suburban shopping centres', the town's newspaper, the *Express and Star*, explained how economic depression had encouraged the unemployed to move into suburban retailing.[58]

Important too were local economic and demographic structures, whose complexities historians are only beginning to fully uncover. In this collection, for example, Andrew Alexander, Gareth Shaw and Deborah Hodson compare the spread of multiple retailers in three regions of England in the half-century before the outbreak of the First World War, and highlight the continued – indeed, in some ways growing – importance of inter- and intra-regional variations in retail provision. Also in this collection, Michael Winstanley, by comparing patterns of retail properties' ownership in three Lancashire towns, demonstrates how these cannot be understood without reference both to national trends in the property market and to local occupational and demographic structures.

More specifically, historians have also observed how the economic disadvantages and cultural discrimination faced by many working-class and minority families encouraged them to enter trades like hawking and peddling and small shopkeeping, which demanded only a small initial investment and provided the opportunity to turn their working-class/minority identity to economic advantage. It was said at the end of the nineteenth century that many working-class consumers chose to patronize working-class hawkers. 'They can't be persuaded that they can buy as cheap at the shops; and besides they are apt to think shopkeepers are rich and street-sellers poor, and that they may as well encourage the poor.'[59] As Peter Mathias suggested in his pioneering study of multiple retailing, working-class shopkeepers enjoyed one significant advantage over middle-class traders: 'Such men knew their future markets instinctively and innately.'[60]

Nor did retailers and would-be retailers operate in a legislative and regulatory vacuum. Those in power locally, regionally and nationally attempted to influence, if not control, the way in which retailing developed. The extent to which livery companies continued to exert influence over urban trades in the seventeenth and eighteenth centuries is a matter of debate. Nevertheless, even where guilds had lost economic control over apprenticeship or entry into the trade, there is evidence that, at least until the end of the seventeenth century, they continued to perform other less prominent functions, such as the provision of charitable donations or the granting of loans to members setting up in business.[61]

During the late nineteenth and early twentieth centuries, regulation tended to discourage very small-scale retailing such as hawking and peddling and suburban shopkeeping. Sometimes it did so inadvertently (for example, by enforcing hygiene or public order regulations), but usually it was deliberate (for example, by enforcing the same closing hours for all types of outlet). In 1883, for instance, Yarmouth Corporation framed a new code of by-laws, including one forbidding the carriage of goods for sale between seven o'clock in the evening and five o'clock in the morning.[62] In this collection, however, Helle Bertramsen's study of municipal street improvement schemes in late-Victorian Manchester shows that regulation could have an equally significant impact on large-scale and well-established retailers, like the department store Kendal Milne. The efforts of Manchester's Corporation to influence the organization of retail space prefigured later attempts. During the second half of the twentieth century, for example, those in power attempted to influence the balance between the redevelopment of city-centre retailing and the development of out-of-town shopping centres. In the 1950s and 1960s, the government concentrated its efforts on redeveloping city centres and creating new and more attractive environments for potential customers.[63] From the mid-1990s there was a fundamental change in the Department of Environment's policy guidance notes towards out-of-town developments. They moved away from the more 'relaxed views' of the 1980s and early 1990s as the environmental consequences of increased traffic congestion began to encourage a more restrictive approach.[64]

✳✳✳

The potential of comparative methodologies should also not be overlooked. It is comparison, after all, which allows us to confirm or refute narratives and explanations that can easily appear self-evident and irrefutable when considered in a single geographical or chronological context.[65] Retailing historians have undertaken a certain amount of geographical comparison, usually in the form of national developments providing the historiographical and empirical context within which, or against which, developments at the regional and/or local level are located. Indeed, this seems to be one of the most popular and productive ways of organizing a PhD thesis on the history of retailing.[66] It is surprising, therefore, that there have been only a handful of studies devoted explicitly (and rigorously) to comparing developments between particular geographical areas. But when such an approach is adopted – be it at the intra-urban, inter-urban, intra-regional, inter-regional or international levels – it can prove extraordinarily helpful. In this collection, for example, Jon Stobart considers retail provision in late nineteenth- and early twentieth-century Hanley not in isolation, but as part of the larger Potteries conurbation, with results that challenge conventional models of city centre retail development.[67]

There are also some indications of what can be achieved by the fusion of geographical and chronological comparison. Diane Collins has compared developments in Wolverhampton and Shrewsbury between 1690 and 1900 as a way of examining – and challenging – the view that eighteenth- and nineteenth-century shopkeeping were as different from each other as late modern historians often suppose. She not only concludes that 'the shops of eighteenth-century Shrewsbury and Wolverhampton cannot be considered primitive', but also states firmly and explicitly that her 'comparative analysis of disparate sources' indicates that 'longitudinal analysis is both possible, and productive in setting short-term change in perspective.[68]

Another study combining geographical and chronological comparison, undertaken by John Benson, provides a way of examining – and challenging – the conventional demand-led model of retail change.[69] He has compared developments in three medium-sized industrial centres in Britain, Canada and Australia (Wolverhampton, England; Hamilton, Ontario; and Newcastle, New South Wales) in the half-century between 1891 and 1941, the years during which permanent markets and small fixed shops are generally supposed to have given way to large department stores and sizeable groups of chain stores.[70] He shows that there were striking differences in the retail development of the three centres: these were marked by the resilience in Wolverhampton of market and co-operative selling; the survival in Hamilton of itinerant and market selling; and the success in Newcastle of the co-operative movement.[71] However, these dissimilarities cannot be explained adequately by differences in the nature of consumer demand, since the major demand-side pressures, such as real incomes and personal mobility (and to a lesser extent population size) developed in broadly similar ways in all three centres.[72]

Differences in the retail development of the three centres can be explained best, he suggests, by differences on the supply side: the proximity of competing retail centres; the impact of legislative and regulatory activity; and the nature of local demographic structures. It is possible, for instance, that the resilience of market and co-operative selling in Wolverhampton was associated with the proximity of Britain's second city, Birmingham, whose large stores both attracted shoppers from Wolverhampton and discouraged retailers from investing in the town.[73] It seems certain that the survival of itinerant and market selling can be explained, in some measure, by the local political environment. On the one hand, the legislation passed in Newcastle (and in New South Wales in general) tended to weaken the competitive advantage that non-fixed-shop selling enjoyed over fixed-shop selling.[74] On the other hand, the legislation passed in Hamilton was often surprisingly favourable to non-fixed-shop selling. The by-laws regulating the operation of the city's market, for example, protected the interests of producers rather than consumers, and 'maintained the existence of an institution which might otherwise have disappeared as it became less and less economically important as a major distributor of food'.[75]

Local demographic structures also played a part in the shaping of local retail systems. Newcastle was very largely an Anglo-Australian city, and students of its demographic and retailing history are in no doubt that it was the presence of United Kingdom-born immigrants and their descendants that goes far towards explaining the success of the co-operative movement. 'It was from the British mining districts that the co-operative tradition came to the Hunter Valley of New South Wales ... The local movement remained very much a transplanted British institution as the societies continued to pay homage to their British origins and to identify themselves with the British Cooperative Movement.'[76] Hamilton was less comprehensively an Anglo-Canadian city. Research undertaken into its ethnic and working-class history suggests that non-fixed shop retailing was central to the survival strategies of immigrants from Southern and Eastern Europe, who played a disproportionate role in the sector's vitality in this part of Ontario.[77] Craig Heron concludes, for example, that the immigrant entrepreneur in Hamilton 'would use his savings to bring out his family and set up a rooming house, or perhaps even a small retail business'.[78]

***

All the chapters in this collection, though rooted in different disciplines and focusing on different periods and retailing forms, examine the complex relationship between the consuming environment and retailing development. The chapters are organized in three sections. The focus of the first section, 'Representations and Self-representations', is largely cultural. These chapters suggest that the creation and expression of cultural identities by commentators concerned with the welfare of the nation, by property developers and by retailers themselves, though not open to quantification, are of considerable importance in explaining patterns of retail change and development. Although acknowledging the impossibility of doing more than speculating about the impact of such climates of opinion, Nancy Cox shows in chapter 1 that in the early modern period, attitudes towards trade and retailing were overwhelmingly – but by no means unchangingly – hostile: intriguingly, most concern seems to have been directed not at the morality of trade itself, but at its effect in supposedly draining riches out of the nation. In chapter 2, Claire Walsh describes how highly successful ventures were often created out of improbable material – plain, tiny wooden stalls – by judicious and knowing use of architectural space. The result in many cases was the association in consumers' minds of these 'shopping galleries' with all that was most exclusive, fashionable and sophisticated. In chapter 3, Laura Ugolini again explores commercial discourses, albeit for a later period. While avoiding deterministic claims about the effectiveness of publicity in influencing consumer behaviour, she shows that retailers' newspaper advertisements exploited widely held notions of desirable male lifestyles, in order to both suggest and endorse acceptable, and supposedly enticing, models of masculine consumption, which, in turn, they offered to cater for.

The chapters in the second section, 'Patterns and Processes', consider the trends underlying the development of retailing forms as diverse as eighteenth-century enterprises run by women, and multiple stores and city-centre retailers in the late nineteenth and early twentieth centuries. Through the use of databases, these chapters are able to map trends that challenge conventional models of retail development. In chapter 4, Sheryllynne Haggerty shows that in the specific social and demographic context of Liverpool's port economy, small-scale women-run enterprises often managed to find a commercial niche within a burgeoning consumer society. In chapter 5, Andrew Alexander, Gareth Shaw and Deborah Hodson draw on the results of a larger research project on the locational strategies of multiple retailers to explore regional variations in multiple provision in England. They emphasize the complexity of variables that can serve to explain the significant diversity in patterns of retailing, including notions of 'core' and 'periphery', demographic density and patterns of settlement. In chapter 6, Jon Stobart's study of retail provision in the Potteries conurbation challenges those models of city-centre retail development that stress the importance of large-scale retailers, such as department and multiples stores, in the creation of 'modern' Central Business Districts. He suggests instead the continuing importance of supposedly 'traditional' spaces, such as the market or the civic offices, as focuses for retail activity. In their different ways, all the chapters in this section show the need for a more nuanced approach to retail 'patterns and processes', with a greater awareness of local circumstances, of small as well as large enterprises, and of the 'traditional' alongside the supposedly 'modern'.

The chapters in the final section, 'Property, Politics and Communities', delve further into specific influences on retail development. In chapter 7, Michael Winstanley uses a hitherto neglected source, a property survey undertaken in connection with the Liberal government's 'People's Budget' of 1909, to compare patterns of retail property ownership in three demographically different Lancashire towns, with results that challenge notions of a rentier class of petit bourgeois property owners. In chapter 8, Helle Bertramsen explores the relationship between municipal politics and the development of Manchester's shopping centre. Focusing on the impact of the Corporation's street improvement schemes on the department store Kendal Milne, she shows that, far from being the result of innovative commercial impulses, the redevelopment of the store as a 'modern' and spectacular shopping environment can, in some respects at least, be understood as the unforeseen outcome of local regulatory activities. In chapter 9, Richard Coopey and Dilwyn Porter examine the role of the agency system as the basis for the success of twentieth-century mail order companies. They emphasize that the smooth functioning of the agency system was dependent on the existence of small-scale local networks of family, work and sociability. Thus the chapters in this section all stress the importance of placing the study of retailing forms (be they Lancashire retailers, prestigious city-centre shops, or mail order firms) in a wider socio-economic and political context, taking into account influences as varied as property development, political pressures (at both national and local levels), and community links.

Taken as a whole, this collection reflects some of the most innovative research currently being undertaken in the field of retailing history, and provides some important pointers for future research into retail development. The contributors stress the need for a more nuanced approach to local peculiarities, for more attention to be devoted to the small-scale alongside the large-scale, and for a greater awareness of the impact of factors such as the property market and the legislative/political environment, as well as the less tangible consequences of cultural constructions of consumption, consumers, retailing and retailers.

Acknowledgements
The editors are extremely grateful to Helen Clifford, Tim Coles, Nancy Cox, Karin Dannehl, Sheryllynne Haggerty, Jonathan Morris and Jon Stobart for their helpful comments and suggestions on the Introduction. Thanks are also due to David Stonestreet and Henry Alban Davies at I.B.Tauris for all their help. Last but not least, many thanks to Philip de Jersey for his generous help in the final stages of the preparation of the manuscript.

Notes

[1] Joan Thirsk, *Economic Policy and Projects: The Development of a Consumer Society in Early Modern England* (Clarendon Press, Oxford, 1978); W. Hamish Fraser, *The Coming of the Mass Market 1850–1914* (Macmillan, London, 1981); Neil McKendrick, John Brewer and John H. Plumb, *The Birth of a Consumer Society: The Commercialization of Eighteenth Century England* (Europa Publications, London, 1982); Lorna Weatherill, *Consumer Behaviour and Material Culture in Britain 1660–1760* (Routledge, London, 1988); Carl Gardiner and Julie Sheppard, *Consuming Passion: The Rise of Retail Culture*

(Unwin Hyman, London, 1989); Carole Shammas, *The Pre-Industrial Consumer in England and America* (Clarendon Press, Oxford, 1990); Beverley Lemire, *Fashion's Favourite: The Cotton Trade and the Consumer in Britain, 1660–1800* (Oxford University Press, Oxford, 1991); Rob Shields (ed.), *Lifestyle Shopping: The Subject of Consumption* (Routledge, London, 1992); John Brewer and Roy Porter (eds), *Consumption and the World of Goods* (Routledge, London, 1993); Gary Cross, *Time and Money: The Making of Consumer Culture* (Routledge, London, 1993); Ben Fine and Ellen Leopold, *The World of Consumption* (Routledge, London, 1993); John Benson, *The Rise of Consumer Society in Britain, 1880–1980* (Longman, London, 1994); Daniel Miller (ed.), *Acknowledging Consumption: A Review of New Studies* (Routledge, London, 1995); Victoria de Grazia and Ellen Furlough (eds), *The Sex of Things: Gender and Consumption in Historical Perspective* (University of California Press, London, 1996); Frank Mort, *Cultures of Consumption: Masculinities and Social Space in Late Twentieth Century Britain* (Routledge, London, 1996); Beverley Lemire, *Dress, Culture and Commerce: The English Clothing Trade Before the Factory, 1660–1800* (Macmillan, Basingstoke, 1997); Elizabeth Kowalski-Wallace, *Consuming Subjects: Women, Shopping and Business in the Eighteenth Century* (Columbia University Press, New York, 1997); Christopher Breward, *The Hidden Consumer: Masculinities, Fashion and City Life 1860–1914* (Manchester University Press, Manchester, 1999).

[2] Geoffrey Crossick and Serge Jaumain, 'The world of the department store: distribution, culture and social change', in G. Crossick and S. Jaumain (eds), *Cathedrals of Consumption: The European Department Store, 1850–1939* (Ashgate, Aldershot, 1999), p. 1.

[3] They have not been so concerned, however, either with the stores' seventeenth- and eighteenth-century predecessors or with their late twentieth-century successors. David Chaney, 'The department store as a cultural form', *Theory, Culture & Society* 1/3 (1983), pp. 22–31; Rachel Bowlby, *Just Looking: Consumer Culture in Dreiser, Gissing and Zola* (Methuen, London, 1985), especially pp. 18–34; Mica Nava, 'Modernity's disavowal: women, the city and the department store', in M. Nava and A. O'Shea (eds), *Modern Times: Reflections on a Century of English Modernity* (Routledge, London, 1996), pp. 38–76; Christopher P. Hosgood, '"Doing the shops" at Christmas: women, men and the department store in England, c. 1880–1914', in Crossick and Jaumain (eds), *Cathedrals of Consumption*, pp. 97–115; Erika D. Rappaport, *Shopping for Pleasure: Women in the Making of London's West End* (Princeton University Press, New Jersey, 2000).

[4] James B. Jefferys, *Retail Trading in Britain, 1850–1950* (Cambridge University Press, Cambridge, 1954). Jefferys' views did not go unchallenged by earlier historians of retailing. Many of the most important contributions to these early debates over the timing and nature of the development of 'modern' forms of retailing have been reprinted in John Benson and Gareth Shaw (eds), *The Retailing Industry* (I. B. Tauris, London, 1999), vol. 2. See also Nicholas Alexander and Gary Akehurst, 'Introduction: the emergence of modern retailing, 1750–1950', *Business History*, 'Special issue on the emergence of modern retailing, 1750–1950' 40/4 (1998), pp. 1–15.

[5] See, for example, Margaret Spufford, *The Great Reclothing of Rural*

England: Petty Chapmen and their Wares in the Seventeenth Century (Hambledon Press, London, 1984); Hoh-Cheung Mui and Lorna H. Mui, *Shops and Shopkeeping in Eighteenth Century England* (Routledge, London, 1989); Lemire, *Dress, Culture and Commerce*; Nancy Cox, *The Complete Tradesman: A Study of Retailing, 1550–1820* (Ashgate, Aldershot, 2000).

[6]   Cox, *The Complete Tradesman*, p. 44.

[7]   Claire Walsh, 'The newness of the department store: a view from the eighteenth century', in Crossick and Jaumain (eds), *Cathedrals of Consumption*, p. 68. See also Mui and Mui, *Shops and Shopkeeping*; Claire Walsh, 'Shop design and the display of goods in the eighteenth century', unpublished MA thesis, V&A/Royal College of Art (1993); Christina Fowler, 'Changes in provincial retail practice during the eighteenth century, with particular reference to Central-Southern England', *Business History*, 'Special issue on the emergence of modern retailing, 1750–1950' 40/4 (1998), pp. 37–54.

[8]   But see David Alexander, *Retailing in England During the Industrial Revolution* (Athlone Press, London, 1970); Barrie Trinder and Jeff Cox (eds), *Yeomen and Colliers in Telford: Probate Inventories for Dawley, Lilleshall, Wellington and Wrockwardine, 1660–1750* (Phillimore, London, 1980); Christina Fowler, 'Robert Mansbridge, a rural tailor and his customers, 1811–1815', *Textile History* 28/1 (1997), pp. 29–38. See also John Rule, *The Labouring Classes in Early Industrial England, 1750–1850* (Longman, London, 1986).

[9]   Martin Purvis, 'Co-operative retailing in Britain', in J. Benson and G. Shaw (eds), *The Evolution of Retail Systems c. 1800–1914* (Leicester University Press, Leicester, 1992), pp. 107–34; Peter Gurney, *Co-operative Culture and the Politics of Consumption in England, 1870–1930* (Manchester University Press, Manchester, 1996); Jayne Southern, 'The co-operative movement in the North-West of England 1919–1939: images and realities', unpublished PhD thesis, University of Lancaster (1996); Johnston Birchall, *The International Co-operative Movement* (Manchester University Press, Manchester, 1997); Ellen Furlough and Carl Strikwerda (eds), *Consumers Against Capitalism: Consumer Cooperation in Europe, North America, and Japan, 1840–1990* (Rowman and Littlefield, Oxford, 1999).

[10]   Hrant Pasdermadjian, *The Department Store, its Origins, Evolution and Economics* (Newman Books, London, 1954); F. W. Ferry, *A History of the Department Store* (Macmillan, New York, 1960); J. H. Porter, 'The development of a provincial department store 1870–1939', *Business History* 13/1 (1971), pp. 64–71; Gareth Shaw, 'The evolution and impact of large-scale retailing in Britain', in Benson and Shaw (eds), *The Evolution of Retail Systems*, pp. 135–65; Bill Lancaster, *The Department Store: A Social History* (Leicester University Press, Leicester, 1995). See also Alison Adburgham, *Shops and Shopping 1800–1914: Where, and in what Manner the Well-Dressed English Woman Bought her Clothes* (Allen & Unwin, London, 1964).

[11]   Peter Mathias, *Retailing Revolution: A History of Multiple Retailing in the Food Trades Based Upon the Allied Suppliers Group of Companies* (Longmans, London, 1967); Andrew Alexander, 'Retail revolution: the spread of multiple retailers in South West England', *Journal of Regional and Local Studies* 13/1

(1993), pp. 39–54; Andrew Alexander, 'The evolution of multiple retailing in Britain 1870–1950: a geographical analysis', unpublished PhD thesis, University of Exeter (1994); Peter Scott, 'Learning to multiply: the property market and the growth of multiple retailing in Britain, 1919–39', *Business History* 36/3 (1994), pp. 1–28; Andrew Alexander, John Benson and Gareth Shaw, 'Action and reaction: competition and the multiple retailer in 1930s Britain', *The International Review of Retail, Distribution and Consumer Research* 9/3 (1999), pp. 245–59; Katrina Honeyman, *Well Suited: A History of the Leeds Clothing Industry 1850–1990* (Oxford University Press, Oxford, 2000).

[12] Richard Coopey, Sean O'Connell and Dilwyn Porter, 'Mail order in the United Kingdom, c. 1880–1960: how mail order competed with other forms of retailing', *The International Review of Retailing, Distribution and Consumer Research* 9/3 (1999), pp. 261–73.

[13] G. W. McClelland, 'The supermarket and society', *Sociological Review* 10/2 (1962), pp. 133–54; Peter Jones, 'Retail innovation and diffusion: the spread of Asda stores', *Area* 13/3 (1981), pp. 197–201.

[14] Keri Davies and Leigh Sparks, 'The development of superstore retailing in Great Britain 1960–1986: results from a new database', *Transactions, Institute of British Geographers* 14/1 (1989), pp. 74–89; Alan G. Hallsworth and John McClatchey, 'Interpreting the growth of superstore retailing in Britain', *The International Review of Retail, Distribution and Consumer Research* 4/3 (1994), pp. 315–28.

[15] Purvis, 'Co-operative retailing'; Gurney, *Co-operative Culture*; Joshua Bamfield, 'Consumer-owned community flour and bread societies in the eighteenth and early nineteenth centuries', *Business History*, 'Special issue on the emergence of modern retailing, 1750–1950' 40/4 (1998), pp. 16–36.

[16] Carol Kennedy, *The Merchant Princes. Family, Fortune and Philanthropy: Cadbury, Sainsbury and John Lewis* (Hutchinson, London, 2000), p. 4. See also Mathias, *Retailing Revolution*, and for an earlier period, see Mui and Mui, *Shops and Shopkeeping*, pp. 268–78. The 'great man' approach is clearest in studies of individual enterprises. See, for example, Richard S. Lambert, *The Universal Provider: A Study of William Whiteley and the Rise of the London Department Store* (George G. Harrap, London, 1938); Asa Briggs, *Friends of the People: The Centenary History of Lewis's* (Batsford, London, 1956); Reginald Pound, *Selfridge: A Biography* (Heinemann, London, 1960); James Mackay, *The Man who Invented Himself: A Life of Sir Thomas Lipton* (Mainstream Publishing, Edinburgh, 1998).

[17] Michael Roper, *Masculinity and the British Organization Man Since 1945* (Oxford University Press, Oxford, 1994); for a quantitative, rather than a cultural approach, see Christine Shaw, 'British entrepreneurs in distribution and the steel industry', *Business History* 31/3 (1989), pp. 48–60. See also D. C. Coleman, 'Historians and businessmen', reprinted in D. C. Coleman, *Myth, History and the Industrial Revolution* (Hambledon Press, London, 1992), pp. 165–78; James R. Raven, *Judging New Wealth: Popular Publishing and Responses to Commerce in England, 1750–1800* (Clarendon Press, Oxford, 1992); Andrew Godley and Oliver M. Westall (eds), *Business History and Business Culture* (Manchester University Press, Manchester, 1996).

[18] Thomas J. Lipton, *Leaves for the Lipton Logs* (Hutchinson, London, 1932), pp. 89–90.

[19] H. Gordon Selfridge, *The Romance of Commerce* (John Lane, London, 1918), p. 13. See also pp. 1–18, 363–5.

[20] Lemire, *Dress, Culture and Commerce*, pp. 86–8. See also the importance of family connections during David Lewis's early years in Liverpool. Briggs, *Friends of the People*, pp. 34–5.

[21] Geoffrey Crossick and Heinz-Gerhard Haupt, *The Petite Bourgeoisie in Europe 1780–1914* (Routledge, London, 1995), pp. 93–4.

[22] *Wolverhampton Chronicle*, 12 November 1999.

[23] Peter Earle, *The Making of the English Middle Class: Business, Society and Family Life in London, 1660–1730* (Methuen, London, 1989); Jonathan Barry and Christopher Brooks (eds), *The Middling Sort of People: Culture, Society and Politics in England, 1550–1800* (Macmillan, Basingstoke, 1994); Margaret R. Hunt, *The Middling Sort: Commerce, Gender and the Family in England, 1680–1780* (University of California Press, Berkeley, 1996).

[24] Geoffrey Crossick and Heinz-Gerhard Haupt (eds), *Shopkeepers and Master Artisans in Nineteenth Century Europe* (Methuen, London, 1984); Frank Bechhofer and Brian A. Elliot, 'The petite bourgeoisie in late capitalism', *Annual Review of Sociology* 11 (1985), pp. 181–207; Crossick and Haupt, *The Petite Bourgeoisie*.

[25] Spufford, *The Great Reclothing*. See also Beverley Lemire, 'Peddling fashion: salesmen, pawnbrokers, tailors, thieves and the second-hand clothes trade in England, c. 1700–1800', *Textile History* 22/1 (1991), pp. 67–82.

[26] Cox, *The Complete Tradesman*, p. 85.

[27] Janet Blackman, 'The food supply of an industrial town: a study of Sheffield's public markets 1780–1900', *Business History* 5/2 (1963), pp. 83–97; Janet Blackman, 'The development of the retail grocery trade in the nineteenth century', *Business History* 9/2 (1967), pp. 110–17. See also Roger Scola, 'Food markets and shops in Manchester, 1770–1870', *Journal of Historical Geography* 1/2 (1975), pp. 153–68; John Benson, *The Penny Capitalists: A Study of Nineteenth Century Working-Class Entrepreneurs* (Gill & Macmillan, Dublin, 1983), pp. 98–127; Martin P. Phillips, 'The evolution of markets and shops in Britain', in Benson and Shaw (eds), *The Evolution of Retail Systems*, pp. 53–75.

[28] Deborah Hodson, '"The municipal store": adaptation and development in the retail markets of nineteenth century urban Lancashire', *Business History*, 'Special issue on the emergence of modern retailing, 1750–1950' 40/4 (1998), p. 99. See also James Schmiechen and Kenneth Carls, *The British Market Hall: A Social and Architectural History* (Yale University Press, New Haven, 1999).

[29] Lemire, *Dress, Culture and Commerce*, p. 114.

[30] Benson, *The Penny Capitalists*, pp. 114–27; Michael J. Winstanley, *The Shopkeeper's World 1830–1914* (Manchester University Press, Manchester, 1983).

[31] Christopher Hosgood, 'The "pigmies of commerce" and the working-class community: small shopkeepers in England, 1870–1914', *Journal of Social History* 22/3 (1989), pp. 439–60.

[32] Mui and Mui, *Shops and Shopkeeping*, pp. 150–1. See also Zoe Lawson,

'Shops, shopkeepers, and the working-class community: Preston, 1860–1890', *Transactions of the Historic Society of Lancashire and Cheshire* 141 (1991), pp. 309–28.

[33] Benson, *The Rise of Consumer Society*, p. 62.

[34] Selfridge, *The Romance of Commerce*. For an earlier period, see also Susan E. Brown, '"A just and profitable commerce": moral economy and the middle-classes in eighteenth-century London', *Journal of British Studies* 32/4 (1993), pp. 305–32.

[35] John Galsworthy, *In Chancery* (Wordsworth Editions, Ware, 1994, first published 1920), p. 196. See also, for example, Geoffrey Mortimer, *The Blight of Respectability* (University Press, London, 1897), pp. 112–13.

[36] Eric Hobsbawm, *The Age of Empire 1875–1914* (Abacus, London, 1999, first published 1987), p. 255. See also Michael J. Winstanley (ed.), *A Traditional Grocer: T. D. Smith of Lancaster 1858–1981* (University of Lancaster, Lancaster, 1991), p. 20.

[37] Fred Gresswell, *Bright Boots: An Autobiography* (David & Charles, Newton Abbot, 1982, first published 1956), pp. 87–8. The classic exposition of the small shopkeeper environment remains Robert Roberts, *The Classic Slum: Salford Life in the First Quarter of the Century* (Penguin, Harmondsworth, 1973).

[38] Winstanley, *The Shopkeeper's World*, p. 11.

[39] Thomas Turner, *The Diary of a Georgian Shopkeeper* (Oxford University Press, Oxford, 1979, based on 1925 edition), p. 6.

[40] Spufford, *The Great Reclothing*, pp. 6–14; Benson, *The Penny Capitalists*, p. 114.

[41] Gerry R. Rubin, 'From packmen, tallymen and "perambulating scotchmen" to Credit Drapers' Associations, c. 1840–1914', *Business History* 28/2 (1986), pp. 206–25; Margot C. Finn, 'Scotch drapers and the politics of modernity: gender, class and national identity in the Victorian tally trade', in M. Daunton and M. Hilton (eds), *The Politics of Consumption: Material Culture and Citizenship in Europe and America* (Berg, Oxford, 2001). See also Lemire, *Dress, Culture and Commerce*, pp. 75–93, for the overwhelmingly negative association of Anglo-Jewry with the itinerant second-hand clothes trade.

[42] Christopher P. Hosgood, '"Mercantile monasteries": shops, shop assistants and shop life in late Victorian and Edwardian Britain', *Journal of British Studies* 38/3 (1999), pp. 322–52.

[43] Matthew Hilton, 'Retailing history as economic and cultural history: strategies of survival by specialist tobacconists in the mass market', *Business History*, 'Special issue on the emergence of modern retailing, 1750–1950' 40/4 (1998), p. 129. On the vagaries of notions of 'independence', see Crossick and Haupt, *The Petite Bourgeoisie*, pp. 60–3.

[44] Hunt, *The Middling Sort*, pp. 141–2. See also Leonore Davidoff and Catherine Hall, *Family Fortunes: Men and Women of the English Middle Class, 1780–1850* (Hutchinson, London, 1987), pp. 272–315; Judith M. Bennett, 'Misogyny, popular culture and women's work', *History Workshop Journal* 31 (1991), pp. 166–88.

[45] Harriet Bradley, *Men's Work, Women's Work: A Sociological History of the*

Sexual Division of Labour in Employment (Polity Press, London, 1989), pp. 175–87. Such census statistics should of course be treated with caution, particularly given the under-reporting of family members as shop workers.

[46] Thomas J. Nossiter, 'Shopkeeper radicalism in the nineteenth century', in T. J. Nossiter, A. H. Hanson and S. Rokkan (eds), *Imagination and Precision in the Social Sciences* (Faber, London, 1972), pp. 407–38; Barbara Taylor, *Eve and the New Jerusalem: Socialism and Feminism in the Nineteenth Century* (Virago Press, London, 1983); Rule, *The Labouring Classes*, pp. 255–378; Anna Clark, *The Struggle for the Breeches: Gender and the Making of the British Working Class* (University of California Press, Berkeley, 1995); Iorwerth Prothero, *Radical Artisans in England and France, 1830–1870* (Cambridge University Press, Cambridge, 1997).

[47] Christopher P. Hosgood, 'A "brave and daring folk"? Shopkeepers and trade associational life in Victorian and Edwardian England', *Journal of Social History* 26/2 (1992), pp. 285–308. See also Mui and Mui, *Shops and Shopkeeping*, pp. 73–105; Geoffrey Crossick, 'Meanings of property and the world of the petite bourgeoisie', in J. Stobart and A. Owens (eds), *Urban Fortunes: Property and Inheritance in the Town, 1700–1900* (Ashgate, Aldershot, 2000), pp. 50–78; Gareth Shaw, Andrew Alexander, John Benson and Deborah Hodson, 'The evolving culture of retailer-regulation and the failure of the "Balfour Bill" in inter-war Britain', *Environment and Planning A* 32 (2000), pp. 1977–89.

[48] For discussions of notions of 'spaces of consumption', see Paul D. Glennie and Nigel J. Thrift, 'Consumers, identities and consumption spaces in early modern England', *Environment and Planning A* 28/1 (1996), pp. 25–45; Paul D. Glennie and Nigel J. Thrift, 'Consumption, shopping and gender', in N. Wrigley and M. Lowe (eds), *Retailing, Consumption and Capital: Towards the New Retail Geography* (Longman, Harlow, 1996), pp. 221–37; Jon Stobart, 'Shopping streets as social space: leisure, consumerism and improvement in an eighteenth-century county town', *Urban History* 25/1 (1998), pp. 3–21.

[49] Quoted in Cox, *The Complete Tradesman*, p. 179. See also pp. 176–80. The extent to which 'people' included men and women on an equal basis is open to argument.

[50] Adam Smith, *The Wealth of Nations* (1776). Quoted in Kevin Jackson (ed.), *The Oxford Book of Money* (Oxford University Press, Oxford, 1995), p. 368.

[51] Anon., *Reminiscences of an Old Draper* (Sampson Low, Marston, Searle & Rimington, London, 1876), pp. 94–5.

[52] Winstanley, *The Shopkeeper's World*, pp. 89–92; Purvis, 'Co-operative retailing', pp. 118–20.

[53] Martin Purvis, 'Stocking the store: co-operative retailers in North-east England and systems of wholesale supply, circa 1860–77', *Business History*, 'Special issue on the emergence of modern retailing, 1750–1950' 40/4 (1998), p. 72.

[54] For Britain, see, for example, Gareth Shaw and Martin T. Wild, 'Retail patterns in the Victorian city', *Transactions, Institute of British Geographers* 4/2 (1979), pp. 278–91; Frank Livesey, *The Distributive Trades* (Heinemann Educational, London, 1979).

[55] See, for example, Sarah Levitt, 'Cheap mass-produced men's clothing in the

nineteenth and early twentieth centuries', *Textile History* 22/2 (1991), pp. 179–92. Significantly, there seems to be no agreement over the timing of these developments.

[56] William Stout, *The Autobiography of William Stout of Lancaster 1665–1752*, edited by J. D. Marshall (Manchester University Press, Manchester, 1967), pp. 157, 165.

[57] Henry Mayhew, *London Labour and the London Poor* (Griffin, Bohn and Company, London, 1861–2), vol. I, p. 177.

[58] *Express and Star*, 12 December 1934.

[59] Mayhew, *London Labour*, vol. I, p. 60. See also Benson, *The Penny Capitalists*, p. 115.

[60] Mathias, *Retailing Revolution*, p. 41. See also *Small Trader*, 15 April 1915.

[61] Cox, *The Complete Tradesman*, pp. 28–37. See also Crossick and Haupt, *The Petite Bourgeoisie*, pp. 23–6; Michael Berlin, '"Broken all in pieces": artisans and the regulation of workmanship in early modern London', in G. Crossick (ed.), *The Artisan and the European Town, 1500–1900* (Scolar Press, Aldershot, 1997), pp. 75–92.

[62] Benson, *The Penny Capitalists*, p. 111.

[63] John A. Dawson, David M. Gransby and Russell Schiller, 'The changing high street', *Geographical Journal* 154/1 (1988), pp. 1–22; Davies and Sparks, 'The developments of superstore retailing'; Ross L. Davies, 'Retail planning policy', in P. McGoldrick (ed.), *Cases in Retail Management* (Pitman Publishing, London, 1994), pp. 230–40.

[64] John Benson and Gareth Shaw, 'Introduction', in Benson and Shaw (eds), *The Retailing Industry*, vol. 3, p. 7. For the relationship between regulation and retailing, see also Neil Wrigley, 'Antitrust regulation and the restructuring of grocery retailing in Britain and the USA', *Environment and Planning A* 24/5 (1992), pp. 727–49; Terry Marsden and Neil Wrigley, 'Regulation, retailing and consumption', *Environment and Planning A* 27/12 (1995), pp. 1899–912; Terry Marsden and Neil Wrigley, 'Retailing, the food system and the regulatory state', in Wrigley and Lowe (eds), *Retailing, Consumption and Capital*, pp. 33–47; Carlo Morelli, 'Constructing a balance between price and non-price competition in British multiple food retailing, 1954–64', *Business History* 40/2 (1998), pp. 45–61.

[65] Ronald Savitt, 'A historical approach to comparative retailing', *Management Decision* 20/4 (1982), pp. 16–23; Stanley C. Hollander, 'A rearview mirror might help drive us forward – a call for more historical studies in retailing', *Journal of Retailing* 62 (1986), pp. 7–10.

[66] See, for example, John Jones, 'The structure, organisation and location of fixed-shop retailing in Wolverhampton, 1870–1914', unpublished PhD thesis, CNAA/University of Wolverhampton (1991); Alexander, 'The evolution of multiple retailing in Britain'; Martin P. Phillips, 'Market exchange and social relations: the practices of food circulation in and to the three towns of Plymouth, Devonport and Stonehouse, 1800–c.1870', unpublished PhD thesis, University of Exeter (1992); Southern, 'The co-operative movement'.

[67] For a comparative approach, see also the chapters by Michael Winstanley and Andrew Alexander, Gareth Shaw and Deborah Hodson.

[68] Diane Collins, 'Primitive or not? Fixed-shop retailing before the industrial

revolution', *Journal of Regional and Local Studies* 13/1 (1993), p. 33.

[69] John Benson, 'Retailing on two continents: Newcastle, New South Wales and Hamilton, Ontario 1891–1941', *Australian–Canadian Studies* 9/1-2 (1991), pp. 21–34.

[70] For retailing in Australia see, for example, H. Wolfers, 'The big stores between the wars', in J. Roe (ed.), *Twentieth-Century Sydney: Studies in Urban and Social History* (Hale & Iremonger, Sydney, 1980); Gail Reekie, 'Sydney's big stores 1880–1930: gender and mass marketing', unpublished PhD thesis, University of Sydney (1987); F. Pollon, *Shopkeepers and Shopkeeping: A Social History of Retailing in New South Wales from 1788* (Retail Traders' Association of New South Wales, Sydney, 1989). For retailing in Canada see, for example, Bank of Montreal, *The Service Industries* (Royal Commission on Canada's Economic Prospects, Ottawa, 1956); B. S. Osborne, 'Trading on a frontier: the function of markets, peddlers and fairs in nineteenth-century Ontario', *Canadian Papers in Rural History* 11(1980), pp. 59–81; Joy L. Santink, *Timothy Eaton and the Rise of his Department Store* (University of Toronto Press, Toronto, 1990); John Benson, 'Small-scale retailing in Canada' and 'Large-scale retailing in Canada', both in Benson and Shaw (eds), *The Evolution of Retail Systems*, pp. 87–101, 186–98; David Monod, *Store Wars: Shopkeepers and the Culture of Mass Marketing, 1890–1939* (Toronto University Press, Toronto, 1996).

[71] Wolverhampton and District Co-operative Society, *Souvenir in Connection with the Extension of Premises ... 1931* (Co-op, Manchester, 1931); W. T. Matthews, 'Local government and the regulation of the public market in Upper Canada 1800–1860: the moral economy of the poor', *Ontario History* lxxix (1987), pp. 297–326; D. Patricia Hampton, *Retail Co-operatives in the Lower Hunter Valley* (Newcastle Region Public Library, Newcastle, 1986).

[72] Tom Brennan, *Midland City: Wolverhampton Social and Industrial Survey* (Dennis Dobson, London, 1948); James C. Docherty, *Newcastle: The Making of an Australian City* (Hale & Iremonger, Sydney, 1983); John C. Weaver, *Hamilton: An Illustrated History* (James Lorimer, Toronto, 1982).

[73] *Express and Star*, 5 February 1917; 8 April 1936.

[74] New South Wales, *An Act for the Early Closing of Shops and to Regulate the Hours of Employment in Shops* (1899), clause 21; *Newcastle Morning Herald*, 9 December 1935; 5 September 1940; 12 December 1940.

[75] *Hamilton Spectator*, 14 August 1919; 16 December 1922; 27 January 1927; L. Van Hoorn, 'The Hamilton central market: an economic anthropological study', unpublished MA thesis, McMaster University (1973), p. 10.

[76] Hampton, *Retail Co-operatives*, pp. 7, 13. See also F. R. E. Mauldon, *A Study in Social Economics: The Hunter River Valley New South Wales* (Workers' Educational Association of New South Wales & Mullens, Sydney, 1927), p. 165.

[77] Jane Synge, 'Immigrant communities – British and continental European – in early twentieth century Hamilton', *Oral History* 4/2 (1976), p. 45.

[78] Craig Heron, 'Working class Hamilton 1895–1930', unpublished PhD thesis, Dalhousie University (1981), p. 330. See also John Benson, 'Hawking and peddling in Canada, 1867–1914', *Histoire Sociale-Social History* xviii/35 (1985), p. 81.

I REPRESENTATIONS AND SELF-REPRESENTATIONS

CHAPTER 1
'BEGGARY OF THE NATION':[1] MORAL, ECONOMIC AND POLITICAL ATTITUDES TO THE RETAIL SECTOR IN THE EARLY MODERN PERIOD[2]
Nancy Cox

The retail sector did not receive a favourable press in early modern England. The quotation in the title of this chapter is only one of many that could have been used to illustrate the low esteem in which shopkeepers were held both by the authorities and by economic and moral thinkers of the day. This attitude penetrated so deeply into the fabric of thought that it found expression in one of the most popular emblem books at the time, Henry Peacham's *Minerva Britanna*. Whence it must have worked its way into the consciousness of every schoolboy who learnt both his Latin grammar and his conceptual understanding of society through an active study of this and similar works.[3]

The reasons for the anxieties were complex. Although some were founded on a distaste for the activities of the shopkeepers themselves, others depended upon issues that only indirectly impinged on the retailing sector. In this chapter, three strands of thinking are investigated in turn. The first, moral anxieties about the dangers of luxury, had the least direct impact on retailing, though it affected a substantial proportion of the wares of many retailers. The second, anxieties about overseas trade and the balance of payments, provoked regulation influencing the availability and price of imported goods, and drew odium upon those who sold them. In each of these strands, the retailer could be seen as acting against the national interest; a perception that was to change as the orthodox theories were challenged. The third strand involved overt attacks on shopkeepers and shopkeeping as such.

Luxury

Moral concerns about the dangers of luxury have a long history.[4] In the fifth century BC, the Greek philosopher Plato had argued that once basic needs were met, any concession to the satisfaction of desire inevitably led to competition, emulation, disharmony and, ultimately, to the destruction of the state.[5] Some Roman moralists, continuing on the same theme, viewed the body and its desires as 'nothing less than a fetter on ... freedom', suggesting that 'the greedy are always in want'. Man should live a 'natural' life controlled by reason and the virtues of justice, courage and temperance. Luxury was seen as the misuse of those intrinsically valueless, but enjoyable, benefits of health, beauty, strength, riches, pleasure and a good reputation.[6] Echoes of these sentiments reverberate down the centuries well after the belief in luxury and immoderation as potent sources of evil had been disarmed. Understated as ever, Jane Austen hinted at contrasts: 'Mr Bingley was good-looking and gentleman-like; he had a pleasant countenance, and easy, unaffected manners. His sisters were fine women, with an air of decided fashion. His brother-in-law, Mr Hurst, merely looked the gentleman.' At a later stage the hero, Mr Darcy, stresses the importance of a well-regulated mind.[7] As the story unfolds, excess, silliness and ill-breeding are contrasted with moderation, gentility and good taste; an eighteenth-century interpretation of the classical ideal.

To the Romans, the dangers of immoderation and luxury were not just to the individual. Self-indulgence led to the emasculation of courage, the essential virtue for the state; it also led to the precedence of private over public interest. Whereas control could be left to the individual in possession of a well-ordered mind, the masses needed to be regulated by the state, hence the Roman sumptuary laws against the excesses of the stomach.[8] Concerns about the well-being of the state were to remain central to the debate about luxury in the early modern period, when those who sold luxury were in danger of being accused of acting against the national interest.

The distinctive addition that early Christians gave to the debate was to confuse vice with sin, and to include luxury, which had acquired overtones of lechery or lust, among the sins to which Man was prone. Furthermore, by drawing attention to the role of Eve in the Fall, Christian thinkers emphasized the potential of emasculation in luxury.[9] St Paul summed up the Christian approach when he wrote: 'For men shall be lovers of their own selves ... lovers of pleasures more than lovers of God', and as such 'lead captive silly women laden with sins, led away with divers lusts.'[10] With such texts in mind, the feminization of luxury was to attract the attention of moralists throughout the early modern period.[11]

Given these connections between luxury and vice, it was only to be

27

expected that moralists in the sixteenth and early seventeenth centuries like Philip Stubbs should have inveighed against luxury. His attack was phrased in gendered terms; the 'two collaterell Cosins, apparel and Pride' were 'the Mother and Daughter of mischiefe'. Interestingly, when he came down to specifics, he attacked articles of apparel worn by both sexes, like feathers and 'great and monstrous ruffes', describing them as 'sternes of pride and ensigns of vanitie'. Stubbs's vituperations against the evils of luxury were weakened partly by the necessity of avoiding offence to his patron, the Earl of Arundel, but also by the general acceptance that displays of luxury were quite properly demonstrations of power. Instead of the maintenance of huge retinues – a practice monarchs had been at pains to discourage – the Tudor nobility, led by those same monarchs, took to maintaining distinctions of status through extravagant dress. This, Stubbs argued, was no more than proper and served 'to ennoble, garnishe, & set forthe their byrthes, dignities, functions, and calling'.[12]

Parliament concurred with the notion that station in life should be marked by appropriate dress, and took action to prevent the lower orders arraying themselves in luxurious fabrics and garments suitable only for their betters. Regulation of apparel stretched back to the fourteenth century and only petered out in the seventeenth.[13] Behind attempts to impose a framework of social grouping distinguished by dress lay continuing anxieties about luxury, exemplified by the preamble to a proclamation of 1574, which talked of 'the superfluity of unnecessary foreign wares ... and other vain devices'.[14] The acts were finally repealed in 1604,[15] although several bills were introduced unsuccessfully during the seventeenth century. In one debate, the statement that 'God did not attire our first parents in the excrement of worms',[16] revealed another strand in the attacks on luxury apart from the moral and religious ones – prejudice against silk.

The frequent repetition of sumptuary regulation points to its ineffectiveness, at least partly due to the lack of any mechanism of enforcement. For this reason it probably had little effect on retail trade. Some sixteenth-century provincial shops, like those of John Beare of Ludham in Norfolk or Anthony Bettenson of Newport in Shropshire, were plentifully stocked with silk ware and other luxuries whose use was supposedly confined to the social elite. Yet as small town tradesmen,[17] their customers cannot have been particularly select and were probably merely the local gentry and tradesmen.[18]

Early in Elizabeth's reign, parliament tried a different tack. Instead of restricting what people could wear, it prohibited the sale of any 'foreign Stuff or Wares ... appertaining to the apparelling ... or the adorning of the Body' except for cash or short-term credit or unless the purchaser was a substantial property owner.[19] It was control of dress under another name, as few luxury wares were of home manufacture.[20] It seems unlikely that this act was any more successful than others at enforcing social distinctions.[21]

A crucial change in thinking about luxury developed during the late seventeenth and early eighteenth centuries. Nicholas Barbon was one of the earliest to question whether luxury was necessarily a threat to society's well-being,[22] but the ideas were most fully developed by Bernard Mandeville in his *Fable of the Bees*,[23] in which he challenged ideas that had barely been questioned since classical times. While recognizing the relationship between luxury and vice, Mandeville insisted, in the words of the subtitle, that 'Private Vices' gave 'Public Benefits'. His arguments were laid out in the much quoted opening poem, and developed in a series of 'Remarks':

> The Root of evil Avarice,
> That damn'd ill-natured baneful Vice,
> Was slave to Prodigality,
> That Noble sin; whilst Luxury
> Employ'd a Million of the Poor
> And odious Pride a Million more.
> Envy itself, and Vanity
> Were Ministers of Industry;
> Their darling Folly, Fickleness
> In Diet, Furniture and Dress,
> That strange ridic'lous Vice, was made
> The very Wheel, that turn'd the Trade.
> ...
> Thus Vice nursed Ingenuity,
> Which join'd with Time and Industry
> Had carry'd Life's Conveniences,
> It's real Pleasures, Comforts, Ease,
> To such a Height, the very Poor
> Lived better than the Rich before;[24]

Mandeville thought it folly even to attempt to distinguish needs from desires, or luxuries from necessities, since none was immutable and all varied over time and between different sections of society.[25] He argued that, however undesirable for the individual's moral fibre, the pursuit of luxury added to the national wealth, encouraged inventiveness and provided employment for many.[26]

Both here and across the Atlantic fears about luxury remained unallayed. An American writer referred in 1747 to luxury as making 'her appearance so engaging' with 'the show of Politeness and Generosity, that we are not aware of Danger, 'till we feel the fatal poison',[27] while a contemporary pamphleteer could write that 'Every

Man has a *natural Right* to enjoy the fruit of his own Labour, both as to the *Conveniences*, and *Comforts*, as well as *Necessaries* of Life' (though not apparently the luxuries).[28] Similar anxieties were expressed this side of the Atlantic. For example, Lord Kames attacked 'the epidemic distempers of luxury and selfishness', suggesting that they were 'above all pernicious in a commercial state' on the grounds that they led to depopulation and the destruction of industry. He even questioned the merit of commerce, arguing that, while it may have appeared advantageous in the short term, it was 'hurtful ultimately by introducing luxury and voluptuousness which eradicate patriotism',[29] thus echoing closely the ideas of ancient philosophers that luxury subverted the national interest.

Adam Smith largely supported the arguments of Barbon and Mandeville. He entered the long-running debate on the distinctions between necessity, convenience and luxury, primarily to question yet again whether it was useful to impose rigid boundaries. He included among necessities 'not only the commodities which are indispensably necessary for the support of life, but whatever the custom of the country renders it indecent for creditable people, even of the lowest orders, to be without'. To illustrate how boundaries could shift, he showed how linen shirts and shoes had become necessities in England, though not necessarily elsewhere.[30]

In two respects Smith remained suspicious about luxury. Firstly, he considered that luxuries 'will always appear in the highest degree contemptible and trifling',[31] though by implication also desirable. Secondly, he believed that for ordinary people, virtue, by which he meant the avoidance of excess, was the true way to fortune, thus mirroring the views of the American pamphleteer quoted above. The corollary was that desire had to be controlled.[32] Despite these reservations, Smith acknowledged, as Nicholas Barbon had done a century before,[33] that satisfying man's basic needs took up only a tiny fraction of trade, and that a far greater proportion was given to 'the amusements of those desires which cannot be satisfied, but seem to be altogether endless'. Smith defined these as 'conveniences and ornaments of building, dress, equipage and household furniture' or any other 'wants and fancies'.[34]

In a sense, Barbon, Mandeville and Smith were doing no more than express a reality already apparent in society. Whatever moralists, the Church and the State may have said about the evils of luxury, little attention seems to have been paid to them either by consumers or by the trading community. Gregory King's estimates of annual expenditure towards the end of the seventeenth century indicate a large consumption of non-essentials; a population estimated at no more than 5.5 million was consuming annually ten million pairs of stockings, four million bands and cravats, as well as 200,000 fans and busks, and 100,000 belts and girdles.[35] Other evidence confirms that most consumers did not concern themselves with the moral danger of luxury; instead they cared only for its desirability.[36] The diarist Samuel Pepys was probably typical of many upwardly mobile Londoners of his day. He revelled in every opportunity for rich living, on one day being 'very merry with a good barrel of oysters', and on another resolving his 'great expence shall be lace-bands'.[37] The satisfaction he felt when he collected from the tailors his fine new suit, with its 'flowered tabby vest, and coloured camelott tunique' is almost palpable, particularly when the 'people did mightily look upon' them.[38] His faint twinges of conscience were caused, not by moral considerations, but by financial ones. Of yet another new suit, he wrote that it cost him much money, and he prayed God to make him able to pay for it.[39]

Pepys's concern as to whether his income could keep pace with his lifestyle suggests that the modern 'paradox of apparently growing unhappiness in the midst of increasing plenty' may not be new.[40] The 'hedonic treadmill' may well not buy happiness, but lead only to more material possessions and more financial anxieties.[41] These ideas were not clearly articulated by economic and moral thinkers in early modern Britain, who did not explicitly consider the concept of happiness as such, nor were they directly expressed by Pepys, though they often seem to lie hidden under his anxieties.

Early modern retailers, who were after all in the business of persuading customers to buy, do not seem to have involved themselves in the debate about luxury. Even nonconformist and Quaker retailers do not appear to have found persuasive the moral arguments against their trade. Benjamin Wright, a seventeenth-century nonconformist mercer in Wellington, Shropshire, sold many of the unnecessary wares disliked by the theorists – taffeta ribbons, silver buttons, lace and playing cards among them.[42] Seventy years later the American Quaker, Jabez Maud Fisher, was no less ready to stock up on luxury goods such as velvet 'fashion caps', women's stockings with 'silk clocks', 'Dutch Lace and Nonsopretties', fans and 'Ribbons of all sorts'. He was always more concerned that his suppliers were men of 'universal Character of Probity and Honour' than with the luxurious nature of their wares.[43] However, by his day luxury was in any case seen less of a threat to the national interest, and as we shall see some tradesmen were beginning to be seen as respectable.

The balance of payments
If the debate about the moral dangers of luxury seems to have had little direct impact on the sale and consumption of luxury goods, a key

element in the stock of most retailing tradesmen, there were other debates at the time that could, and sometimes did, threaten retail trade. The 'Mercantile Theory', a term coined by Adam Smith and adopted by historians, was far broader than he chose to admit, but one of its central tenets was that money alone constitutes wealth. With this in mind, orthodox economic thinkers in much of the early modern period saw the balance of payments, or rather the perceived imbalance, as one of the key challenges to the wealth of the nation. It was a recurring theme, addressed in the eighteenth century no less than in the sixteenth. The theory was summarized in 1664 by Thomas Mun: 'The ordinary means ... to increase our wealth and treasure is by Forraign Trade, wherein wee must ever observe this rule; to sell more to strangers yearly than wee consume of theirs in value.'[44] Since many of Britain's imports consisted of perceived luxuries that were not balanced by British exports of equivalent value, concern for the economic wellbeing of the nation thus became inextricably bound up with moral anxieties about luxuries. And, given that shopkeepers were responsible for selling these goods to the consumer, their activities were equally suspect.

One early exposition along these lines was probably written in about 1549, though it was actually published in an extended form in 1581 under the pseudonym of a writer usually identified as William Smith.[45] W. S. divided tradesmen into three groups. The first, consisting of 'mercers, grocers, vinteners, haberdashers, mileyners' and the like, sold foreign goods such as 'drinkinge and lokinge glasses, paynted clothes, perfumed gloves, daggers, kniues, pinnes, pointes, aglets, buttons, and a thowsand things of like sort'. They were condemned, because they encouraged money to go out of the country and thereby did 'but exhause the treasure out of the Realme'. Although with other writers this perception became entangled with concerns about luxury, this was not the case with W. S., who appears to have had no anxieties about the nature of such goods, merely about their importation. His solution was to advocate the establishment and active encouragement of 'projects' in this country, whereby such goods could be manufactured at home rather than imported from abroad. He envisaged a utopian England in which towns were revived and 'replenished with all kind of artificers ... cappers, glovers, paper makers, glasiers, pointers, goldesmithes, blackesmithes of all sortes, coverlet makers, nedle makers, pinners and such other', thus reducing if not eliminating the undesirable mercer and others of his kind.[46] Correcting the balance of payments in this way would also solve unemployment, another major concern of the Tudor authorities.

Tudor governments took action. They attempted to establish the scale of the imbalance; for example, by drawing up lists of imports into

London. One was significantly entitled 'The Particular Value of certain necessary and unnecessary Wares brought into the Port of London ... the overquantity whereof most lamentably spoileth the realm yearly.'[47] Governments also attempted to reduce imports by encouraging home manufacture, largely through the establishment of monopolies, such as the one aimed at addressing deficiencies in the home production of brass.[48] But governments then as now had mixed and sometimes confused motives, so that they used patents to foster the production not only of essentials but also of some of those 'Unnecessary Wares'.[49] Parliament was likewise confused, passing a series of acts banning the importation of such obvious luxuries as girdles and other silk wares, whilst declaring their aim was to encourage their manufacture at home.[50] Probably governmental action of this sort had little effect on retailers, though any shift from imports to home manufacture would have inevitably led to some realignment of supply lines.

The argument about imports became more complicated in the seventeenth century, when recently established and powerful trading companies made their profits from the importation of luxury foreign goods for which they had an unfavourable balance of payments. The East India Company was incorporated at the end of 1600 with a monopoly secured by charter for 15 years.[51] A director of the Company, Thomas Mun, was one of the most influential economic thinkers of the seventeenth century and the author in 1664 of a coherent account of exchange mechanisms in trade, from which I have already quoted.[52] In an earlier work published in 1621, he defended the East India Company,[53] and in so doing had to face a real dilemma. The Company at this stage in its history imported far more than it exported and its trade was a constant drain on England's treasure. Mun resolved the dilemma neatly. He categorized goods in the orthodox way into the essential, 'such as are foode, rayment, and munition for warre and trade', the desirable, such as those wares 'fitting for health and arts', and the unnecessary 'which serue for our pleasure, and ornament'. It was in his interpretation of these categories that his argument twisted the classification of essential, desirable and unnecessary beyond what it could sustain. In so doing he inadvertently made a chink that was to be opened wide by later thinkers, who abandoned the theory of imbalance altogether.

In his vindication of the Company, Mun defended 'the necessary use of Drugges, Spices, Indico, Raw-silke, and Callicoes',[54] all goods of particular concern to retailers. On the 'moderate use of wholesome Drugges and comfortable Spices' he was on relatively sure ground, as he was with raw silk and indigo, both valued raw materials in British manufacture. Calicoes were less defensible and required a different approach. Passing rapidly over the fact that their importation profited 'Infidells', Mun argued rather speciously that it must also 'abate the excessive price' of alternative competitive imports such as 'Cambricks, Holland, and other sorts of Linnen-cloth', an argument trotted out subsequently by other writers.[55] It was accepted by parliament several decades later, when plain calicoes were exempted from prohibitive legislation.[56] As a further argument, Mun maintained that the importation of all calicoes was beneficial to the nation in that it increased trade generally in foreign parts. In so doing he was using one of the core arguments of later economic thinkers and was fundamentally calling into question the whole theory of the balance of trade, although he does not seem to have appreciated what he was doing.[57]

In passing, Mun gave a sideways swipe at 'unnecessary' imports from other parts of the world such as 'Tobacco, Cloth of gold and Silver, Lawnes, Cambricks, Gold & Silver lace, Velvets, Sattens, Taffaties, and diuers other manufactures yearely brought into this Realme, for an infinite value; all which as it is most true, that whilst wee consume them, they likewise deuoure our wealth'. Even here, honesty compelled him to admit that their moderate use 'euer suted well with the riches and Maiestie of this Kingdome'.[58]

Governments generally agreed with Mun about unnecessary imports, though they did not exempt decorative calicoes as he suggested. They adopted an aggressive policy of discouraging foreign trade that did 'but exhause the treasure out of the Realme', either by direct prohibition or by high duties. There was, for example, a string of acts stretching from the fifteenth century to the eighteenth prohibiting the importation of silk goods such as girdles, ribbons, laces, stockings and gloves.[59] The dilemma for governments was always that other European countries shared the same orthodoxy, so that prohibitive measures frequently led to retaliation – as in the disastrous attempt to prohibit the importation of French lace in 1698.[60] In an attempt to stem the flow from the Far East, parliament first banned the use of Indian decorative textiles,[61] and then their importation, except for re-export.[62] Parliament also imposed high duties, often with the dual aim of improving the balance of payments and of protecting home industry. The best known set of regulations concerned tea. The East India Company imported tea from the 1660s, but it was only after 1713, when the company established direct trade with Canton in China, that importation became both substantial and regular. The authorities imposed heavy duties; the public strenuously evaded them by purchasing smuggled tea, so that by the 1740s it was estimated that only about 25 per cent of tea was acquired legally.[63] The case against these prohibitive duties was gradually appreciated, and they were removed in 1784.[64]

While the authorities struggled to combat the drain on the nation's treasure, economic thinkers were exploring Mun's conclusions. Lewes Roberts wrote positively about 'trafficke, and forraigne trade' as 'the most certain, easiest, and soonest way ... whereby a Kingdome may be inriched', but he also drew attention to the dichotomy that a trade that 'impoverisheth a Kingdome', could nevertheless 'inrich the trader, and Merchant'.[65] In this recognition of potentially conflicting private and public interests, he predated Mandeville by over half a century. Samuel Fortrey was of much the same opinion as Mun and Roberts on the merits of trade in general, but he singled out France as the bogeyman, claiming that by the French trade 'at least sixteen hundred thousand pounds a year, [was] clear lost to this Kingdome ... Hereby it may appear how insensibly our treasure will be exhausted, and the nation begger'd'.[66] Another contemporary went much further in challenging orthodoxy on the balance of payments and the thinking of these writers. The 'real and hearty Lover of his King and Countrey' defended both trade with France and the importation of useless luxury, claiming it mattered not whether the goods were 'Apes and Peacocks' or Norwegian deals, all trade with whatever foreign lands enriched the nation. 'Take away our supernecessary trades,' he wrote, 'and ... our City of London will in a short time be like an Irish hut.'[67]

The old orthodoxy, however, resisted assaults on its purity. As late as the 1750s, Malachy Postlethwayt was advocating the balance of payments without qualification. To attain superiority in trade 'a society should have in proportion to it's populousness and the extent of its lands, a greater number of men able to consume the productions of art, than another has: 2dly, that it consumes less than the other does of the produce of foreign ingenuity.'[68] He propounded a 'fundamental maxim, that there is a beneficial national trade, and a national trade that is not so', and as an illustration of this he asserted that the 'importation of foreign commodities of mere luxury, in exchange for money, is a real loss to the state'.[69]

None of these writers appreciated fully that the volume of trade had more impact on the wealth of the nation than the balance of payments in any group of commodities or with any one country. It was Adam Smith who finally laid bare the fallacies inherent in the balance of payments. He exposed item by item the damage done by governments over the previous 200 years by implementing such beliefs. Prohibitions, bounties on exports, high duties, commercial treaties and all the other restraints of trade were examined and condemned in turn. 'The laudable motive of all these regulations', he argued, 'is to extend our own manufactures, not by their own improvement, but by the depression of those of all our neighbours, and by putting an end, as much as possible, to the troublesome competition of such odious and disagreeable rivals.'[70]

Having demolished the arguments in favour of the balance of payments, Smith made a further attack on orthodoxy by questioning whether the interests of manufacturing should hold such a central place in government policy. He suggested that, since 'Consumption is the sole end and purpose of all production ... the interests of the producer ought to be attended to only in so far as it may be necessary for promoting that of the consumer.'[71] Although Smith did not develop the implications of his theory for the retailing sector, they should be obvious to us. If the wealth of the nation lay, not in a favourable balance of payments but in free trade, a major cause of odium was removed from shopkeepers and they could no longer be accused of exhausting the national treasure. Instead, as agents of consumption, they increased the volume of trade to the benefit of efficient manufacturers and producers no less than importing merchants, and thereby to the nation as a whole.

Prejudice against retailers

A third strand in early modern discourses related directly to the retail sector. While concerns about the moral dangers of luxury and an unfavourable balance of payments threatened the nation's political economy, they rarely caused direct action against the retailing tradesman. However, some of their practices did engender frontal assaults, which were no doubt strengthened by the anxieties about luxury and the balance of trade already discussed. When the assumptions behind these issues were addressed and challenged, attitudes to retailing changed, though it is not possible to say whether this was consequential or coincidental.

Prejudice against the retail sector has a long history. The classical delineation of society included at the top a class of noble warriors, whose appropriate virtue was courage and whose way of life transcended self-interested appetite. Inferior to them was the class of tradesmen, bodily weak and inevitably ruled by the demands of economic life.[72] Such sentiments found echoes in the early modern period, though the terms were somewhat modified. By then the warrior had lost some of his former glory,[73] and had been replaced at the top of the hierarchy of virtue by the landed gentleman. Property in land was widely seen as giving its owner independence and opportunities for public service. Postlethwayt, for example, suggested that

it is scarce possible that the landed gentleman should not glaringly discern how his own prosperity is interwoven with that of the national commerce ... For the more useful and estimable production the land affords, the greater will be the gain of the land-holder, and the greater treasures will be brought into the kingdom from our foreign negoce.[74]

In this line of thought, the interests of land and the nation coincided. By contrast, trade was seen as less admirable, depending on profit and opportunism, with its participants necessarily governed by self-interest. Seen in the most unfavourable light, as in Thomas Wilson's *Discourse upon Usury* (1572), retailers were no better than 'hucksters, or chapmen of choyce, who retaying small wares, are not able to better their own estate but wyth falsehode, lying and perjurye'.[75] Opinion had hardly changed when in 1680 an anonymous writer attacked those 'home-Traders ... whom we call Shopkeepers', because they added to their own wealth by 'buying cheaper and selling dearer' without adding 'a peny to the National Riches'.[76]

Opprobrium of the trade was the greater, according to the anonymous sixteenth-century economist, W. S., because retailers such as 'mercers, grocers, vinteners, haberdashers, mileyners, and such' threatened not only the moral fabric of society, but also its economic health, since they were involved primarily in selling goods imported from beyond the seas. Furthermore, because these imports affected detrimentally the interests of the more worthy manufacturing tradesmen, who alone 'doe bringe in any treasour', W. S. could not see what mercers, haberdashers and the like 'doe in any towne, but finde a livinge to v. or vj. howsholdes, and in steade thereof impoverished twice as manie'.[77]

Another later anonymous writer reiterated some of these anxieties, drawing attention to the dichotomy between national and personal trade. Whereas the former was almost by definition desirable, the latter might 'be very beneficial to the private trader,' but 'harmful, nay of very ruinous Consequence to the whole National' interest. By dealing 'over-much in Consumptive Foreign Wares' such tradesmen were assisting in 'the beggary of the Nation'. Like W. S., he concluded that 'one poor Manufacturer ... adds more in a year to the Wealth of the Nation then all such Retailers and Shop-keepers in England.'[78]

Concerns about the questionable morals and self-interested activities of the retailing tradesmen were fuelled by suspicions concerning some of their practices, such as a preference for trading from within fixed premises and the almost universal use of credit. The thinking behind these concerns was not new. Prejudice against trading from fixed shops originated in the attempts of the Church to develop an ethic of trade in the Middle Ages, and of governments to implement it. Central to the idea was the concept of the just price, which 'the buyer was willing to pay and the seller was willing to accept'.[79] The idea was simple; interpretation and implementation were more difficult. The Church accepted that victims of fraud and misrepresentation should have remedy in the civil courts and that the concept of the just price implied the existence of the unjust. It recognized too that, when one party to the deal was stronger than the other, all sorts of undesirable practices could arise, and it condemned monopoly and the artificial fixing of prices, as well as such practices as forestalling, regrating and engrossing.[80]

The simplest method of implementing these concepts was to ensure that as much selling as possible took place in the open market. Here were two safeguards: it was easier to regulate and police, and the watchful eye of the public could protect the purchaser from the sharp dealing of the seller. Sale from inside the fixed shop, by contrast, was open to abuse, since regulation and policing were difficult to enforce on private property and the public was unable to oversee the deal.

Parliament attempted to strengthen the open market,[81] and it did not hide its suspicion of retail outlets sited away from the marketplace, such as those 'late newly set up ... in Back-lanes, Corners and suspicious places'.[82] In the London of the 1660s, streets like Cheapside, lined with fixed shops, were part of fashionable life. The rebuilding of London after the Great Fire of 1666 was used as an opportunity to regularize street design, but no attempt was made to enforce a plan wholly orientated towards the markets. Instead the act for the rebuilding of London designated four categories of street, each regulated according to width of carriageway and standards of building. Shops were apparently expected only in the 'high and principal streets', but not in the 'By lanes' or 'streets and Lanes of Note', presumably because these were less open to public scrutiny.[83]

Suspicion of retailing from fixed shops may have discouraged the movement of such outlets away from the marketplace, where a shopkeeper could use his fixed premises more or less for warehousing and use a stall in the street on market day for trade, like any other stall holder. It may also have encouraged the survival of the hybrid shop, where most sales took place through an unglazed shop window to passers-by in the street. However, there is evidence for the continued use of the open window at least until the end of the eighteenth century, long after writers and government had ceased to promulgate the market as the ideal. It seems probable, therefore, that there were other reasons, such as customer preference, for perpetuating what might appear to have been an archaic practice.[84]

It is impossible to say whether these concerns, and governmental action to enforce them, delayed the development of select shopping areas away from the market, or the redesigning of some shops to exploit fully the advantages of glazing. It seems unlikely. Shopkeepers

who benefited from the association with the market were no doubt
unwilling to forego the advantages of selling through the window even
if they also developed other strategies for selling within the shop. On
the other hand, shopkeepers who wished to attract customers from the
social elite or to develop different selling strategies found a glazed
window and a carefully designed interior more appropriate to their
needs. Examples of both types of shop can be found in the provincial
towns of the seventeenth century no less than in London. For
example, Joshua Johnson of Wellington in Shropshire, whose estate
was appraised in 1695, had several counters suggesting sale to
customers within the shop. But he also had a lattice for the window,
whether for security or for the display of goods is not clear, suggesting
sale through the open window. Markedly different is the shop
belonging to his contemporary, Richard Motley of Newport,
Shropshire, who died in 1709. The interior of his shop, with its desk
and drawers, cane chairs, silk cushions, looking-glass and pictures, was
designed for a style of shopping in which customers browsed, selected
and purchased in comfort and at leisure. Although there can be no
proof, surely such valuable fittings were protected from the weather
by glazed windows.[85]

Another practice of retailers, disliked by many, was the use of
credit. This was seen as a form of lending upon usury, which,
following biblical teaching,[86] was discouraged. In fact, most shop credit
in the early modern period was quite unlike modern hire purchase and
did not, at least openly, involve the payment of interest. Overt
concern about the possibilities of abuse surfaced in the late sixteenth
century and was directed against the shop book, that is, a record of
debts owing to the shopkeeper and made by him.[87] Evidence
concerning the medieval practice is scant, but by the late sixteenth
century surviving probate records reveal the emergence of the shop
book as a genre of credit distinct from personal loans.[88] No doubt this
method of recording the day-to-day debts of customers was open to
abuse, and such debts fell uncomfortably between those recoverable at
law (because there was an authenticated written record) and those not
so protected. Parliament acknowledged the problem in 1609,
perceiving it as one for the customer who might be charged a second
time by careless bookkeeping or fraudulent practice. The act laid down
that the shop book could only stand as evidence for a debt for one
year unless there was 'a Bill of Debt' – an unlikely eventuality for
much shop credit.[89] Although by imposing a time limit on the
recovery of debts recorded in the shop book, the act appeared to
increase the difficulties of shopkeepers and their executors or
administrators, this may not have been the case. For the first time the
shop book was recognized, albeit with qualifications, as a legitimate

record of debt; an interesting example of government interference having unlooked-for consequences.

As late as the early eighteenth century, some writers were still inveighing against the use of credit. For example, Charles Davenant claimed that credit, having 'existence only in the mind of man, nothing is more fantastical and nice ... it hangs upon opinion; it depends upon our passions of hope and fear'.[90] Such views were increasingly out of tune with current opinion and practice. For example, Daniel Defoe, writing in 1726, took a more neutral view of credit as a necessary evil. He accepted the tradesman 'that takes credit may give credit,' but warned that 'he must be exceedingly watchful, for it is the most dangerous state of life that a man can live in'.[91] His views seem to have accorded with those of parliament, which by the mid-eighteenth century was prepared to legislate on small debts. From 1750 a series of private acts, each relating to a particular town or district, was passed by parliament to facilitate the collection of small debts and to protect the well-intentioned small debtor from the rigours of the existing law. The earliest noted acts were for Westminster and Tower Hamlets in 1750, and over the next 25 years some 20 more were passed covering large towns like Liverpool and Birmingham, county towns like Shrewsbury, Exeter and Canterbury and places like Old Swinford and the Holland district in Lincolnshire.[92] In 1807 such acts were extended to cover all debts up to £5.[93] However, even in these acts, parliament seems to have been at least as concerned to assist the 'poor honest Persons', who were 'obliged to contract Small Debts' as they were to protect the tradesman whose business was threatened by those who could not, or would not, pay.

The imperatives of business nevertheless seem to have required retailers to give credit, however poorly the practice was protected by law.[94] The experience of Thomas Turner, an eighteenth-century Sussex shopkeeper, epitomizes the reason why retailers used credit and the dangers of so doing. The saga began in 1758 as he contemplated the default of one of his long-standing customers:

> Oh what a confusion and tumult there is in my breast about this affair! To think what a terrible thing it is to arrest a person, for by this means he may be torn to pieces, who might otherwise recover himself ... But then ... some of this debt hath been standing above 4 years ... I have tried very hard to get it these two years, and cannot get one farthing. They have almost quite forsaken my shop ... but every time they want anything of value, they go to Lewes.[95]

Clearly credit as a means of encouraging sales and fostering the loyalty of a customer had broken down, and Turner did eventually go to law to recover the debt of £18. However, four years later, after a bill of sale, a bond given as security and countless visits, he had still not recovered £16 of it.[96]

Although prejudice against trade and tradesmen really only began to dissolve in the late seventeenth century, there was one solitary sixteenth-century voice challenging the orthodoxy of the day. The anonymous 'great Marchant Dives Pragmaticus' had no uncertainty about the value of trade. Not for him the moral anxieties expressed by Philip Stubbs, nor even the economic concerns of W. S. or Thomas Mun. Instead, Dives declared that 'Now truly for to bye and truly to sell, Is a good thyng' and 'Both God and man, in it doeth delyght'. Indeed, he claimed that 'God the great gever of vertue and grace, hath planted man here ... to bye and to sell.'[97] Probably Dives was referring to overseas trade, with which the term 'Merchant' was usually associated, and in this his encomiums were in line with those of Mun a century later, when he wrote of 'The Qualities which are required in a perfect Merchant of Forraign Trade' and of 'the nobleness of this Profession', claiming that the Merchant could 'worthily be called The Steward of the Kingdoms Stock'.[98] Equivalent praise for those involved with internal trade was slower in coming, and then at first only for a select few.

In the 1670s and 1680s anxieties about the number of shopkeepers, and their usefulness to the community, provoked a rash of pamphlets offering solutions to the problem. The most popular was to corral all tradesmen into the towns and to oblige them to belong to a trade association, rather along the lines of the system in force in Stockholm, though not apparently inspired by it.[99] 'H. N., Merchant in the City of London' started in a similar vein; there were too many shopkeepers.[100] However, rather than tarring the whole retail sector with the same brush, as others had done, he supported what he perceived as the respectable end of the internal market. At least the 'mercers, and haberdashers, vinteners and grocers' so disliked by W. S. contributed something to the common weal; they payed taxes and rents, took local offices, kept 'good Houses, relieved the poor at their door, and bought meat for which they payed in ready money'. Since their status and probity, he believed, was already established and protected to some extent by entry through apprenticeship, he suggested, among other proposals, that this requirement should be extended to all retailers.[101] His arguments were more cogently laid out than those in some of the other pamphlets and they represent an early recognition on economic grounds of the value of retailing and distributing, even if the corollary was the supposed existence of a murky lower end of the trade, which must be regulated and controlled, if possible to extinction.

Although writing just prior to H. N., the anonymous 'real and hearty Lover of his King and Countrey' developed further ideas about the potential value of internal trade. His response to the question of what he would do against the 'multitude of Trades-men' was unequivocal: encourage more and by competition increase the total wealth:

> Do not some of our Trades-men spend one or two hundred pounds a year, whose parents never saw forty Shillings together of their own in their lives? Doth it not make the Capons and the Custards go off at a good rate? Doth it not mightily encrease his Majesties revenue, by Customs, Excise, and Chimney-Money? Doth it not make a tax light, by having many Shoulders to bear the burden?

He thus extended to all the riffraff in trade the benefits accorded by H. N. only to the established retailing tradesman of the town. His vision of the future was of 'six times the Traders and most of their Shops and Ware-houses better furnisht than in the last Age', with 'many of our poor Cotagers children ... turn'd Merchants and substantial Traders'.[102]

Daniel Defoe went even further. In *The Complete English Tradesman*, first published in 1726, he entitled one of his concluding chapters, 'Of the inland trade of England, its magnitude, and the great advantage it is to the nation in general.'[103] His language verged on the ecstatic. This inland trade was, he averred, 'the wonder of all the world of trade' and by 'this prodigy of trade, all the vast importation from our own colonies is circulated and dispersed to the remotest corner of the island, whereby consumption is become so great'.[104] The final link in the chain from producer or importer through to the consumer was the retailer, so that 'in every town, great or little, we find shopkeepers, wholesale or retail, who ... hand forward the goods to the last consumer.' The chain stretched from London to the 'great towns' and from thence to the 'smaller markets' and even to the 'meanest villages ... every body here trades with every body' so that it was impossible to calculate the number of shopkeepers – 'we may as well count the stars'.[105] For all its exaggerations, Defoe's analysis re-emphasized two significant concepts: firstly, that a flourishing internal market encouraged consumption; and secondly (though this was not made so explicit), that consumption contributed to the nation's wealth.

The final defeat of prejudice against the retail sector came with Adam Smith's theoretical exposition of the cost of distribution. Since this was an element in the price of any commodity, there was no merit, rather the reverse, in the long-cherished model of the producer dealing directly with the consumer. This form of distribution would be inefficient, since the responsibility for it lay in the hands of the producer whose skills and capital ought to be devoted to production.

In arguing thus, Smith acknowledged the positive contribution to the national economy of retailers and the network of distribution, since it was they who ensured that commodities came to the consumer most efficiently and at least cost.[106]

Conclusion

Substantial shifts in moral, economic and political thinking during the early modern period have been observed and analysed by historians, and it has been widely recognized that these shifts severally and combined played their part in facilitating the development of a consumer culture in Great Britain and Europe from 1650 onwards.[107] What has less often been acknowledged is the hostile intellectual and regulatory environment in which retailing tradesmen had to operate during the sixteenth century and much of the seventeenth. Anxieties about the moral and political dangers of luxury and about a balance of payments perceived as unfavourable gave rise to a stream of polemical literature and a formidable body of restrictive legislation. A long-standing belief in the virtues of the open market may have discouraged, but certainly did not prevent, the development of fixed-shop retailing, while a perception of the dangers of credit, though not of its advantages, led to legislation favourable to the purchaser rather than the seller.

It is not possible to assess how far changes in thinking and in governmental action were instrumental in fostering the development of the retail sector during the eighteenth century, though it seems probable that the two were linked, if only indirectly. The consumer culture described in many texts was undoubtedly underpinned by an active and innovative retail sector. Yet the possible effects of a hostile intellectual climate and restrictive action by the authorities in the first half of the early modern period remain unexplored and the evidence elusive. Daniel Defoe's eulogy affirming that the inland trade was 'the wonder of all the world of trade', with outlets in even 'the meanest villages' postulated a very active retail sector in the early eighteenth century, at a time when shifts in the intellectual climate can hardly have made themselves felt. Adam Smith's more sober analysis of the contribution made by retailers, written some 50 years later, suggests that Defoe had been either wildly optimistic or merely prophetic. Common-sense persuades us that the hostile environment must have retarded the development of the retail sector, but the evidence supporting this is rarely, if ever, objective.[108] Much work still needs to be done to investigate the link – if any – between an expanding and innovative retail sector and the shift in attitude from hostility to recognition by government and by influential thinkers like Mandeville, Defoe and Smith.

Notes

[1] Anon., *Britannia Languens, or a Discourse on Trade* ... (printed for Tho. Dring, London, 1680), reprinted in John R. McCulloch (ed.), *A Select Collection of Early English Tracts on Commerce* (Political Economy Club, London, 1856), p. 301. The author was possibly William Petyt (1636–1707), author of *Jus Parliamentarium* and Keeper of the Records at the Tower of London.

[2] This chapter further develops ideas first explored in the author's *The Complete Tradesman: A Study in Retailing, 1550–1820* (Ashgate, Aldershot, 2000).

[3] Henry Peacham, *Minerva Britanna or a Garden of Heroical Devises, Furnished and Adorned with Emblems and Impressa's of Sundry Natures* (Walter Dight, London, 1612, modern edition by Scolar Press, Menston, 1973). Discussed in Michael Bath, *Speaking Pictures: English Emblem Books and Renaissance Culture* (Longman, London, 1994), pp. 100–1, which contains an extensive study of emblems and their place in early modern thought. Henry Peacham (1578–1643?) was a schoolmaster and probably a courtier in the entourage of Prince Henry, the ill-fated eldest son of James I. Emblem books, which comprised collections of symbolic images coupled with epigrammatic texts, were much used to teach the young.

[4] For a longer exposition on the history of attitudes to luxury, see Christopher Berry, *The Idea of Luxury: A Conceptual and Historical Investigation* (Cambridge University Press, Cambridge, 1994).

[5] Berry, *The Idea of Luxury*, chapter 2, particularly p. 51.

[6] *Ibid.*, pp. 65, 67, referring to Seneca, *Epistles*, no. 65, Horace, *Epistles*, no. 1.2 and Diogenes Laertius, *Life of Zeno*.

[7] Jane Austen, *Pride and Prejudice* (J. M. Dent, London, 1900, first published 1812), particularly vol. I, pp. 8, 57.

[8] Berry, *The Idea of Luxury*, chapter 3, particularly pp. 72, 84–5. The control of excesses of the table was not a feature of early modern regulations in this country.

[9] *Ibid.*, p. 89.

[10] Paul's second Letter to Timothy, chapter 3, verses 2–6. Authorized Version.

[11] Some of these issues are further explored in Elizabeth Kowalski-Wallace, *Consuming Subjects: Women, Shopping and Business in the Eighteenth Century* (Columbia University Press, New York, 1997); Maxine Berg and Helen Clifford (eds), *Consumers and Luxury: Consumer Culture in Europe, 1650–1850* (Manchester University Press, Manchester, 1999).

[12] Philip Stubbs, *The Anatomie of Abuses, Contayning a Discoverie or Briefe Summarie of such Notable Vices and Imperfections, as now Raigne in Many Christian Countreyes, but especiallie in this realme of England ... Verie godly to be Read of all True Christians* ... (1581), modern edition, Frederick J. Furnivall (ed.), New Shakespere Society Publications, series VI, no. 4 (1877), particularly pp. 33, 44, 51. Philip Stubbs (*fl.* 1581–1593) was a Puritan pamphleteer.

[13] For a full account of the acts and proclamations regulating apparel, see Negley B. Harte, 'State control of dress and social change in pre-industrial

England', in D. G. Coleman and A. H. John (eds), *Trade, Government and Economy in Pre-Industrial England* (Weidenfeld & Nicolson, London, 1976), pp. 132–65.

[14] Paul L. Hughes and James F. Larkin (eds), *Tudor Royal Proclamations* (Yale University Press, Newhaven, 1964–9), no. 601. Quoted in Harte, 'State control of dress', p. 138.

[15] 1 JAC1 c 25 (1604).

[16] *House of Commons Journal*, vol. III, p. 449, quoted in Harte, 'State control of dress', p. 61.

[17] I have adopted the gendered term 'tradesmen' because that matches my sources. Writers appear to have seen shopkeepers as exclusively male, though there were female shopkeepers throughout the period. Curiously enough, women probably constituted a large proportion of the small shopkeepers so disliked by many writers, but they do not appear to have become a focus of direct concern.

[18] Probate inventories, respectively INV 5.139, Norwich Record Office, and calendared under 1580, Lichfield Joint Record Office.

[19] 5 ELIZ c 6 (1562).

[20] Silk manufacture in London was supposedly protected by acts such as 33 HEN6 c 5 (1455/6) 'for the encouragement of Silkwomen and Throwsters'.

[21] See Beverly Lemire, *Fashion's Favourite: The Cotton Trade and the Consumer in Britain, 1660–1800* (Oxford University Press, Oxford, 1991), pp. 3–21, for a further discussion of dress.

[22] Nicholas Barbon, *A Discourse of Trade* (printed by Tho. Milbourn for the author, London, 1690), modern edition, J. Hollander (ed.), (John Hopkins Press, Baltimore, 1905). Nicholas Barbon, M.D. (1640?–1698), was instrumental in setting up the first fire insurance office in London after the Great Fire of 1666, and was one of the projectors for the short-lived National Land Bank.

[23] Bernard Mandeville, *The Fable of the Bees, or Private Vices, Public Benefits* (printed for J. Roberts, London, 1714), modern edition, Philip Harth (ed.), (Penguin Books, Harmondsworth, 1970). Harth gives a history of this complicated and much altered text. Bernard Mandeville (1670–1733) was a Dutch physician who moved to England. He is largely known for *The Fable*. His un-English background may have contributed to the horror with which his ideas were received by some in this country.

[24] *Ibid.*, pp. 68–9. The poem itself, entitled 'The grumbling hive', was first published in 1705, but was subsequently incorporated in *The Fable*.

[25] *Ibid.*, Remark L, particularly pp. 136–7.

[26] For discussions of the background to Mandeville's ideas and the reactions to them, see Berry, *The Idea of Luxury*, chapters 5 and 6; Berg and Clifford (eds), *Consumers and Luxury*, Introduction.

[27] *Boston Gazette*, 17 November 1747. Quoted in Timothy H. Breen, 'The meaning of things: interpreting the consumer economy in the eighteenth century', in J. Brewer and R. Porter (eds), *Consumption and the World of Goods* (Routledge, London, 1993), p. 255.

[28] *The Good of the Community Impartially Considered* (1754), pp. 18–9. Quoted in Breen, 'The meaning of things', p. 258. Breen does not name the

author.

[29] Henry Homes, Lord Kames, *Sketches on the History of Man* (printed for J. Williams, Dublin, 1779, first published 1774), pp. 63–4, 473–4, 477. Quoted and discussed in Berry, *The Idea of Luxury*, pp. 175–6. Lord Kames (1696–1782) was a Scottish gentleman, who wrote extensively on law and jurisprudence.

[30] Adam Smith, *The Wealth of Nations* (J. M. Dent, London, 1910, first published 1778), vol. II, pp. 351–2. Adam Smith (1723–1790), was a Scottish philosopher and economist and Professor of Moral Philosophy at Glasgow University from 1752.

[31] Mary Douglas and Baron Isherwood, *The World of Goods: Towards an Anthropology of Consumption* (Allen Lane, London, 1979), p. 98, show that such reservations have continued into this century with some economists still implying that 'expenditure on luxuries is slightly immoral'.

[32] Adam Smith, *Theory of Moral Sentiments* (printed for A. Millar, London, 1759). Discussed by Neil De Marchi, 'Adam Smith's accommodation of "altogether endless desires"', in Berg and Clifford (eds), *Consumers and Luxury*, pp. 18, 19.

[33] Barbon, *A Discourse of Trade*, pp. 13–14; see also Berry, *The Idea of Luxury*, pp. 108–11.

[34] Smith, *The Wealth of Nations*, vol. I, pp. 150, 149. Smith's ideas are further explored by De Marchi, 'Adam Smith's accommodation'.

[35] *MSS Burns Journal*, folio 203, London Metropolitan Archives. Quoted in Joan Thirsk, *Economic Policy and Projects: The Development of a Consumer Society in Early Modern England* (Clarendon Press, Oxford, 1978), p. 176. A transcript of the manuscript appears in Negley B. Harte, 'The economics of clothing in the late seventeenth century', in N.B. Harte (ed.), *Fabrics and Fashions: Studies in the Economic and Social History of Dress* (Pasold Research Fund, London, n.d. c.1986), pp. 277-96, appendix pp. 293-4. A 'busk' is a piece of stiffening passed down the front of a corset or, as is probably meant here, the garment itself.

[36] It is inappropriate here to set out at length the evidence on the luxury market in the early modern period. Recent works on this subject include Ann Bermingham and John Brewer (eds), *The Consumption of Culture: Image, Object and Text* (Routledge, London, 1995); Berg and Clifford (eds), *Consumers and Luxury*.

[37] A band was a collar or ruff worn round the neck, often ornamental. Pepys apparently wanted his to be of lace.

[38] Samuel Pepys, *Diary of Samuel Pepys F.R.S. Secretary to the Admiralty in the Reigns of Charles II & James II* (J. M. Dent, London, 1906), respectively, 5 April 1661, vol. I, p. 145; 19 October 1662, vol. I, p. 296; 1 May 1669, vol. II, p. 682.

[39] *Ibid.*, 1 July 1660, vol. I, p. 78.

[40] Robert E. Lane, *The Loss of Happiness in Market Democracies* (Yale University Press, New Haven, 2000), p. 4.

[41] *Ibid.*, chapter 4, particularly p. 76.

[42] Barrie Trinder and Jeff Cox, *Yeomen and Colliers in Telford: Probate Inventories for Dawley, Lilleshall, Wellington and Wrockwardine, 1660-1750*

(Phillimore, London, 1980), pp. 23–4, 314–21.

[43] Kenneth Morgan (ed.), *An American Quaker in the British Isles: The Travel Journals of Jabez Maud Fisher, 1775–1779* (Oxford University Press, Oxford, 1992), pp. 282–319.

[44] Thomas Mun, *England's Treasure by Forraign Trade, or the Balance of our Forraign Trade is the Rule of our Treasure* (printed by J. G. for Thomas Clark, London, 1664), reprinted in McCulloch (ed.), *A Select Collection of Early English Tracts on Commerce*, p. 125. An earlier work by Mun is discussed below. Thomas Mun (1571–1641), was a noted merchant and a Director of the East India Company.

[45] W. S., *A Compendious or Brief Examination of Certayne Ordinary Complaynts of Divers of our Country Men in These our Dayes: which although they are in Some Part Uniust and Friuolous yet they are All by VVay of Dialogues Throughly Debated and Discussed* (printed by Thomas Marshe, London, 1581), reprinted as Elizabeth Lamond and William Cunningham (eds), *Discourse of the Common Weal of this Realm of England* (Cambridge University Press, Cambridge, 1929). The work has also been attributed by various authors to William Stafford, John Hales or Thomas Smith.

[46] *Ibid.*, particularly pp. 91, 125, 129.

[47] Respectively State Papers 12/8, no. 31 (1559) and Lansdowne MSS 8/17 (1565), both Public Record Office, London. They were collated into a single list in Thirsk, *Economic Policy and Projects*, pp. 181–5.

[48] Monopolies of mining and production were granted to the Company of Mines Royal and the Company of Mineral and Battery Works by Royal Charters in 1568. For a history of these companies, see Henry Hamilton, *The English Brass and Copper Industries to 1800* (Frank Cass, London, 1967, first published 1926), chapters 1–3; Maxwell B. Donald, *Elizabethan Monopolies: The History of the Company of Mineral and Battery Works from 1565 to 1604* (Oliver & Boyd, Edinburgh, 1961).

[49] For example, playing cards were on the list of 'Unnecessary Wares', but the government also encouraged their home manufacture. See Thirsk, *Economic Policies and Projects*, pp. 49–57. Thirsk discusses the use of patents of monopoly and outlines the whole history of governmental support for home industries by the Tudors and Stuarts. See particularly chapters 2–4.

[50] For example, 22 EDW4 c 3 (1482) 'preventing the importation of silk manufactures'. It was renewed several times, but imports continued to find their way in.

[51] William H. Woodward, *A Short History of the Expansion of the British Empire, 1500–1902* (Cambridge University Press, London, n.d., c.1902), pp. 71–3. The imports of one of the other companies, the Levant Company, formed in 1581 to trade with Turkey, Syria and Egypt, were to some extent balanced by exports of kerseys and other textiles; Ralph Davis, *English Overseas Trade 1500–1700* (Macmillan Press, London, 1973), pp. 18–19.

[52] Mun, *England's Treasure*.

[53] T. M., *A Discourse of Trade, from England unto the East-Indies* (printed by Nicholas Okes for John Pyper, 1621), reprinted in McCulloch (ed.), *A Select Collection of Early English Tracts on Commerce*, pp. 1–48. T. M. was a thinly disguised pseudonym for Thomas Mun.

[54] *Ibid.*, p. 3.

[55] For example, Anon., *England's Great Happiness: or a Dialogue between Content and Complaint wherein is Demonstrated that a Great Part of our Complaints are Causeless* (printed by J.M. for Edward Croft, London, 1677), reprinted in McCulloch (ed.), *A Select Collection of Early English Tracts on Commerce*, pp. 259–60. The work is usually attributed to John Houghton (1640–1705). He was a member of the Royal Society and best known for the weekly letters published from 1692 to 1703, later collected and revised by Richard Bradley as *Husbandry and trade improv'd: being a collection of many valuable materials relating to corn, cattle, coals, hops, wool, &c.* (printed for Woodman and Lyon, London, 1727).

[56] 11 & 12 GUL3 c 18 (1700) and 7 GEO1 statute 1 c 7 (1720).

[57] T. M., *A Discourse of Trade*, pp. 9–10.

[58] *Ibid.*, pp. 8–9. Many of these goods came from France, the trade with which was later to attract particular odium, as outlined below.

[59] The earliest noted was 33 HEN6 c 5 (1455), and the latest 5 GEO3 c 48 (1765).

[60] 9 & 10 GUL3 c 9 (1698). The act led to retaliatory measures by France and was repealed in 11 & 12 GUL3 c 11 (1700).

[61] 11 & 12 GUL3 c 18 (1700).

[62] 7 GEO1 statute 1 c 7 (1720).

[63] Carole Shammas, *The Pre-Industrial Consumer in England and America* (Clarendon Press, Oxford, 1990), pp. 83–5.

[64] 24 GEO3 session 2 c 38 (1784). The act applied only to customs duties; the burdens of Excise remained.

[65] Lewes Roberts, *Treasure of Trafficke, or a Discourse of Forraigne Trade wherein is shown the Benefit and Commoditie arising to a Commonwealth or Kingdom, by the Skilfull Merchant, and by a Well Ordered Commerce and Regular Trafficke* (printed by E. P. for Nicholas Bourne, London, 1641), reprinted in McCulloch (ed.), *A Select Collection of Early English Tracts on Commerce*, pp. 58, 76. Lewes Roberts (1596–1640) was a merchant and a member of both the Levant Company and the East India Company. He is better known as the author of *The Merchant's Mappe of Commerce*, published in 1638.

[66] Samuel Fortrey, *England's Interest and Improvement consisting in the Increase of the Store and Trade of this Kingdom* (printed for Nathaneal Brook, London, 1673), reprinted in McCulloch (ed.), *A Select Collection of Early English Tracts on Commerce*, pp. 231–4. Samuel Fortrey (1622–1681) was a Gentleman of the King's Bedchamber. He is known almost entirely for this influential tract, which did much to raise and perpetuate prejudice against trade with France.

[67] Anon., *England's Great Happiness*, pp. 260, 262.

[68] Malachy Postlethwayt, *Britain's Commercial Interest Explained and Improved in Series of Dissertations on Several Important Branches of her Trade and Police* (printed for D. Browne, London, 1757), reprinted in facsimile (Augustus M. Kelly, New York, 1968), vol. II, pp. 394–5. Malachy Postlethwayt (1707?–1767) was a well-known mercantilist writer.

[69] *Ibid.*, pp. 368, 371.

[70] Smith, *The Wealth of Nations*, vol. II, p. 154.

[71] *Ibid.*, vol. II, p. 155.

[72] Berry, *The Idea of Luxury*, p. 56.

[73] But see Randle Holme, *Academy of Armory* (printed for the author, Chester, 1688), book III, p. 69. His attributes of a gentleman included manly and honourable behaviour in battle. Randle Holme (1627–1699) was a noted antiquary and heraldic painter, who made a huge collection of documents, which now form part of the British Library Harleian collection.

[74] Postlethwayt, *Britain's Commercial Interest*, vol. I, p. 245. The terms 'commerce' and 'foreign negoce' here may cause confusion to the modern reader. Postlethwayt was viewing England as an exporter of agricultural produce rather than as the importer it was to become in the following century.

[75] Quoted in Thomas S. Willan, *The Inland Trade: Studies in Internal Trade in the Sixteenth and Seventeenth Centuries* (Manchester University Press, Manchester, 1976), p. 50.

[76] Anon., *Britannia Languens*, p. 301.

[77] W. S., *A Compendious and Brief Examination*, pp. 91, 125, 129.

[78] Anon., *Britannia Languens*, pp. 289, 301–2.

[79] James A. Brundage, *Medieval Canon Law* (Longman, London, 1995), pp. 75–6, 237–8.

[80] John Gilchrist, *The Church and Economic Activity in the Middle Ages* (Macmillan, London, 1969), pp. 59–61.

[81] For example, by exempting from regulation goods sold in the open market, as in 23 ELIZ c 8 (1581) (bees wax) or by prohibiting sale anywhere but the open market, as in 6 HEN8 c 9 sect 3 (1514) (coloured wool and yarn).

[82] 7 EDW6 c 5 (1553).

[83] 19 CAR2 c 3 section 14 (1667).

[84] For example, the Customer Ledger of William Wood, 1786–91, piece number MS F942, Manchester Public Library.

[85] Both from the archive of probate records at Lichfield Joint Record Office. For a discussion of shop design, see Claire Walsh, 'Shop design and the display of goods in eighteenth-century London', *Journal of Design History* 8/3 (1995), pp. 157–76.

[86] Deuteronomy, chapter 23, verse 19.

[87] It may be that similar anxieties contributed to the restrictions placed on the use of credit in the sale of some goods to customers of inferior status. See note 19.

[88] The earliest recorded is the entry of 'Such Sperat dettes as were owinge ... as appereth by the shoppe bokes' in the inventory of Thomas Harrison, girdler of Southampton, 1554 (B wills 1554/126–7, Hampshire Record Office, Winchester), in Edward Roberts and Karen Parker (eds), *Southampton Probate Inventories, 1447–1575*, Southampton Records Series XXXIV (1992), pp. 53–61. It should not be assumed that this is the first noted instance of shop debts as such. Few inventories survive for retailers before 1550, so conclusions on earlier practice must be tentative.

[89] 7 JAC1 c 12 (1609).

[90] Charles Davenant, *The Complete and Commercial Works*, edited by Charles Whitworth (printed for R. Housfield, London, 1771), vol. I, p. 151. Quoted in Berry, *The Idea of Luxury*, p. 121. Charles Davenant (1656–1714) was a Commissioner of Excise, an MP and a political pamphleteer.

[91] Daniel Defoe, *The Complete English Tradesman* (Alan Sutton, Gloucester, 1987, based on the 1839 edition, first published 1726), particularly pp. 48–9, 71, 188. Defoe (1660–1731) was an English novelist, pamphleteer and journalist, who is probably best known as the author of *Robinson Crusoe*.

[92] All private acts, respectively 23 GEO2 c 27 (1750) Westminster; 23 GEO2 c 30 (1750) Tower Hamlets; 25 GEO2 c 43 (1752) Liverpool; 25 GEO2 c 45 (1752) Canterbury; 26 GEO2 c 34 (1753) Birmingham; 13 GEO3 c 27 (1773) Exeter; 17 GEO3 c 19 (1777) Old Swinford; 17 GEO3 c 32 (1777) Holland district; 23 GEO3 c 73 (1783) Shrewsbury. Each act set up a 'Court of Requests' in the town, composed usually of the mayor and several named commissioners, who were to sit regularly and deal with claims of less than £2.

[93] 47 GEO3 session 1 c 4 (1806–7).

[94] For a fuller discussion of shop credit, see Cox, *The Complete Tradesman*, chapter 5, particularly table 5.1.

[95] Thomas Turner, *The Diary of Thomas Turner, 1754–1765*, edited by David Vaisey (Oxford University Press, Oxford, 1984), 22 May 1758, p. 149.

[96] *Ibid.*, 4 and 6 July 1762, p. 252.

[97] Dives Pragmaticus, *A booke in Englysh metre, of the great marchaunt man called Dives Pragmaticus* (1563), reprinted in facsimile (Manchester University Press, Manchester, and Bernard Quaritch, and Sharratt and Hughes, London, 1910), Preface, lines 28–31.

[98] Mun, *England's Treasure*, chapter 1, particularly p. 122.

[99] A brief description of the Swedish system was given by Mats Fagerberg, in 'Traditional retailers and innovative manufacturers in the hardware market of Stockholm in the 1880s', unpublished paper presented at the 'Petty Traders and Captains of Commerce, 1500–2000: Retailing and Distribution' conference, University of Wolverhampton, 13–14 September 2000. For a typical exposition of the proposal to corral all tradesmen into towns, see Anon., *The Trade of England Revived: and the Abuses Thereof Rectified in relation to Wooll and Woollen-Cloth, Silk and Silk-Weavers, Hawkers, Bankrupts, Stage-Coaches, Shopkeepers, Companies, Markets, Linnen-Cloath; also what Statutes in Force may be Injurious to Trade and Tradesmen, with Several Proposals* (printed for Dorman Newman, London, 1681), reprinted in Joan Thirsk and J. P. Cooper (eds), *Seventeenth-Century Economic Documents* (Clarendon Press, Oxford, 1972), pp. 389–403.

[100] H. N., Merchant in the City of London, *The Compleat Tradesman or the Exact Dealers Daily Companion: instructing Him Throughly in All Things Absolutely Necessary to be Known by All Those who would Thrive in the World and in the Whole Art and Mystery of Trade and Traffick* (printed for John Dunton, London, 1684), p. 1.

[101] *Ibid.*, pp. 17–26.

[102] Anon., *England's Great Happiness*, pp. 251–74, particularly pp. 270–1.

[103] Defoe, *The Complete English Tradesman*, chapter 22.

[104] *Ibid.*, p. 223.

[105] *Ibid.*, pp. 225–30.
[106] Smith, *The Wealth of Nations*, vol. II, pp. 28–32.
[107] For example, Berg and Clifford (eds), *Consumers and Luxury*.
[108] For example, the cries of anguish from shopkeepers against the proposals to introduce a shop tax in the 1750s and the 1780s are discussed in Hoh-Cheung Mui and Lorna H. Mui, *Shops and Shopkeeping in Eighteenth Century England* (Routledge, London, 1989), chapter 4.

CHAPTER 2
SOCIAL MEANING AND SOCIAL SPACE IN THE SHOPPING GALLERIES OF EARLY MODERN LONDON
Claire Walsh

Introduction

In this chapter I analyse the shopping galleries of early modern London as a particular retail phenomenon. The first section considers the factors that made the galleries so popular and distinct from other retail outlets of the period. These factors include the architectural design of the galleries and their management by owner-entrepreneurs, which affected, in particular, consumers' sociability and movement inside the galleries. The second section considers the interpretation of the galleries by those who visited them, and shows how consumers were able to extend their use of these spaces beyond the objectives of managers and retailers, and to create venues that were more important for leisure and sociability than for shopping. I argue that while retailers could offer particular narratives about the retail site and the goods sold, these only became meaningful to consumers once they had been mediated by the consumers' own narratives and values. The shopping galleries of the early modern period provide an example of co-agency between retailers and consumers, rather than a confirmation of the power of retail manipulation.

The shopping gallery of early modern London was a distinctive retail format, which gained a similar iconic cultural significance in the retail landscape of the period, as did the department store of the nineteenth century.[1] Shopping galleries were not simply a phenomenon of London, but appeared also in Paris, Antwerp, Prague and Amsterdam, where they were usually associated with the city's stock exchange or law courts, and were renowned as elite shopping centres. These galleries were covered shopping areas, purpose-built and designed, and containing a large number of different shops lined along walkways. The shops sold different types of goods, but of a high and fashionable quality, and were frequented by the upper levels of society. The shopkeepers paid high rents for a position in what were the most fashionable and expensive shopping locations in London. Shoppers could roam freely around the stalls, taking in the displays and the varieties of goods, without any obligation to buy. The manner of leisurely promenading and self-display characteristic of visitors to the galleries is captured in the term 'walk' applied to the rows of shops.

From the seventeenth to the early eighteenth century London possessed five shopping galleries: the Royal Exchange, built in the heart of the City of London in 1568 and rebuilt after the great fire of London, opening again to shopkeepers in 1671; Westminster Hall, situated outside the City of London and the site of the principal law courts, whose central hall had been lined with shops since the sixteenth century; the New Exchange, built in 1609 to compete with the Royal Exchange, and pulled down at its decline in fashionability in 1734; Exeter Exchange, built in 1676 on the back of the late surge in popularity of the New Exchange and declining from around 1710, although the building itself survived into the nineteenth century; the Middle Exchange was likewise built in the wave of commercial optimism created by the resurgence of the New Exchange in 1676, but suffered from competition from the nearby Exeter Exchange and was pulled down in 1694. These last three were all built in close proximity to one another on the Strand. It has been possible to accumulate some information about the Royal and New Exchanges, but very little is known about the other three.[2] The number of shopping galleries in London in the late seventeenth century was a reflection of the capital's ever-increasing wealth, as well as of a spirit of competitive commercialism, responding to the evident initial success of the Royal Exchange.

The shopping galleries of early modern London were so successful that they were included in itineraries of guidebooks and appeared in poems and as the settings of innumerable plays of the period.[3] The Royal Exchange was referred to in the 1630s as 'the Eye of London',[4] and was the resort of businessmen, who visited the trading floors and the shops, and of wealthy female shoppers, providing a complete range of goods directed at both genders. Westminster Hall was seen to cater predominantly for the male shopper, with its preponderance of bookshops and stationers. The galleries on the Strand were particularly associated with fashionable merchandise and female shoppers,[5] and the New Exchange in particular, in its heyday, was associated with elite women, as a sociable rendezvous and fashionable promenade, containing shops stocked with wares aimed specifically at female shoppers to a greater degree than other galleries.

Like the department stores of the nineteenth century, despite their iconic status, shopping galleries were not the only places where people could shop. This chapter will investigate why people were particularly drawn to the shopping galleries, why such an enormous cultural emphasis was placed on these sites, and how retailers and consumers developed and used these distinctive spaces.

Retail design

In all the galleries, the shops were smaller and structurally more limited than shops on the street. They consisted of a simple wooden frame and wooden partitions that could be put up by a joiner. Uniform in nature, they could not support much decoration, and were really simply frames for the containment and display of goods, with wooden shutters to lock them up at the end of the day like a fair booth or bulk[6] (Figure 1). In comparison with the extensive decoration and display possibilities of upmarket shops on London's key shopping streets, the design potential of the gallery shops was very limited. Upmarket shops in London deployed up-to-the-minute styling in their facades and interiors, incorporating classical columns or gothic arches as leading fashions dictated. Signs, fascia boards and window displays were used to hallmark a particular shop and establish its market level. Mouldings, gilding, display cases and extensive glazing were necessary features of interior design, as well as elaborate furnishings such as padded chairs, sconces, curtains, mirrors and pictures for ambience and customer comfort.[7] Unlike street-fronting shops, the galleries did not have a shop facade as such, and while attempts were made to differentiate the uniform wooden frames, little could be done because of the flimsy nature of the structure. Thus shops that were uniform in size and appearance were mainly distinctive through their wares and sales staff, a principle that went against the modern retail strategies of their street-fronting counterparts.

In addition, the availability of space sharply differentiated gallery shops from their street-fronting counterparts. While shops on principal streets would commonly be at least 10 to 15 ft in width, with the depth dependent on the amount of internal space put to retail use, extending to as much as 40 or 50 ft in the eighteenth century (without including storage space),[8] the dimensions of the gallery shops were considerably less. The shops on the ground floor of the New Exchange were recorded as being only 5 1/2 ft deep,[9] and their width was probably around 6 ft, creating frontage longer than the depth.[10] The first floor shops may have been the same size or even smaller,[11] and the first tenants complained of 'the shopps being, as it were, smale chests rather than shopps'.[12] Customers could not enter the shops in Westminster Hall. They merely consisted of a counter behind which

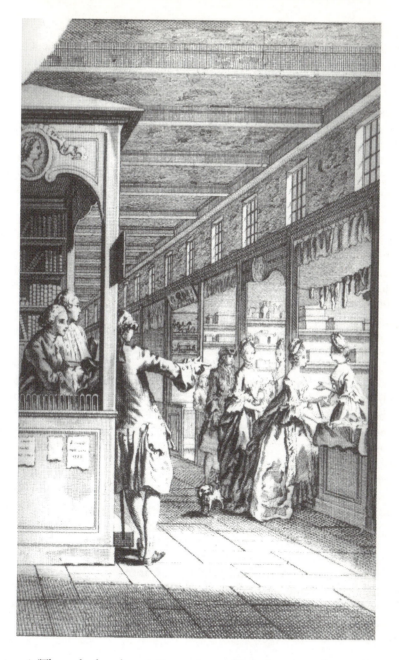

Figure 1 'The unlucky glance'. Engraving attributed to Gravelot, and said to represent the New Exchange. Originally published in *Town and Country Magazine*, 1772.
Reproduced by permission of Guildhall Library, Corporation of London.

stood the shopkeeper and a press of wares, which was perhaps less extensive than the goods a market stall might have displayed (Figure 2). In all the gallery shops storage space would have been at a premium, and in those that planned to draw customers inside, space for sales staff and customers would have been very limited.

Despite their popularity then, the shops within the galleries were shadows of their street-front counterparts. So why did the shopping galleries attract retailers and customers alike so successfully? An important element of their success was the fact that each (with the exception of Westminster Hall) was purpose-designed as a shopping gallery, and that all (including Westminster Hall) benefited from the prestige and grandiosity of the buildings they were housed in.[13]

The Royal Exchange was developed by Sir Thomas Gresham and was based on the idea of the Antwerp Exchange, which also contained a shopping gallery. Both pre- and post-fire exchanges possessed a dramatic arcaded entrance to the courtyard that housed the merchants' trading floor. The design of both pre- and post-fire facades were commented on as examples of modern design, and were meant to impress and convey status. Nathan Bailey's guide to London of 1722, for example, described the rebuilt facade as the best in Europe.[14] Sweeping staircases lined with carvings, moulded work and statuary led to the upper shopping walks.[15] Shopkeepers approved of these, as they would be 'for the more state and magnificence of the said place (wch would be also very commodious for the Shop-keepers, in relation to their Customers)', though they would have preferred four staircases rather than two, as shops did particularly good trade at the staircase heads.[16] Balconies were built into the post-fire shopping floor so that customers could look down onto the trading activity below them, increasing the drama of the overall space. Above the walkways were large glazed windows allowing light to fall not only on the shops and walks, but also on the structure vaulting this enormous space, supported by columns. Guide books and tourist accounts commented on the interior structure and drama of the building. A French visitor described it in 1685: 'On two sides of this main entrance ... two very large stone staircases descend which lead above to the arcades. This upper level is made up of four double galleries, where there are 190 shops filled with haberdashery, gloves, linen-drapery.'[17] A French guidebook of 1693 advised tourists to see it as part of their very first visit on arrival in London:

> On the upper floor there is a very beautiful and rich Exchange filled on all sides with all sorts of curious wares for sale and 4 beautiful balconies from where you can see the people in the Bourse below ... as you go down, you see at the foot of the two beautiful staircases two

Figure 2 'Westminster Hall: the first day of term'. Engraving by Mosely, eighteenth century.
Reproduced by permission of Guildhall Library, Corporation of London.

doors through which you can enter into the vaults below the Bourse.[18]

As no other shopping area and few other buildings at the time provided such an impressive and grandiosely decorated space, the impact of the galleries on their visitors must have been comparable to that of department stores' entrance halls, or that of the great Italian shopping arcades of the late nineteenth century. The galleries took on the same cultural iconic status within the city as did the department stores and arcades; all three were distinctive as retail structures and as urban constructions, and were central to contemporary discourses about consumption and urban prestige. It is important to emphasize, however, that despite the renown and distinctiveness of the galleries in the retail landscape, compared with the number of shops, stalls, bulks, markets and established shopping streets, they were, like the nineteenth-century department stores, very few in number, forming only a minimal percentage of retail activity.[19] Yet historians and social theorists have tended to concentrate on the department store to the exclusion of other retail outlets, without considering consumers' familiarity with a range of establishments, and without considering what was different (or similar) about the experience of shopping in the new outlet.[20]

The space for perambulation and the way it was carefully handled was central to the way the galleries worked. Westminster Hall was the smallest of the galleries, accommodating only 69 shops. However, these were situated within a massive, elaborately decorated and roofed hall, the 'hall of Rufus', built in the late eleventh century, a tourist attraction in its own right, and thought of as the nation's most magnificent and historic building.[21] It possessed enormous glazed windows, and the walls were hung round with royal coats of arms and ancient banners.[22] The fact that there were two lines of shops along each wall emphasized the space for sociability between them.

The New Exchange was based on a very similar plan to the Royal Exchange and sought to emulate it in style, format and commercial success. Like the Royal Exchange, the New Exchange was a two-storied building, whose lower floor was entered through immense arcading. It deployed the new classical style, and Inigo Jones was considered at one point for its architect, indicating the importance accorded to a fashionable appearance.[23] The final design echoed that of the Royal Exchange, with the facade punctuated with niches and statuary, the whole of the street front faced in stone, and the arcade floor lined in black and white marble.[24] Both galleries made use of the modern classical style throughout, and expensive stone paving was laid down on the street in front of both buildings.[25] Though the New Exchange was built in a long rectangle rather than a square, sweeping staircases at either end copied those at the Royal Exchange and led up to the upper shopping floor. This was a lofty, immensely long gallery, lined with purbeck marble. As with the other galleries, large high windows, here marked with the royal and Salisbury family coats of arms, emphasized the size of the structure.

It was the surrounding space that made an impact on visitors to the galleries, with the shops a part of that impression. Gallery managers were willing to make considerable investment to upgrade their interior fitting and accentuate the sense of space. In 1639 £1030 was spent on structural alterations to the main shopping floor at the New Exchange, which included a central balcony, large new windows and re-roofing.[26] With the growing commercial success of the New Exchange came the developments of Exeter Exchange and the Middle Exchange, both, significantly, built on the site of, or within, aristocratic mansions.

Their developers intentionally exploited the buildings' aristocratic origins and style, in the same way that the retailers renting shops there utilized the architectural renown of Westminster Hall. Jouvin de Rochefort described Exeter Exchange in 1676 as 'a sort of palace, adorned with numerous columns, large doorways, distinguished by decorations and statues'.[27] François Colsoni noted of it in 1693 that 'on the uppermost floors there are ongoing auctions of excellent paintings, and below numerous beautiful shops with all sorts of fashionable items for the convenience of the ladies'. In his opinion the Middle Exchange was 'not much different from the Royal Exchange in terms of its grandeur and its riches, as there are as many shops on the upper levels as below which are just as beautiful as precious, where the Ladies can be found buying their millinery'.[28] A guidebook of 1790 still recalled Lord Shaftsbury's London house, Exeter House, as the site of the gallery, despite the fact that it had ceased to operate 70 years earlier and the building had been demolished: 'on its site was erected Exeter-exchange. It had been a very handsome pile with an arcade in front, a gallery above, and shops in both.'[29] These ancient aristocratic mansions were reborn in a new commercial form, carrying with them their prestigious associations, and providing the architectural statements and grandiose space that were necessary to create a shopping palace from a row of wooden booths.[30]

The shopping gallery was designed to symbolize nobility and grandeur. Shops on London's most expensive shopping streets, taken in combination, produced an effect of wealth and fashionability that foreign visitors remarked on, but these shops had individually designed frontages that fought for distinction, rather than achieving the uniformly styled appearance of the shopping galleries. The aim of the lavish architectural planning of the shopping galleries, in contrast, was not to accentuate the individual shops within it, but to suggest that the site as a whole had a unified character and an ambience of wealth and distinction. Gallery shops were not even allowed to use the shop signs that were such crucial distinguishers on the streets outside.[31] It was the overall design – the incorporation of individual shops into a single concept – that created the impression for visitors that they were somewhere special. Instead of being presented with a choice of different shops, as on a shopping street, they could grasp this environment as a unit that surrounded them with atmosphere and status, and of which they partook simply by being there. This superimposed atmosphere of grandeur and fashionability on an overwhelming scale was unavailable to other shopkeepers. The large upmarket shops of the city enclosed their customers in their own individually constructed retail world, producing their own drama, but the galleries subordinated individual retail experiences to offer a single sensation of grandeur.

Glazed windows appeared in the street-fronting shops of London's principal streets from the late seventeenth century, providing seclusion from the bustle and social mix of the street, while still allowing personal display. But in the galleries the principle of seclusion through glazed shop windows (such an imperative for upmarket shopkeepers) was turned on its head. In the gallery, the absence of glazing created a sense of immediacy for customers, which worked with the smallness of the shops and the narrowness of the walks, and a sense of intimacy with the sales staff and goods, which could not have been achieved on a busy street. This sense of intimacy must have been greatly accentuated if the customers entered the shops, which, from contemporary comment, it seems they did.[32] The appeal of such intimacy to customers must have been considerable. In the galleries, because of the restrictions on space, the customer was very much the focus of the shopkeeper's attention, and also the focus of the attention of the social elite passing along the walks such a short distance away. Personal display was heightened by the intimacy of the gallery's internal layout and by small, shallow, single-storey shops, while personal prestige was heightened by its overall grandiose design. While glazed shops offered seclusion, they could not match the intimacy and visibility provided by the galleries. In a scene set in the New Exchange in Sir George Etherege's 1676 play, 'The Man of Mode; or Sir Fopling Flutter', both Dorimant, a young beau, and Harriet, a young, sensible gentlewoman, accuse each other of attracting and enjoying the glances of the opposite sex, the mall being the place to elicit them. Dorimant exclaims, 'I know y'are greedy of the praises of the whole Mail.'[33]

The difference in the environmental arrangement of the galleries also made a difference to customers' sense of movement. In the gallery, the shopper did not move along a street that branched out into many other streets, lined with stylistically differentiated shops, choosing at certain points to enter and be enveloped by the strategically designed interior of a single shop. Instead, customers were contained in a single enclosed space, experiencing a flow of goods displayed in undifferentiated shops that blended into a single perception of fashionability and richness; they were channelled by the interlinked walkways in a circular path without destination. This reordering of movement, space and experience created a kind of perambulation that was not experienced on the street or inside a street-fronting shop. It gave the impetus towards more leisurely movement, to a roaming that was not about discovering the city, but about idly absorbing its amassed and finest products. Four of the galleries (with the exception of Westminster Hall, which was arranged on an open plan) deployed the arrangement that was called by retailers and managers a 'double pawn'. This consisted of two parallel rows of shops, back to back, creating two narrow parallel walks, increasing the number of shops that could fit in the space available, and channelling the visitor round in a never-ending circle, as the end of one row turned seamlessly into the next. It is notable that on the rebuilding of the Royal Exchange after the fire, the committee wished to maintain the structure of double pawns all round the four sides of the building, despite the petitions of shopkeepers, who argued for larger, deeper shops.

The lofty exclusiveness intended at the Royal Exchange was summed up in a poem of 1668, which envisaged two young ladies strolling in the gallery, enjoying 'Upon a Summers day / The Walks above amidst the throng'.[34] The inner row of shops, which allowed visitors to gaze down on to the trading floor below, was the most popular.[35] The idea of being distant from the busy world of trade and money added to the associations of leisure and sociability connected with the galleries. The galleries may also have drawn on associations with the long galleries or picture galleries built in aristocratic houses from the Renaissance onwards as areas to walk in, talk and consider aesthetics. Certainly, they were more akin to the long galleries in their structure than to any other commercial building or leisure site that existed at the time. Moreover, the terms applied to the passages between the shops in guidebooks and travel accounts, such as 'walk' or 'gallery', and 'mail' or 'mall' for the site itself, emphasized these elite associations and the idea of promenading. Such terms embodied the ways visitors used the rows of shops, rather than the way retailers (who used the word 'pawn') saw them. They were terms that emphasized an understanding of these spaces as being primarily about leisure, rather than about shopping.

The galleries of the early modern period, like the department stores of the nineteenth century, established themselves as distinct from other shops. Although there were differences in the respective sizes of the galleries, each was clearly identifiable as a shopping 'gallery', because each adhered to the gallery format. They were different from conventional shops in a homologous way. Gallery developers either believed that the identity of the new leisure and commercial site pioneered by the Royal Exchange was too well-established to be interfered with, or they were too uncertain of which factors contributed to the galleries' success to start to diverge too much from the functioning model.

Across the five galleries the uniformity of format is clear: in each, the shops were simple wooden structures, subordinate in their decoration to the surrounding building. Throughout, the shops were kept small and unglazed. The four galleries with 'walks' used the 'double pawn' arrangement.[36] All the galleries sought to create the effect of both a bazaar and a promenade. The key shopping floor of the galleries was on the first floor, benefiting from extra light and from associations with the precept of aristocratic reception rooms (the exception was Westminster Hall, which only had one floor, but the same principles of light and dramatic space were sustained).[37] The shopping floors in all these establishments were both large and spanned by a single roof, creating a single cohesive space. In each, aristocratic connections were signalled.

Galleries successfully established themselves as distinct from street-fronting shops, and their real competition lay with other galleries rather than with other shops.[38] Speculators and retailers at the Royal and New Exchanges constantly made alterations to the internal appearance of the buildings and the arrangements of shops in order to maximize trade, but they were reluctant to deviate from the overarching format once its success was established.[39] Visitors to the galleries likewise knew what was meant by, and what to expect from, one of the new Strand 'exchanges', which had absolutely nothing to do with the stock exchange.

Social meaning and social use

The exclusivity of the galleries was managed by the buildings' owners or by management committees, who were able to dictate which trades could set up shop. The visibility of artisanal production was not an issue for high-class London shops in this period, as sales areas had already been divided off from production areas, and many shops in any case sold bought-in stock, rather than making their own.[40] But in any shopping street a mix of retail outlets could develop, which might place a butcher, who flung down waste products in the street, next to a china seller retailing valuable porcelain produced in the Orient. The gallery managers had the opportunity to exercise total control over the retail environment, and this they did, laying down complex regulations for retailers' behaviour and the control of waste and noise, in order to maintain an atmosphere of politeness and refinement to a degree that was not possible outside. Most relevant was the control of the type of merchandise sold in the galleries. Retailers were confined to the sale of luxury products, such as high-quality textiles, apparel and haberdashery, perfume, jewellery, china and books. The regulations of the New Exchange specified not only luxury, but also fashionable goods, restricting the retailers to haberdashers, stocking-sellers, linen-drapers, seamstresses, goldsmiths, jewellers, milliners, perfumers, silk mercers, tiremakers, hoodmakers, stationers, booksellers, confectioners, girdlers and those who sold china ware, pictures, maps and prints.[41]

The enclosed structure of the galleries meant that social exclusion operated more effectively than elsewhere. Unlike the open street, where a range of people might be attracted by the different kinds of retail outlet, and where everyone could walk, even if they might feel uncomfortable about entering a particular shop whose goods were beyond their means, the shopping galleries signalled their codes of social acceptability at their grandiose entrance portals, aiming to deter those who were considered socially inappropriate from entering not just the shops, but the shopping area itself. Together with the intimidating effects of styling and reputation, beadles were employed by the galleries to discourage undesirables from entering, in the same way that they were used in the arcades of the nineteenth century.[42]

In fact, the full range of early modern society, eager for betterment and new experiences, was not totally kept out of these sites. However, social elites read into these sites an air of exclusivity that they wished respected, even if in practice it was not. Sir George Etherege used such values to comic effect in his portrayal of four tradesmen ruffling the sensibilities of the gentry strolling in the New Exchange in 'The Man of Mode':

Sir Fopling: ... there never was so sweet an evening.
Belinda: 'T has drawn all the rabble of the town hither.
Sir Fopling: 'Tis pity there' not an order made, that none but the *beau monde* should walk here.
Mrs Loveit: 'Twould add much to the beauty of the place: see what a sort of nasty fellows are coming.
Enter four ill-fashioned Fellows singing, "Tis not for kisses alone', &c.
Mrs Loveit: Foh! Their periwigs are scented with tobacco so strong -
Sir Fopling: It overcomes our pulvilio - methinks I smell the coffe-house they come from.
First Man: Dorimant's convenient [mistress], Madam Loveit.
Second Man: I like the oily buttock with her.
... all of them coughing; exeunt singing.[43]

The enclosed structure of the galleries contributed to an elite atmosphere and a social cachet akin to an exclusive club, which appealed to consumers used to thinking about the shopping-cum-promenading behaviour of the galleries in terms of personal display. Belinda in 'The Man of Mode' preferred the type of display she could make in the New Exchange to that on a shopping street: 'I hate to be hulched up in a coach; walking is much better.'[44] In the early modern period, the role of socializing was inherent within the activity of shopping for both men and women. However, the management of the galleries facilitated socializing further, and enhanced its effect, making the galleries places simply to go to in order to pass time and meet people. This applied to both genders, with the

Royal Exchange and Westminster Hall having a bias towards male sociability, while the New Exchange – a place of social rendezvous for both sexes – was seen as geared towards female consumption because of the range of merchandise sold there.[45]

In their heyday, all the guidebooks to London, of every nationality, referred to the Royal Exchange and to the Strand galleries, even when they did not necessarily make any mention of the shops on the principal streets of the city; the galleries were considered sites to be visited in their own right (the Royal Exchange and Westminster Hall specifically because of their architecture), and came to stand for London shops and shopping in general.[46] The richness of the wares on sale and the number of shops were emphasized, without reference to shop size – the gallery shops were perceived, or recorded, as shops rather than as booths or stalls.[47] The early guides mentioned the shops of London's shopping streets as part of the description of the wealth and status of the city, without specifically leading the reader to them. But the galleries appeared on specific itineraries, as sites that should be visited as part of acquiring knowledge and experience of London.[48] They featured as prominent landmarks in the city, and this explains why they were mentioned in guidebooks long after they had ceased to function as shopping galleries.

The fashionability of the galleries was established by a combination of the quality and type of merchandise sold, the architecture, the air of social exclusivity, a regular wealthy clientele and, over the years, growing mystique. The role of the galleries as the most fashionable rendezvous in the city was recognized by the guidebooks and tourist accounts. Samuel de Sorbière remarked in 1664 that the area of town around the Royal Exchange, 'where I fixed appeared to me by much the best, because 'tis that which is frequented by our Countrymen, and also by People of Quality, and is the Finest and most Regular Building in London'.[49] *The Foreigner's Guide* of 1729 directed the tourist to the New Exchange, 'a large Building consisting of two large Walks full of Mercers and Milleners Shops, where the Ladies may be provided with all Things according to the newest Fashion'.[50] A German guide of 1706 called it 'the New Exchange or the Fashionable Exchange'.[51] Contemporaries recognized that the fashionability of the merchandise could be conveyed as much by its location as anything else. A verse from 1723 compared the New Exchange with the Royal Exchange, but considered that at the New Exchange the goods were made even more fashionable, because this was the place 'Where all Things are in Fashion'.[52]

The shopping galleries of the early modern period relied on a fairly small group of people with time and money to spend and who revelled in the social cachet and social connections that could be played out in such a small, contained environment. In 'The Man of Mode', young Bellair idly commented of the New Exchange, 'Most people prefer High Park to this place.' Harriet rejoindered, 'It has the better reputation I confess: but I abominate the dull diversions there, the formal bows, the affected smiles, the silly by-words, and amorous tweers, in passing; here one meets with a little conversation now and then.'[53] From the 1660s the Royal Exchange was the resort for Restoration fops,[54] and it was the socially distinct atmosphere of the place that allowed it to be used by certain social groups, such as the fops, to make statements about their lifestyles that would have been lost in the social melting-pot of the street.

For the social elite as a whole, however, the shopping galleries became places where it was proper, and perhaps necessary, to be seen. Visiting the galleries became a leisure event appropriate to a certain station in life, and was one enactment in many different leisure possibilities used to maintain that station. Lady Mary Wortley Montagu, in her poem 'Toilette', woke in the morning and wondered how to spend her day. She decided against going to chapel and instead: 'Strait then I'll dress, and take my wonted range/ Thro' India shops, to Motteux's, or the Change.'[55] Shopping at the galleries appealed to the varied social demands of an elite group who were eager to be feted by the galleries' exclusive atmosphere, and conversely, their frequenting of the galleries meant that these spaces came to carry strong social meanings. A space can come to signify a whole sector of human activity, with its appropriate dress, gestures and decorum, though that activity has to be generated by the users, within an appropriate space, rather than being imposed on them by architects or managers. But once such a site has generated a particular range of social meanings, continued use reasserts these: loyalty to a place means loyalty to its values, and vice-versa.

Other leisure opportunities in early modern London were numerous, and many used the same strategies of aristocratic associations and suggestions of elitism as did the galleries. They were certainly thought of in the same connection. In William Wycherley's comedy 'The Country Wife' of 1675, Mrs Pinchwife was newly arrived in London and wanted to know what there was to do in the city. 'Mrs Pinchwife: Pray, Sister, where are the best Fields and Woods, to walk in in London? Alithea: A pretty Question; why, Sister! *Mulberry Garden*, and *St James's Park*; and for close walks the *New Exchange*.' They then went on to discuss the theatres of London.[56] The galleries were not exceptional sites; they grouped together with assemblies, pleasure gardens, theatres and promenades, which also carried strong social meanings for their users. And like other commercial leisure sites such as the theatres or pleasure gardens, they were encroached on by members of the lower classes exactly because of their claims to entertainment and refinement and their easy accessibility.[57]

There was one way, however, in which the galleries did subtly differ from these other related sites. Theatres and pleasure gardens were commercially managed leisure sites, while the galleries, although they were also commercially managed, aimed not to provide for the consumption of leisure, but for the consumption of goods within a leisure context. This was also the case for those high-class shops on shopping streets that used leisure as a sales tactic. But in these shops consumers could not operate with the same kind of freewheeling sociability enabled in the galleries. In contrast with other shops, the heightened leisure context of the galleries was a distinctive feature, and in contrast with other leisure sites, it was the purchasing context that was distinct. Consumers, always immensely adaptable, probably took easily to the galleries, despite their newness, because of the familiarity of their associations with established patterns both of retailing and of leisure and sociability. The distinctions between the galleries and other retailing and leisure sites were probably of little concern or relevance to them.

This provides us with an important clue to the power of consumers in early modern London. That the galleries were so renowned as a social rendezvous indicates that visitors saw them as primarily about socializing (as opposed to primarily about shopping). In 'The Man of Mode', Dorimant, the young beau, detains Lady Woodvill at the New Exchange by telling her: 'Tis now but high Mail madam, the most entertaining time of all the evening.' And to Mrs Loveit he comments:

> Dorimant: I hope this happy evening, madam, has reconciled you to the scandalous Mail we shal have you now hankering here again -
> Mrs Loveit: Sir Fopling will you walk -
> Sir Fopling: I am all obedience madam -
> Mrs Loveit: Come along then – and let's agree to be malicious on all the ill-fashioned things we meet.
> Sir Fopling: We'll make a critick on the whole Mail madam ... We'll sacrifice all to our diversion.[58]

Even when inside a street-fronting shop, people did not necessarily make any purchases, but were at least potential consumers. Inside a gallery, however, people were not even necessarily potential consumers, but simply visitors. The social elite of early modern London were not only willing to transfer socializing to the new venue of the gallery that appeared on their everyday horizon, but were also able to extend its use to their own ends, rather than to be entirely managed by the aims of the retailers and speculators who set it up.

Michel de Certeau, in *The Practice of Everyday Life*, counters the orthodoxy (particularly found in writing about the department store and the shopping mall) that sees the shopper as the passive victim of retailers' and planners' strategies of management and manipulation. Instead, he calls for the recognition of consumers' ability to take control of retail settings by the use of their own subversive 'tactics'. He believes that there has been 'too much emphasis on strategies of control and too little emphasis on tactics.'[59] In particular, de Certeau highlights consumers' practices of reappropriating space for purposes that exceed those of designers. Such consumer tactics may indeed have been employed in the early modern period, although no evidence survives to us. However, de Certeau's concept of tactics only envisages consumers subverting the retail system for their own, and entirely different, ends from those of retailers and planners.

In the case of the shopping galleries of the early modern period, this chapter suggests instead the application of sociability (users' ends) to a retail site *beyond* its intention, rather than its subversion in a completely different direction. This could only happen because the galleries functioned (and intended to appeal) by providing a superior leisure facility to that of an ordinary shopping street. Therefore, rather than subversion, this uncommercial use of a commercial space came about through the nexus of both visitors and retailers, rather than as the result of the power of one side or the other. As Meaghan Morris has said of the shopping mall, management organizes and unifies the site and provides aesthetic control, but this does not mean that managers succeed in managing either the total spectacle or the responses it provokes.[60]

However, although the galleries had a very strong profile and reputation, and enormous appeal as a leisure environment, we know they were also used for shopping as well as for socializing, because retailers traded there successfully. How, then, did the early modern shopper negotiate the discourse of the galleries in order to make a purchase? Did shoppers abandon shopping skills and experience acquired on an everyday basis in the vast range of London's retail outlets once they entered the heady atmosphere of the galleries? As theorists of the department store have claimed, did the glamour of the retail environment dupe the galleries' customers into unwise purchases?[61]

The high profile of the shopping galleries among the city's shopping options does not mean that the wealthy and socially aware only shopped at the galleries and not elsewhere. Samuel Pepys recorded how different locations could be used depending on what was wanted:

> So home to dinner, and thence by coach to the Old Exchange, and there cheapened [haggled down the price of] some laces for my wife, and then to the great laceman in Cheapside, and bought one cost me £4, more by 20s than I intended, but when I came to see them I was resolved to buy one worth wearing with credit.[62]

Pepys made the choice to go to Cheapside when he wanted to buy his own lace, and was not averse to spending more outside the Royal Exchange than in it. The Royal and New Exchanges had the most renown and were the most fashionable shopping sites in London in the period, and though enjoyable to frequent, this does not necessarily mean they were known as the best places to shop. Many users of the galleries, like Pepys, would have been cautious about when to buy there and when not.

In particular, the small size of gallery shops meant that they contained only a limited stock, and shops elsewhere, especially on the surrounding key shopping streets, had a much greater range to offer, and probably more specialized expertise from a larger number of staff. Alison Adburgham suggests that some shops in the galleries were merely branch shops of larger shops elsewhere in the city (and usually manned by a female relative of the shopkeeper).[63] This seems possible, considering that in the eighteenth century successful London retailers sometimes had a branch shop in Bath, benefiting from the seasonal trade there.[64] The practice of keeping a branch shop (although it is uncertain how widespread this was) would have made sense, providing retailers with a fashionable profile in the gallery and a contact point to channel customers to their larger shop. This form of advertising would have redressed to an extent the disadvantages of having such a small space for stock in the gallery shops. The customers would have approached a branch shop in the gallery with a different understanding: they were not now entering a shop with a small stock to choose from, but a shop where a choice selection of the best had been made from a much larger stock. In many cases the limitation of stock may well have sent consumers elsewhere – I argue for the capacities of consumers to reason (though their reasoning may often be very personally or emotionally based and defy conventional economic 'rational' behaviour), and to differentiate between the discourse of fashionability and quality surrounding the gallery shops and their practical limitations. Consumers such as Pepys would have been capable of choosing the moment when to go for selectivity and when for a broader range. The contemporary characterization of the galleries was that they were used for the purchase of fancy items, for light browsing or impulse buys. Equally, this did not mean that the shopping galleries could not be used for quality and considered purchases when it suited customers, once they had built up their knowledge of what was available there.

Nigel Thrift's understanding of the concept of social knowledge can be applied to the process of shopping: as well as the ability to build up banks of knowledge about different shops, shoppers are also able to establish the standing of different shops as a part of their store of 'social knowledge'.[65] While they would not all have entered the galleries, many Londoners would have known of their standing within the range of retail outlets in the city. Consumers would have gained knowledge that placed shops and shopping sites in particular orders empirically, by a constant process of visiting and testing. They compiled, organized and circulated this knowledge within society, so that attributions and meanings were shared.[66] The meanings associated with particular shopping sites must have been generally known, even if most people could not enter the shopping galleries or would not want to spend time looking in the shop windows on Cheapside. It would have been this social knowledge, or rankings of shops and sites, which helped consumers make the range available to them manageable. But these hierarchies would not have been rigid, and not necessarily adhered to by individuals, and they would have been numerous and overlapping. On any shopping trip consumers could create different hierarchies under different criteria, depending on their changing shopping needs.

In all probability, those who did buy in the shopping galleries knew that they were paying high prices for fashionable association, and chose to do so because they wished to indulge in that particular experience at that moment in time, or could afford to do so. And it should not be denied that shopping had a value as an experience, and not simply as a means of acquiring something. Purchasing could occasionally be motivated by the enjoyment of joining in with the sheer drama of the situation. To purchase on a regular basis, however, there had to be some other motivation for the visitor to the gallery to become a customer. This brings us to the problem of how the connection was made between the atmosphere of the gallery and the goods the consumer saw and bought. How were social cachet and fashionable reputation conveyed on to the goods themselves – or rather, how did the consumer perceive that this was what took place?

Many sociologists of consumption have assumed that the important factor in shopping is the relationship between a person's identity and the goods they choose, the one being able to be read from the other. This means that shoppers' motivations for acquiring fashionable goods should be interpreted as a striving for a fashionable identity or lifestyle. This theory asserts that consumers will buy any goods defined as fashionable – a definition created in the modern period by manufacturers and advertisers and in the early modern period by retailers. This parallels the orthodoxy of retail historians studying the department store and the shopping mall, where an overarching emphasis is placed on the power of the retail environment to convey a lustre directly onto the goods for sale, making them irresistible, although it is not explained how this process of transference takes place. This once again places the power over consumers' purchasing decisions in the hands of advertisers and retailers. In his discussion of the shopping mall, Daniel Miller argues instead that 'identities are multiple, contested and discursively constituted through narratives of the self, constructed in relation to socially significant others and articulated through relations with particular people, places and material goods.' Miller calls for the focus to shift away from an assumed direct interaction between consumers and place or presentation, which supposedly 'makes' people select certain goods. Of greater interest, he considers, is the way that different groups of shoppers construct different discourses and narrative identities, as they relate to particular types of goods, in particular kinds of places.[67]

Comparatively little evidence survives relating to the early modern shopping galleries, so conclusions about consumers' responses to them and to the goods they sold can only be speculative. However, the case of the early modern shopping gallery presents a chance to focus on a very particular kind of retail environment, and to consider the way that networks of discourses, narratives and social relationships may operate in retail environments in general (today and in the past), rather than to fall back on assumptions about shoppers' unfettered absorption of externally produced messages.

A fairly small group of wealthy consumers was drawn to the galleries by their air of exclusivity and nobility, established through social knowledge. This group, however, would have comprised varied occupations and social backgrounds within the bracket of 'wealth'. They would have included the business community, the aristocracy, the well-to-do middling sort, young and old, male and female, fops, liberals and conservatives – small in numbers but varied in outlook. The broad narrative offered by the building and its shopkeepers was one of elitism, fashionability and wealth, yet each of these groups could interpret this in many different ways. The associations that the gallery and its staff could apply to the goods on offer were imprecise, to say the least, consisting of general suggestions of glamour and status. The visitors to the gallery were not a homogenous body, and the galleries would have been unable to tailor their 'messages' or associations to individuals or specific groups. The associations could only be tailored by the consumers themselves. If consumers wished to draw on these messages, they had to construct their own narratives in tandem with them, otherwise these messages were meaningless and ineffectual.

I argue that relationships with goods are formed by a combination of the personal, the social, the environmental and the goods themselves. Undoubtedly people would have been predisposed to examine and buy more expensive goods by their decision to enter a renowned retail environment such as the galleries in the first place, and by the atmosphere they encountered once inside. My conjecture is that atmospheres of grandeur or exclusivity would not so much transform people's perceptions of the goods they bought, leading them to purchase something that appeared glamorous in the shop yet was revealed as tawdry once taken home. Rather, it would lead them to speculate on, or enlarge their thinking about, those aspects of their lives that responded to the atmosphere around them. In the light of their personal narrative operating at that moment, shoppers might purchase something slightly different or more expensive than was usual, or they might feel it was appropriate to buy an object in this location rather than elsewhere. This item would then seem suitable on arriving back home only if the consumers wished to continue the narrative they had entered into in the gallery, shop, department store or mall. If the item did not seem suitable, then the disparity between the narrative developed at the retail site and that matched with the more familiar narrative (rather than the failure of the object itself) would create a learning experience. Some customers may have strong personal narratives that are heightened by repeatedly frequenting a particular site in the same way each time, producing familiarity and contentment by shopping there. But as Miller points out, most people have multiple and continually contested narratives, and in any shopping trip these will flow and change and contradict one another, and purchases will be made at some point in this process.[68]

Most importantly, narratives of self (and purchase decisions) are constructed in relationship with socially significant others, and are not formed in isolation. It is the interrelation of context and action that produces effect, not the application of one upon the other. Miller interprets shopping malls not as places that make either passive or subversive shoppers, but as 'a part of the process by which goods communicate, and are communicated as social relationships'.[69] As Miller shows, in the modern period the act of shopping is carried out in the company of others – family or immediate social contacts – rather than, as so often is assumed in the literature on consumption and shopping, by the lone individual.[70] Not only do people shop with others, but most often they buy things for others, rather than for themselves. Shopping is not, therefore, an individualistic act of identity expression. This was likewise the case in the early modern period, more particularly so when those who lived in London or visited it would shop on behalf of friends and family elsewhere, as well as their immediate family.[71]

Purchase decisions made by early modern shoppers, and the narratives shoppers explored, were mediated and made meaningful by whomever they were shopping with and shopping for. In the shopping galleries the interpersonal significance of shopping would have been intensified. Unlike street-fronting shops, where socializing could go hand in hand with shopping, visitors to the galleries used them as sites primarily for socializing, and saw them as leisure and cultural venues more than as commercial ones. Thus, of all the places where elite consumers could make purchases, this was one with the most heightened social implications. No other shopping site was so loaded with social values. In this setting, narratives of self may have been more open to being influenced at that moment by messages about social position than in other retail environments.

It is significant, however, that these social values were constructed by social groups in society at large, rather than by retailers or managers. They were applied and developed within the galleries by the galleries' users, although retailers and commercial entrepreneurs may have channelled their physical expression. These social values were maintained in the galleries only through users' constant attendance. Such retail strategies cannot unequivocally be said to manipulate consumers, because everything within this retail environment is developed as part of an interrelated social web.

In practical terms, too, there could not have been too great a discrepancy between ambience and value for money in the galleries, and gallery shops, in the main, did provide top-quality goods and a selection of their best wares. It was undoubtedly possible for anyone, in any historical period, to fantasize about different lifestyles when shopping, but actual purchase requires some engagement with a realistic framework, such as the practicalities of financing, and use after purchase. This usually reveals the discrepancy between fantasy and possibility. The approach taken in this chapter is a bid to see the retail environment not as an all-powerful manipulator of consumers, or as merely a passive backdrop to human activity, but as an element in the interactive process by which consumers experience and understand themselves.[72]

Conclusions

The shopping gallery of early modern London was a particular retail type, distinctive among contemporary retail outlets. Large numbers of these sites could not be sustained in one centre, and their appeal was based on their distinctiveness within the range of retail sites available.

As unusual sites, they were used only periodically by consumers who were informed about and had access to a wide range of retail outlets across London.

A consideration of the way that consumers used the shopping galleries of early modern London suggests that while retailers and managers sought to use social exclusivity and renown, and to create an arena for promenading and social display in order to increase the commercial viability of the galleries, visitors themselves saw the galleries as primarily about socializing as opposed to primarily about shopping. Consumers were able to extend the use of the galleries beyond that intended by their designers. Because consumers had knowledge of a variety of other retail sites and other leisure venues, they could approach the shopping galleries with self-conscious awareness, which could include accepting high prices and small stocks as an intrinsic part of the way that the galleries met the social demands of their users. Use of the galleries carried strong social meanings, but it was the users who generated these meanings. Narratives that retailers tried to associate with the goods on sale only had relevance for consumers through their own interpretation, which could differ for each consumer or social group. The galleries enabled consumers to speculate on, or to enlarge their thinking about aspects of their lives resonant with the atmosphere, the social situation, their wider social relations and the types of goods on sale, but they could not directly manipulate the meanings consumers placed on goods.

Notes

[1] This chapter is based on part of my PhD thesis, 'Shopping in early-modern London, c. 1660–1800', unpublished PhD thesis, European University Institute, Florence (2001). I have coined the term 'shopping gallery' to characterize these sites, but they were known at the time by their individual names, such as 'the Royal Exchange', which was also known as 'the Old Exchange', or simply 'Change', and Westminster Hall, which was often referred to as 'the Hall'. These are terms used by Samuel Pepys and others. See Samuel Pepys, *The Diary of Samuel Pepys*, edited by Robert C. Latham and William Matthews (Bell and Hyman, London, 1983), vol. 10, pp. 357–8.

[2] The only works dealing directly with the history of the galleries are Laurence Stone, 'Inigo Jones and the New Exchange', *Archaeological Journal*, 114 (1957), pp. 106–21; London County Council, *Survey of London* (Ams Press, New York, 1971, first published 1937); Ann Saunders, *The Royal Exchange* (Royal Topographical Society, London, 1998). The galleries have not been considered in unison before. Other information comes from primary sources such as guidebooks, tourist accounts and contemporary comment.

[3] Plays with scenes set in the galleries include: William Wycherley, 'The Country Wife' (1675); William Wycherley, 'The Plain Dealer' (1676), both in

The Complete Plays of William Wycherley (New York University Press, New York, 1967), [Westminster Hall]; Sir George Etherege, 'The Man of Mode; or, Sir Fopling Flutter' (1676), in *The Plays of Sir George Etherege* (Cambridge University Press, Cambridge 1982), [New Exchange]; Sir Richard Steele, 'The Lying Lover' (London, 1704), [includes references to the New Exchange]. Poems that mention galleries are included in: Edward Ward, *London Spy* (London, 1698), [New Exchange]; Anon., *The Second Part of Pleasure for a Minute* (London, 1723), [New Exchange]; Anon., 'Ehver Kynd', *London's Nonsuch, or the Glory of the Royal Exchange* (London, 1668).

[4] Quoted in Henry B. Wheatley and Peter Cunningham, *London Past and Present: Its History, Associations, and Traditions* (John Murray, London, 1891), vol. III, p. 182.

[5] A greater proportion of the shops at the New Exchange sold millinery or mercery than any other merchandise. In 1708, 76 of the c. 150 shops were let to milliners and mercers. Edward Hatton, *A New View of London* (London, 1708), p. 612.

[6] This was also the case of the post-fire shops. Pepys refers to the shutters being taken down and stowed during the day. Alison Adburgham, *Shops and Shopping 1800–1914: Where, and in what manner the Well-Dressed English Woman Bought her Clothes* (Allen & Unwin, London, 1964), p. 15.

[7] For more details, see Claire Walsh, 'Shop design and the display of goods in eighteenth-century London', *Journal of Design History* 8/3 (1995), pp. 157–76.

[8] This is evident from maps and ground plans for shops in the City of London from the Comptroller City Land Deeds, Corporation of London Record Office; see, for example, James Price, Cheapside, 1746–7, and Robert Gihon, 128 Bond Street, 1795.

[9] Stone, 'Inigo Jones and the New Exchange', p. 112.

[10] I have based this calculation on the fact that when a second row of shops was added on the ground floor, it contained 30 separate shops, while the arcade was 201 ft in all.

[11] The dimensions of the upper chamber were 201 x 24 ft, and there was a double pawn of shops.

[12] Stone, 'Inigo Jones and the New Exchange', p. 117. They were complaining about the 'want of stowage'.

[13] In the case of Westminster Hall the shops were inserted into the hall, which was the chief building of the palace of Westminster. The Middle Exchange was the result of the conversion by the Earl of Salisbury of a long upper room in Little Salisbury House. The shopping area itself was therefore purpose-designed, while the building that housed it was pre-standing.

[14] Nathan Bailey, *The Antiquities of London and Westminster* (London, 1734, first printed 1722), p. 144. Samuel de Sorbière referred to it in 1664 as 'the Finest and most Regular Building in London'. Samuel de Sorbière, *A Voyage to England* (1664, translated Graverol, London, 1709), p. 14.

[15] London County Council, *Survey of London*, pp. 94–7. See also Saunders, *The Royal Exchange*, for details about the construction of the building, the trading courtyard in particular.

[16] Anon., *London's Nonsuch*; Anon., *A Brief Memorial wherein the present Case*

of the Antient Leasees ... of the Royal Exchange ... (London, 1674), p. 6, in which there was concern about the 'turning' of the north stairs. The shops nearest the stair-head were worried that they would lose trade.

[17] M. de Sainte-Marie, *Un Voyageur Français à Londres en 1685*, edited by Georges Roth (Didier, Paris, 1968), letter 4, 11 May 1685, pp. 64–5: 'Aux deux côtés de cette principale entrée dont je bous ai parlé, tombent deux très grands escaliers de pierre qui conduisent au-dessus des arcades. Ce dessus est composé de quatre galeries doubles, où il y a 190 boutiques remplies de merciers, gantiers, lingères.'

[18] François Colsoni, *Le Guide de Londres pour les Estrangers ...* (London, 1693), reprinted in facsimile (Cambridge University Press, Cambridge, 1951), p. 2: 'En la partie superieure il y a une tres belle et riche Bourse remplie tout à l'entour de toutes sortes de curieuses Marchandise à vendre & 4 beaux balcons d'ou l'on peut voir le monde qui est à la Bourse d'en bas ... quand vous en descendrez, vous verrez aux pieds de deux beaux escaliers deux portes par où l'on entre dans les voutes de dessous la Bourse.'

[19] For a recent revision of ideas about the history of the department store, see Geoffrey Crossick and Serge Jaumain, 'The world of the department store: distribution, culture and social change', in G. Crossick and S. Jaumain (eds), *Cathedrals of Consumption: The European Department Store, 1850–1939* (Ashgate, Aldershot, 1999), pp. 1–45.

[20] See, for example, Michael Miller, *The Bon Marché: Bourgeois Culture and the Department Store 1869–1920* (George Allen & Unwin, London, 1981); Rosalind Williams, *Dream Worlds: Mass Consumption in Late Nineteenth Century France* (University of California Press, Berkeley, 1982); Rachel Bowlby, *Just Looking: Consumer Culture in Dreiser, Gissing and Zola* (Methuen, London, 1985); Elizabeth Williams, *Adorned in Dreams: Fashion and Modernity* (Virago, London, 1985); Thomas Richards, *The Commodity Culture of Victorian England: Advertising and Spectacle 1851–1914* (Verso, London, 1990); Elizabeth Wilson, *The Sphinx in the City* (Virago, London, 1991); Rudi Laermans, 'Learning to consume: early department stores and the shaping of modern consumer culture 1860–1914', *Theory, Culture & Society* 10/4 (1993), pp. 79–102; Allan R. Pred, *Recognising European Modernities: A Montage of the Present* (Routledge, London, 1995); Mona Domosh, 'The feminized retail landscape: gender, ideology and consumer culture in nineteenth-century New York City', in N. Wrigley and M. Lowe (eds), *Retailing, Consumption and Capital: Towards the New Retail Geography* (Longman, Harlow, 1996), pp. 257–70.

[21] The magnificence of the building was often commented on by tourists. See, for example, Sainte-Marie, *Un Voyageur Français*, pp. 53–4. Contemporaries did not comment upon the application of modern commercial use to these ancient structures, and did not apparently see it as anomalous.

[22] The Restoration in 1660 was followed by a notable programme of repair and renovation to the hall, which included moving the courts of King's Bench and Chancery from the sides to the south end of the hall, repaving much of it, and introducing a doorway at the south end. This was followed by a thorough overhaul for the coronation. The hall was damaged by fire in 1834, after which it was used as a vestibule. Pepys, *Diary*, vol. 10, p. 358.

[23] Stone, 'Inigo Jones and the New Exchange', pp. 106–21. In the end Jones's design was probably thought too classical and thus 'un-Jacobean', but it seems likely that some of his ideas were incorporated in the final design.

[24] *Ibid.*, pp. 113–16. Alterations were made to the facade in the course of the seventeenth century.

[25] *Ibid.*, p. 116.

[26] *Ibid.*, p. 119. These changes were made when the upper floor was turned back into shops from flats, but the cost did not include joinery work for the shops, as the partitions and shop fittings were paid by the shopkeepers for a reduced 'fine', or lease fee.

[27] Jouvin de Rochefort, *Le Voyageur d'Europe* (Paris, 1676), p. 440: 'Exeter exchange, dans lequel sont des boutiques de Marchands, qui vendent ordinariement quelque chose de curieux & de rare, comme en une foire, semblable à cette petite bourse, qui est en façon d'un palais, paré de plusieurs colomnes, de grands portiques, distinguez de figures, & de statues.'

[28] Colsoni, *Le Guide de Londres*, pp. 8–9: 'au haut de la quelle il y a une Auction continuelle d'excellentes peintures, et en bas plusieurs belle boutiques de toutes sortes de choses à la mode pour la Commodité des Dames ... Poursuivez votre route le long du Strand, jusqu' à ce que vous arrivez à une autre Bourse, appellée Middle-Exchange, la quelle ne differe pas beaucoup de la Bourse Royale, tant pour sa grandeur que pour ses richesses, car il y a autant de boutiques en haut qu'en bas, aussi belles que pretieuses, où les Dames se trouvent pour acheter leurs Garnitures.'

[29] Thomas Pennant, *Some Account of London* (London, 1790), p. 148. This is also true of the other galleries; for example a Dutch guide of 1759 described the 'magnificent stone building' of the New Exchange: 'This Exchange being deserted by the Mercers and others who kept shops therein, it was taken down in the Year 1737, and is now replaced by several handsome Houses.' And of the Royal Exchange: 'The upper part of the Royal Exchange (till of late) was completely filled with shops, stored with the richest and choicest sort of merchandize; but the same are now forsaken.' Anon., *De Leydsman der vreemdelingen of, nodig en nuttig ... Wandeling door de steden Londen en Westmunster* (Dirk onder de Linden, Amsterdam, 1759), pp. 76, 114.

[30] Exeter Exchange was built by Lord Shaftsbury on the site of Exeter House (also called Burghley House). The New Exchange was built on the site of Durham House stables. The Middle Exchange was developed within Little Salisbury House. The Strand – the site of a number of galleries – was an area on which noblemen's houses had been situated since the mid-sixteenth century. Wheatley and Cunningham, *London Past and Present*, vol. III, pp. 320–1.

[31] However, they could use conventional shop names, such as The Blue Anchor, used by the bookseller Herringham at the Royal Exchange. The importance of shop signs in retailers' publicity strategies is outlined in Walsh, 'Shop design and the display of goods', pp. 27–30.

[32] Pepys recorded that counters were introduced inside shops after the fire and that the shops were much more comfortable than previously. Liza Picard, *Restoration London* (Weidenfeld & Nicolson, London, 1997), p. 140. Merchants returned to the newly built Royal Exchange in 1669, but the shops

were first opened in 1671.

33 Etherege, 'The Man of Mode', Act 3 Scene 3.

34 Anon., *London's Nonsuch*.

35 Anon., *A Brief Memorial*, p. 6.

36 Three of the galleries adhered to the structure of two walks on the ground floor and two above. These were the three purpose-built shopping galleries. Westminster Hall's gallery was only on the ground floor, and the Middle Exchange's only on the first floor. Westminster Hall presumably could not deploy a double pawn because the space also had to be used for legal business.

37 The use of the first floor and the emphasis on light and dramatic space in the galleries may have fed into the development of showrooms in London's key shops from the mid-eighteenth century. These showrooms, most often in upstairs rooms and lit by large windows or skylights, allowed the customer to browse, did not have counters and displayed their wares in a more or less domestic setting. For further details, see Claire Walsh, 'The newness of the department store: a view from the eighteenth century', in Crossick and Jaumain (eds), *Cathedrals of Consumption*, pp. 46–71.

38 There was considerable anxiety among the Royal Exchange shopkeepers at the development of the New Exchange. They feared it would draw trade away, and that the market was not large enough to sustain two galleries. The New Exchange was built very quickly, despite high labour costs, in the main to avoid a build-up of opposition from the City. During the Great Fire of London many Royal Exchange shopkeepers relocated to the New Exchange while they awaited rebuilding, and some of them remained there when it proved a profitable location. See Stone, 'Inigo Jones and the New Exchange', p. 114.

39 At various times in the post-fire Royal Exchange balconies were introduced, stairs were turned, posts were taken down and the size and numbers of shops were changed. Anon., *A Brief Memorial*, pp. 6 and 20. Internal changes to the New Exchange are mentioned above.

40 See Helen Clifford, 'Parker and Wakelin, the study of an eighteenth century goldsmithing business with particular reference to the Garrard Ledgers 1770–1776', unpublished PhD thesis, V&A/Royal College of Art (1989); Emma Packer, 'Refining the goldsmith: the London goldsmiths' trade seen through inventories 1698–1732', unpublished MA thesis, V&A/Royal College of Art (1992); Claire Walsh, 'Shop design and the display of goods in the eighteenth century', unpublished MA thesis, V&A/Royal College of Art (1993).

41 London County Council, *Survey of London*, pp. 94–7. In lean times, control over the type of merchandise sold slipped, and was commented on by contemporaries. The management control over the shops within the gallery extended to opening hours, matters of cleanliness, sanitation, the rowdy behaviour of shopkeepers and assistants, and potential shop-lifting. Stone, 'Inigo Jones and the New Exchange', pp. 116–17. These forms of control were maintained through a complex system of regulations, fines and punishments. At the New Exchange a fine of 1s a time was imposed on shopkeepers who 'throw or poure out into the walk or range or outt att any of the windowes any piss or other noysome thing'. *Ibid.*, p. 117.

[42] Beadles at the galleries were referred to in *The Spectator*, 14 October 1712.

[43] Etherege, 'The Man of Mode', Act 3 Scene 3.

[44] *Ibid.*

[45] Hatton, *A New View of London*, p. 612.

[46] For example, see Anon., *The Foreigner's Guide: or, a necessary and instructive companion ... through the cities of London and Westminster* (London, 1729). Similarly in Paris, guides concentrated on the Palais de Justice and the Palais Royal, perhaps even more to the exclusion of other shopping areas than was the case in London.

[47] Travel accounts and guides in French used the term 'boutique'; those in German use the terms 'laden' and 'boutiquen'.

[48] See, for example, Colsoni, *Le Guide de Londres*; Anon., *Die Sehens-Würdigkeiten der weltberuhmten Stadt Londen in Engelland* (Thomas von Wiering, Hamburg, 1706); Bailey, *The Antiquities of London and Westminster*; Johann Basilius Kuchelbecker, *Der nach Engelland reisende curieuse Passagier ...* (Nicolaus Förster, Hanover, 1726); Anon., *A New Guide to London: or directions to strangers; shewing the Chief Things of Curiosity and note in the city and suburbs* (London, 1726).

[49] Sorbière, *A Voyage to England*, p. 14.

[50] Anon., *The Foreigner's Guide*, p. 52.

[51] 'Die neue Exchange, oder die Alamodische Borse'. Anon., *Die Sehens-Würdigkeiten der weltberuhmten Stadt Londen*, p. 38.

[52] 'Commodities of the New Exchange', in Anon., *The Second Part of Pleasure for a Minute*.

[53] Etherege, 'The Man of Mode', Act 3 Scene 3.

[54] Dorothy Davis, *A History of Shopping* (Routledge, London, 1966), p. 125.

[55] Lady Mary Wortley Montagu, *Six Town Eclogues* (London, 1747), pp. 28–9. The 'Change' here is the New Exchange.

[56] Wycherley, 'The Country Wife', Act 2 Scene 1.

[57] For other sites, see John Brewer, *Pleasures of the Imagination: English Culture in the Eighteenth Century* (Harper Collins, London, 1997), p. 96.

[58] Etherege, 'The Man of Mode', Act 3 Scene 3. High Mail was the most fashionable time of day to visit the gallery or mall.

[59] Michel de Certeau, *The Practice of Everyday Life* (University of California Press, Berkely and Los Angeles, 1984), pp. 110–12.

[60] Meaghan Morris, 'Things to do with shopping centres', in S. Sheridan (ed.), *Grafts: Feminist Cultural Criticism* (Verso, London, 1988), p. 204.

[61] Miller, *The Bon Marché*; Williams, *Dream Worlds*; William R. Leach, 'Transformations in a culture of consumption: women and department stores, 1890–1925', *Journal of American History* 71/2 (1984), pp. 319–42; Bowlby, *Just Looking*; Wilson, *Adorned in Dreams*; Richards, *The Commodity Culture of Victorian England*; Laermans, 'Learning to consume'; Domosh, 'The feminized retail landscape'; Lisa Tiersten, 'Marianne in the department store: gender and the politics of consumption in turn-of-the-century Paris', in Crossick and Jaumain (eds), *Cathedrals of Consumption*, pp. 116–34.

[62] Quoted in Adburgham, *Shopping in Style*, p. 12, no reference given.

[63] *Ibid.*, p. 14, no reference given.

[64] Trevor Fawcett, 'Eighteenth-century shops and the luxury trade', *Bath*

History 3 (1990), pp. 52–3.

[65] 'Social knowledge' denotes the continual process of creating stocks of knowledge on which actors (who are always members of various social groups) can draw in the production of their lives and the reproduction or transformation of social groups and ultimately society. Nigel Thrift, *Spatial Formations* (Sage, London, 1996), p. 97. The application of this to shopping is explored in Walsh, 'Shopping in early-modern London', chapters 1 and 2.

[66] Thrift, *Spatial Formations*, p. 102; Walsh, 'Shopping in early-modern London', chapter 1.

[67] Daniel Miller, *Shopping, Place and Identity* (Routledge, London, 1998), p. 23.

[68] *Ibid.*

[69] *Ibid.*, p. 26.

[70] On shopping in the company of others see *ibid.*, p. 17. The model of the lone shopper arises from the concept of the *flâneur* and has fed into the history of the department store and the notion of the lifestyle shopper. See Rob Shields (ed.), *Lifestyle Shopping: The Subject of Consumption* (Routledge, London, 1992); Susan Buck-Morss, *The Dialectics of Seeing: Walter Benjamin and the Arcades Project* (MIT Press, Cambridge MA, 1989); Tiersten, 'Marianne in the department store'.

[71] Walsh, 'Shopping in early-modern London', chapter 1.

[72] See Thrift, *Spatial Formations*, p. 3: 'I take context to be a necessary constitutive element of interaction, something active, differentially extensive and able to problematise and work on the bounds of subjectivity'.

CHAPTER 3
MEN, MASCULINITIES, AND MENSWEAR ADVERTISING, c. 1890–1914
Laura Ugolini

In his best-selling novel *The Man of Property*, first published in 1906, John Galsworthy used the image of a hat, 'a soft grey hat, not even a new one – a dusty thing with a shapeless crown', to symbolize the difference between Philip Bosinney, the hat's owner, and his fiancé's family, the upper middle-class Forsytes. It was this 'significant trifle' that to the Forsytes provided 'the detail in which was embedded the meaning of the whole matter'. Bosinney's insistence on wearing a shapeless old hat not only encapsulated the problem of the young man's uncertain status as a struggling architect, but also raised suspicions concerning his moral and psychological make-up.[1]

Historians have in recent years devoted a good deal of attention to the relationship between femininity and the purchase and use of consumer goods, but have only recently begun to explore male patterns of consumption. It is in this context that Philip Bosinney's hat acquires significance beyond that of a 'trifle': the investigation of men's relationship with consumer goods – including clothing – provides new insights into masculine identities. Of equal importance is the understanding of male purchasing habits, about which we still know relatively little: to date, most attention has focused on the importance of shopping as a female activity, and on retailers' – particularly department stores'– attempts to attract women's custom.[2]

By investigating menswear retailers' press advertisements, this chapter seeks to shed some light on male consumption and shopping habits, and on their relationship with masculine identities. The purpose is not to formulate generalizations concerning menswear retailers' marketing techniques. Rather, advertisements will be considered in their role as intermediaries between the retailer and the potential purchaser, as a 'common sartorial language'[3] that encouraged and justified male consumption. The focus is on the last decade of the nineteenth and the early years of the twentieth century, and the chapter begins by exploring the models of masculinity proposed and endorsed by most advertisements, a model that was based on notions of 'gentlemanly' lifestyles. I will suggest that advertisements promised success to those men who purchased the 'correct' goods, and at the same time played on the apparently widespread desire among middle-class men to escape the confines of family and domesticity. I will also argue that advertisements proposed an undoubtedly narrow model of masculinity, a model that did not really reflect the diversity of contemporary male clothing styles and identities. Nevertheless, they derived their appeal from drawing upon widely shared understandings of the role and function of commodities (in this case, clothes) in sustaining and endorsing desirable male lifestyles. As such, they provide valuable insights into the ideals and perceptions that acted as the background against which men lived their lives and developed their identities at the turn of the century.

***

Recent historians of advertising in Britain have tended to concentrate their attention on the ways in which late Victorian and Edwardian advertisements were directed at women, in their twin role as purchasers of family goods and of goods for personal consumption.[4] Nevertheless, the enormous variety of advertisements that appeared in magazines devoted mostly to a male readership, selling 'masculine' goods, and using images of satisfied male consumers, suggests that men's spending power was targeted as strongly as women's, although possibly in different ways.[5] In a 1902 interview with the magazine *Progressive Advertising*, Jaeger's advertising manager confided that he had decided to buy space for the firm's range of men's clothing and underwear only in 'ladies' papers', since 'nowadays, ladies buy the greater part of their husbands' clothing, or, at all events, underclothing.' Nonetheless, judging by the evidence of the advertisements in the many magazines directed at a male readership, he seems to have been the exception, rather than the rule.[6]

That menswear retailers made use of advertisements, in the press and elsewhere, does not of course mean that anybody necessarily took any notice. Historians have now come to reject simplistic notions that potential customers were in a straightforward way manipulated by advertisements, or that advertisers created needs for specific goods, where none had previously existed.[7] Evidence of contemporary cynicism towards the excessive claims of advertisers is certainly not difficult to find. In his classic account of life in a Salford slum at the end of the nineteenth century, Robert Roberts described the local store's claim: '"Turpin's 10/6 Trousers Astonish the World!" ... Unamazed, we bought them – heavy, rebarbative garments that would stand erect even without a tenant.'[8] Having rejected notions of 'manipulation', however, the relationship between commercial forces and the consumer – particularly in the pre-First World War period – remains difficult to disentangle.

A useful approach to advertising is suggested by the fact that for the most part it consciously tried to present images of 'desirable' lifestyles, rather than lifestyles actually available to the majority of the population. As a contributor to *Progressive Advertising* pointed out in 1902, it was much better to use 'the ideal human nature', rather than 'the real': 'Any observant man can see that it would be absolutely futile, if not, in some cases, foolhardy, to introduce the real humanity that exists around us into his advertising.'[9] An investigation of menswear advertising, therefore, is revealing of masculine models of purchase and consumption that were generally viewed by contemporaries – including retailers and their prospective customers – as desirable. As Christopher Breward puts it:

> Advertising ... offers an indication of the codes adopted by sellers to convince potential customers that the business methods or stock of a company conformed to pre-existing expectations or would furnish the desired fashionable image. Pre-existing expectations were themselves reliant on established commercial or vernacular rhetorics that might be honed by the retailer to isolate the more idiosyncratic tastes of the local audiences.[10]

As will be seen, in the case of advertisements in the national press, the 'commercial rhetoric' assumed a considerable degree of standardization, to a far greater extent than the more local advertisements analysed by Breward.[11]

Just as potential customers could view advertisements with a degree of cynicism, and without necessarily developing a desire to purchase the commodity on offer, conversely, not all retailers were convinced of the need to advertise. Writing in his regular feature in *The Wide World Magazine*, 'The Captain' complained in 1913 that there were still too many tailors who 'consider it rather beneath their dignity to advertise'. They relied on word-of-mouth recommendations from their customers, and on the attractiveness of their windows, 'and then wonder why turnover does not increase'.[12] It was certainly the case that in the minds of many in the menswear trade at the turn of the century, advertising – particularly newspaper advertising – was associated with a lower class of trade and with cheap 'show' shops, patronized by working-men and 'would-be swells'.[13]

The notion that aggressive advertising was the province of shops selling low quality merchandise was also widespread among those not involved in the menswear trade. In the concluding chapters of Arnold Bennett's 1908 novel, *The Old Wives' Tale*, for example, The Midland Clothiers Co., part of a regional chain of stores, takes over Baines's drapery shop, a family-run and old-established shop, situated in the most exclusive shopping area of the fictional Potteries town of Bursley. The Midland Clothiers Co. proves a new departure in the staid atmosphere of Bursley's 'Square'. It erects an enormous shop sign, and covers the whole frontage with coloured posters. The front page of the local paper is plastered with advertisements, announcing the sale of 10,000 overcoats for 12s 6d each: 'The tailoring of the world was loudly and coarsely defied to equal the value of these overcoats.'[14]

In the novel, the opening of the new shop represented the culmination of a process of 'modernization' that had been gathering pace over the previous half-century, and was symbolized by changing retailing practices. The ultimate outcome of this process was the sale of cheap, poor quality items to gullible customers duped by brash advertising. The Midland Clothiers Co. was described as 'something between a cheapjack and a circus'.[15] The notion that unscrupulous advertisers were not simply vulgar, but actually intent on misleading consumers, was echoed by large sections of the menswear trade. In a letter to the tailoring journal, *The Weekly Record of Fashion*, in 1890 'Xenophon' remarked that it was no wonder that 'sloppers and outsiders' were making inroads into the tailoring trade, if one compared 'the modesty so often displayed by the good practical tailor' in his advertisements, with the 'blazing impudence' and – it was implied – the outright lying of the others.[16] According to John Glass, giving a lecture in 1889 to an organization of foremen tailors in South Shields, in recent years the tailoring trade had seen the incursion of 'an army of unscrupulous men ... greedy for gain'. They had succeeded in getting a large trade 'by deceiving the public with untruthful advertisements'.[17]

It would nevertheless be a mistake to assume that advertising was in fact limited to cheap establishments, or that it was a new phenomenon at the end of the nineteenth century. Retailers, including tailors, already enjoyed a long tradition of printed advertisements, dating back to the eighteenth century and earlier.[18] It is also clear that most complaints focused on what was seen as the misleading nature of certain advertisements, not on advertising per se. By the end of the nineteenth century, for example, the importance of window displays as a form of advertisement was generally recognized, even if it is difficult to establish the extent to which the most ambitious schemes suggested by the trade press were actually put into practice.[19] Furthermore, there is no doubt that a wide range of retailers *did* advertise in the press, both at a local and at a national level, from the most exclusive tailoring shops advertising in *The Fortnightly Review* (a monthly magazine priced at 2s 1d), to much cheaper establishments advertising in *Comic Cuts* (a popular halfpenny weekly). Therefore, the menswear advertisements analysed in this chapter, appearing in a range of national periodicals directed either at a masculine audience, or at a mixed one, include a significant cross-section of clothing establishments, appealing to widely different spending powers, from the well-to-do to the relatively impecunious. As a contemporary observed, 'There is ... no class of consumers which cannot be affected through the medium of some section or other of the press.'[20]

***

The year 1909 saw the opening of Gordon Selfridge's purpose-built London department store, following an extensive publicity campaign in the national press. There is little doubt that most of this publicity was aimed at attracting women to the store. Selfridge prided himself on his success in attracting female customers, and was said to have claimed in later years that he had opened his shop just at the time when women started to want 'to step out on their own ... they came to the store and realized some of their dreams'.[21] Nevertheless, press advertisements also stressed Selfridge's hope of gaining the reputation of 'The Man's Best Buying-Place'.[22] Unlike women, however, men were not enticed by 'the lingering pleasures of shopping'. On the contrary, men were supposed to like Selfridge's because it cut down, rather than extended, the time they had to spend shopping.[23] It was the store's 'admirably displayed' stocks of gentlemen's clothing, outfitting and other manly accessories, their high quality, and 'London's lowest prices' that was to act as a magnet for male customers.[24]

An emphasis on the qualities of the goods for the sale, rather than on the shopping 'experience' was the pattern most often repeated in menswear (and in most other) retailers' advertisements. Samuel Brothers, a London-based firm of 'merchant tailors, juvenile and general outfitters', invited prospective customers to browse in their 'spacious show rooms', where in Autumn 1895 could be found on display a 'Choice Assortment of the Most Fashionable Materials' of the season.[25] Nevertheless, advertisements usually focused on the goods, not on the pleasures of buying. A 1912 advertisement for Pettigrew & Stephens, a Glasgow department store ('one of the largest ... in the kingdom'), was echoed by numberless others in claiming that 'Their enormous trade is done on the basis of high-grade dependable goods at strictly popular prices.'[26] The selling point of mail order departments, apart from their relative cheapness,[27] was the convenience of not having to shop at all. Curzon Brothers, a firm that claimed branches in London, as well as Paris, Brussels, Liege, Antwerp, Toronto and Cape Town, stated that thanks to the detailed instructions they sent out, customers could measure themselves 'as accurately as any tailor', and could select the fabric they required 'right in the privacy of your own home'.[28]

Part of the explanation for the lack of emphasis on the shopping environment may lie in the assumption that men did not in fact 'shop' in the same way as women, the whole package of spectacular displays and attractive decor therefore having little attractions for them. Men were believed to make their purchases only when strictly necessary, in haste and with reluctance. Christmas shopping, in particular, was portrayed by contemporary commentators as degrading and emasculating to men, reducing them to the status of beasts of burden if they shopped with women, or of easily manipulated incompetents if alone. By 1915, it could be asserted as a matter of common sense observation that 'Most women like to shop. Only a few men, relatively speaking, enjoy shopping.'[29]

Nevertheless, this seems at best only a partial explanation. There is, in fact, plenty of evidence that menswear retailers were just as keen as other traders to create a 'spectacular' shopping environment for their customers. As early as 1849, in one of his letters to *The Morning Chronicle*, Henry Mayhew described a class of 'show' shop where 'every art and trick that scheming can devise or avarice suggest, is displayed to attract the notice of the passer-by … the quiet, unobtrusive place of business of the old-fashioned tailor is transformed into the flashy palace of the grasping tradesman.'[30] At the same time, the lack of extensive plate glass windows or luxurious decor does not necessarily imply a lack of attention to creating an environment conducive to parting the customer from his money. In the years immediately preceding the First World War, Siegfried Sassoon's literary alter ego, George Sherston, travelled up to London from his aunt's house in the country to buy hunting clothes and boots, as well as to attend a concert. Sherston's clothes were purchased not in one of the great department stores, but in a quiet and immensely dignified high-class tailor's shop. Here he was not dazzled by spectacular displays, and was certainly not allowed to browse, but instead was carefully shepherded, or as he put it, 'wafted', through the shop by 'the presiding presence'. Sherston's experience may have been more nerve-racking than enjoyable, and may not have conformed to definitions of 'shopping' associated with department stores. However, it did not imply a lack of interest in clothing on his part, or in making a profitable sale on the part of the tailors. Indeed, his visit was orchestrated in such a manner as to make him feel that 'To have asked the price of so much as a waistcoat would have been an indecency.'[31]

On the whole, it seems unlikely that menswear retailers' advertisements stressed the goods for sale, rather than the 'shopping experience', simply on the assumption that reluctant male customers were indifferent to the environment in which they made their purchases. Rather, they did so at least partly because of the centrality and power of the commodity itself in late Victorian and Edwardian culture and society. As Thomas Richards observes with characteristic hyperbole, by the late nineteenth century 'the commodity had become a cynosure, a monument, a palace, and a shrine, and soon it would set about remaking the world in its spectacular image.'[32] The autonomous power and authority of the commodity should nevertheless not be exaggerated: leaving it to speak for itself was actually seen by advertisers as fraught with dangers. Writing in 1910, C. F. Clark advised clothiers and outfitters that the most effective way to advertise was to describe thoroughly the goods for sale, therefore enabling the prospective customer 'to see the goods in his mind's eye'. At the same time, however, the commodity was to be presented in the way most likely to 'appeal to the imagination', carefully excluding any 'undesirable features'.[33] In the case of men's clothing, therefore, the commodity was not left to speak for itself, but acquired its significance and appeal (at least as far as advertisements in the national press were concerned) when it was associated with male identities and lifestyles that can best be described as 'gentlemanly'.

***

By the end of the nineteenth century, as contemporaries recognized, the notion of a British 'gentleman' had become difficult to define with precision. It was clear, however, that education, breeding, manners, and of course income and social background all played a part.[34] In her advice manual, 'Mrs Humphry' suggested a definition that mixed qualities of character and of manners. In her opinion, a gentleman should possess 'gentleness and moral strength combined ... together with that polish that is never acquired but in one way: constant association with those so happily placed that they have enjoyed the influences of education and refinement all through their lives.' At the same time, the true gentleman would never be careless in 'dress and personal appearance'.[35] A distinctive – if at times rather blurred – visual image of the 'gentleman' would have been recognized by contemporaries; an image based not only on the style, cut and quality of his clothes, but also on a variety of smaller details: his headgear, a walking cane, a well-kept moustache, a cigar or cigarette negligently held in a gloved hand, and so on.

Although most contemporary novelists and commentators chose to emphasize the 'sterling' value of the true (English) gentleman's character and morals,[36] the elegance and well-dressed appearance of this figure could easily take precedence in popular representations over any moral content, and become associated with a lifestyle characterized by ease, pleasure, and the ability to purchase a variety of desirable consumer items. Such a hedonistic lifestyle, characterized by 'material satisfaction'[37], clearly exerted a powerful pull for many, including individuals with no interest in the high-minded qualities supposedly also associated with the gentlemanly status. The 'High Mobsmen' depicted in Arthur Morrison's *A Child of the Jago*, 'swaggering in check suits and billycocks, gold chains and lumpy rings', provide an extreme but nevertheless interesting example. Neither in their own eyes, nor in those of the inhabitants of the Jago, one of London's poorest slums, was there any doubt about the symbolic meaning attached to these criminals' ownership of gentlemanly accoutrements of fur coats, top hats, umbrellas or cigars. To the envy of Jago residents, the appearance of these 'resplendent ones' made it clear that they had escaped from poverty and hardship, and now were 'bursting with high living, drunk when ... [they] like, red and pimply'.[38]

Menswear advertisements, in their turn, made unashamed use of such symbolism and the pleasures associated with it. Advertisements divested the image of the gentleman of any nostalgic or backward-looking connotations, replacing these with an enthusiastic engagement with the 'modern' world of consumer goods, travel and leisure. In an advertisement of 1894 for the International Fur Store, for example, the door of a first-class train carriage, the top hat, cigar, riding crop and boots all served to create the image of an elegant sporting gentleman. Customers spending a minimum of £10 on a fur-lined overcoat – the image suggested – would be able to enjoy the pleasures of a gentlemanly lifestyle[39] (Figure 1). Almost 20 years later Gooch's, a 'very old-established firm' that catered 'for the best class of trade only', advertised their 'Ideal' motor coat, priced from a very expensive five guineas, by using a similar image: a gentleman casually leaning against a car, cigarette in hand, the coat opening to reveal a glimpse of a smart suit, and both man and car appearing as the very epitome of luxurious ease.[40] Men able to afford these prices may also have been able to enjoy the lifestyles suggested by the advertisements, or at least an approximation of them. Significantly, though, such images were not used only by the more expensive menswear shops, but can also be found endorsing a whole range of establishments, down to the very cheapest end of the market.

The advertisements of Charles Baker & Co., a store whose various London branches (ten in 1910) specialized in both made-to-measure

Figure 1 The International Fur Store advertisement, *Illustrated London News*, 10 November 1894.
Reproduced by permission of Bodleian Library, University of Oxford, shelfmark N 2288 b.6.

and ready-to-wear clothing for men and boys, emphasized as selling points both the reasonableness of the prices and the availability of clothes to suit men 'of every occupation'. Nevertheless, the images followed the same 'gentlemanly' pattern as those used by more high-class establishments. Whether offering (moderately priced) morning coats and vests, suits or overcoats, the images came complete with walking canes, gloves, cigarettes, collars and ties, the correct headgear for the various outfits, and shiny shoes[41] (Figure 2). At the still cheaper end of the market, Thompson Bros. described itself as 'an old-established West End firm, with a reputation to maintain', and claimed that 'the best gentlemen in the land can wear our suits, overcoats, boots or watches'. Illustrations also showed a well-groomed and debonair figure, with all the hallmarks of a gentleman: one who could, however, buy his suits ready-made for as little as 27s 1d.[42]

Bespoke tailoring, these cheaper firms suggested, was not essential

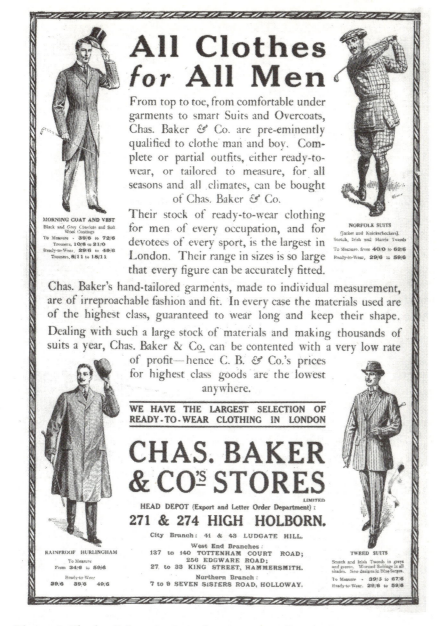

Figure 2 Charles Baker & Co. advertisement, *Illustrated London News*, 30 April 1910.
Reproduced by permission of Bodleian Library, University of Oxford, shelfmark N 2288 b.6.

for a gentlemanly appearance. As a Charles Baker & Co. advertisement emphasized, 'The day of ill-cut, ill-fitting [ready-to-wear] garments has passed.' Their ready-made suits were 'all scrupulously cut and finished with character and distinction'.[43] This was an appeal that may have had particular resonance for those men struggling at the lower end of the middle class, with incomes of £200 or less per year, but who still had an image of respectability to maintain, or to aspire to. Men employed in the lower paid reaches of white-collar occupations are the most obvious examples.[44] At the same time, despite advertisements' claims, it is at least debateable whether much of this cheaper clothing would have been socially and aesthetically acceptable for men wishing to make any claim to status. In 1905 *The Tailor and Cutter* (a tailoring trade journal, so admittedly hardly a disinterested observer) reported gleefully the case of a man in a good white-collar job, employed as the manager 'of a large body of men in the building trade', who had gone to 'one of the shoddy houses for a "rig-out" of a holiday suit'. The whole outfit, which included hat and tie, had cost less than 20s. It seems that when the labourers came to hear of their manager's thrifty purchase they teased him so unmercifully that in the end he was forced to get rid of the suit.[45]

Moreover, in the context of renewed calls for an end to the scandal of 'sweating', it may have become more desirable not to be seen to wear a cheap garment. As newspapers uncovered more and more stories of low wages, harsh working conditions and underemployment among home workers, including those in the needle trades, it would have become increasingly difficult to ignore sweating's frequently reiterated connection with cheap clothing.[46] Furthermore, at least according to Beatrice Webb, the origins of a garment produced by sweaters could not be disguised. Anybody walking behind the wearer of a 'sweater's coat' would have been able to notice – with disapproval, presumably – that 'if the material be light, it will sway to and fro with a senseless motion; if heavy, it bulges out first here, then there.'[47] If it was not already bad enough that by purchasing and wearing a cheap outfit a man could be marked as a supporter of sweating, cheap clothes were also associated with connotations of 'swelldom' and vulgar working-class dandyism, as immortalized in contemporary comic papers and music hall song. As Webb bluntly put it, endorsing a more general contemporary perception, the purchasers of cheap and badly put-together clothing made by workers 'struggling and striving for a mere subsistence wage', were 'the African gold digger, the East End lounger, or the agricultural labourer'.[48] It was assumed that few men would have wished to be identified with any of these groups.

For their part, perhaps at least partly in response to these concerns, menswear advertisers did not stress the cheapness of their products (although cut-price firms made sure their prices were clearly visible), but rather their supposed quality and good value. According to Samuel Brothers' advertising manager, the most effective advertisements by tailors and outfitters appealed to the public on the basis of 'the special value that he offers, and ... the exceptional character of the cutting or tailoring at his command'.[49] Indeed, as one of many contemporary advice manuals for shopkeepers pointed out, 'Any extraordinary parade of cheapness ought always to be looked upon with an eye of suspicion, as no such establishment can be supported honestly without suffering taking place somewhere.'[50]

The more exclusive firms used the notion of quality to justify their higher prices. Burberry raincoats, for example, were made – it was claimed – of such 'fine and strong threads ... welded so closely that each cloth is a veritable shield against the wind'.[51] Despite the warnings of the better establishments about the exaggerated claims and special offers of 'cheap-jack tailors',[52] the emphasis on quality was not exclusive to high-class goods. The department store Robinson & Cleaver tried to convince potential customers to buy their linen collars rather than the cheaper cotton ones, since theirs were whiter, stronger, and 'possessing that brilliancy and lustre which imports to Menswear that look of distinction not found in the cheaper article'.[53] Nevertheless, they were only one voice among a chorus that emphasized that it was possible to have 'the highest class workmanship and the soundest materials' without paying 'extravagant prices'.[54] The wool overcoat advertised by Curzon Bros. in 1913 offered 'perfect style, perfect cut, perfect finish, perfectly trimmed' for 30s,[55] while Henochsberg & Ellis, a Liverpool-based firm, advertised a 'complete cyclist's outfit' for only 21s, warning potential customers not to 'allow our marvellously low price to mislead you into thinking it impossible to obtain sound material and good workmanship from us'.[56] The ready-to-wear shirts advertised for 2s 3d each by Henry Blyth, 'shirt-maker and draper' of Edinburgh, may have been 'a marvel of cheapness', but they were also 'really good ... the shape perfect'.[57]

On the whole, customers were promised a good bargain. Significantly, and contrary to what Beatrice Webb stated in her study of the tailoring trade, they were reassured that however low their price, the advertised garments would not *look* cheap. A 30s overcoat bought, possibly in instalments, from Catesby's, promised to provide the wearer, whatever his social and economic background, with 'a well-dressed – a gentlemanly appearance'.[58] In a more outspoken way, the Sheffield-based mail order firm of J. G. Graves stated that 'It is very generally believed ... that reasonably priced clothing always betrays itself by obvious commonness and inferiority of both cut and style ... the Graves 35/- suit embodies all the essentials of a great popular priced tailoring success, good style, good taste, good value' all on 'Easy Terms'.[59]

***

The desire to look like a 'gentleman', which advertisements promised to fulfil, cannot be explained simply in terms of social emulation and a desire to ape the fashions of those higher in the social hierarchy. As has been suggested above, part of these images' attraction would have been the way in which the clothing advertised embodied a lifestyle of luxury and pleasure, a lifestyle clearly available only to a minority of the male population. Significantly, however, advertisements also warned of the penalties if this lifestyle was rejected. As numberless commentators agreed, the 'right' choice of clothes was essential for men's success in life, while a disregard for appearances was a sure recipe for disaster.

As *The Wide World Magazine*'s 'The Captain' stressed in 1912, the opportunities for sartorial *faux pas* were numerous. Coloured handkerchiefs, for example, were acceptable, but those in 'violent-coloured fabrics' risked making the wearer look like a 'workman'. In choosing to buy one of the newly fashionable soft hats, a British man had to take care not to end up looking 'a little too continental', or worse, like an 'undesirable alien'. If the dangers of looking like a workingman or a foreigner were not frightening enough, an unfortunate purchase could lead a hapless man to lose his very masculinity. On the matter of trimming the belts or the cuffs of overcoats with velvet, 'The Captain' was unequivocal: 'No really manly man wants ... these effeminate little adornments.' A proper attention to attire, he explained, was necessary not only in order to avoid social blunders; it was actually indispensable to success in life: at a time of 'keen competition no man can afford to be slovenly or ill-turned-out, and a smart appearance is a most excellent asset to anyone who has his way to make in the world'.[60]

The words of W. H. Davenport Adams, published in *The Young Man*, seem to have expressed a widely held opinion: 'If you see a man untidy in his personal appearance ... you may reasonably conclude that he will be loose and disorderly in his mental habits.'[61] In the same vein, an advertisement for Catesby's warned that it was the height of foolishness to 'appear unprosperous'. Addressing the customer directly, it warned that 'by so appearing your chances are handicapped, and people seem less willing to aid and trust you'.[62] Almost ten years earlier, Cuer & Mundy, tailors based in the City of London, had given a similar warning: 'No young man can afford to neglect his personal appearance, and the importance of dressing well can hardly be overestimated.'[63]

Richard Sennett has suggested that, during the nineteenth century, clothing was perceived as a reflection of the individual's 'private character ... private feeling, and ... individuality'. In the context of the anonymous urban landscape, the 'details' of one's clothing were seen as revelatory, and served to chart individuals' relationships with the strangers of which the city was mostly composed: the quality of the fabric, of the leather of boots, the way of tying a cravat, the type of watch worn, the way of buttoning one's coat, and so on, all held a deeper moral and psychological meaning. To ignore this could spell disaster.[64]

At the same time, however, men were warned there was a fine line separating a justifiable concern over one's appearance from an excessive concern. Conformity and an avoidance of 'singularity' were recommended. According to Davenport Adams, 'the rule to be observed by every gentleman ... is *to dress so that no one shall notice how you are dressed*. A prevailing air of modesty, neatness and simplicity should disarm curiosity and baffle attention.'[65] Roland Marchand has shown how the notion of the individual as constantly under the critical scrutiny of others, haunted by anxiety and fear of failure, either in personal relations or in the workplace, was a dominant theme of American advertisements directed at men in the inter-war years.[66] Turn-of-the-century advertisements for men's clothes in Britain also acknowledged the presence of others' gaze, but rather than stress its potentially devastating effects, claimed to be able to transform it into a benign look of approval. The man leaving home wearing the shoes, hat and coat sold by Jacksons could do so feeling confident of being well-dressed, and of making 'a favourable impression on everybody'.[67] The dominant image of these advertisements was of success and satisfaction, endorsed by approving onlookers. The friends of a man who wore a suit by J. G. Graves would 'notice that you have suddenly taken on a more successful appearance; you find yourself recognized with more cordiality and respect than usual, and you feel a new confidence in your ability to ... take advantage of the opportunities of advancement which come your way.'[68]

***

Menswear advertisements promised and endorsed masculine lifestyles of ease and comfort, sometimes even of luxury: for those men who bought and wore the 'correct' clothes, success in life was assured. Such models of male lifestyles were undoubtedly narrow. Clearly, for example, advertisers in the national press were not interested in representing the working clothes of men employed in manual occupations.[69] Nevertheless, the masculine image promoted by advertisements was not an entirely inflexible one. It was remarkably successful, in particular, in incorporating certain notions of masculinity that ostensibly rejected conventional notions of a correctly attired, formal, urban manhood.

The historian John Tosh has suggested that, by the end of the nineteenth century, British middle-class men – young men in particular – were experiencing what he has termed a 'flight from domesticity'; a desire to escape, both metaphorically and physically, the confines of home, family and marriage.[70] At the same time, for many men, the workplace (particularly 'the office') and the urban environment as a whole increasingly acquired prison-like connotations. As Harold Begbie put it in 1904:

> Four grey walls and a dusky ceiling ...
> An ink-smudged desk with the ledge in splinters ...
> And I'm sick and shamed of this cursed adding;
> I! To be chained to this office dreary
> With the blood of my veins of sea and prairie ...[71]

These men could seek refuge in overwhelmingly male enclaves, including those of organized sport, travel and, for the most daring, the world of imperial adventure. In all these cases advertisers were on hand to supply suitable clothing. The waterproofs offered by J. and G. Ross, 'court tailors, military and colonial outfitters', based both in London and in Exeter, were sold as suitable 'on the Indian frontier, the African veldt, the American prairies, in the Cathay, the frozen North, as well as the Homeland ... in the late Boer war many an officer used his instead of a blanket'.[72] Apart from an emphasis on the practical qualities of the clothes on offer, less tangible dreams of escape and adventure, as well as imperialist and war fervour, can be found reflected – and legitimated – in certain retailers' advertisements.[73] In 1890 the London firm of Oliver Brothers attempted to associate their stock with notions of imperial endeavour by claiming that their 'cellular' underclothing had been endorsed by the popular journalist and explorer Henry Stanley, who had just returned from Africa to a hero's welcome.[74] Among the many retailers even more brazenly exploiting the wave of nationalistic fervour during the South African war, Thompson Bros offered 'A startling novelty. The rage of London. Khaki fancy vests, with Union Jacks.' Cautious potential customers were reassured that the vests were 'patriotic, but not vulgar'.[75]

More prosaically, an enormous variety of retailers recognized that 'There are many men, and women too, who require garments of special cut and material for most of their amusements',[76] and offered outfits suitable for activities that took men (and increasingly women) outside the confines of the home, the workplace and the city: cycling,[77] hunting and shooting,[78] holiday-making,[79] playing tennis, golf, cricket and a variety of other sports.[80] Gamage's, a well-known store based on Holborn in London, for example, made the sporting man its niche market, describing itself at various times as the 'cheapest, largest, and best house in the world for all sports', as well as 'the world's great motor house' and 'the leading Sports and Recreations House in the World'.[81] Not surprisingly, it specialized in clothing suitable for all sorts of sports, cycling and motoring.[82]

Nevertheless, the differences between the gentlemanly image proposed by most menswear advertisements, often placed in an urban or domestic environment, and the sportsman/adventurer, should not be exaggerated. As Graham Dawson has suggested, the worlds of urban (or suburban), domestic masculinity and of outdoor and imperial adventure were not entirely separate.[83] The transformation of the hero from foppish city boy to hardened man, unconcerned with appearances, was of course a standard device of contemporary adventure fiction. In Erskine Childers' best-selling novel *The Riddle of the Sands*, for example, the protagonist, a Whitehall clerk, gradually hardened to life on board a small yacht, in 'pursuit of perilous quest'. He 'grew salt, tough, and tolerably alert', discarded his 'faultless' white flannels, 'cool white ducks ... [and] neat blue serge' in favour of 'rough woollen garments ... breeches, jerseys, helmets, gloves; all of a colour chosen to harmonize with paraffin stains and anchor mud'.[84] This break, no doubt, did not take place in most men's experience, particularly when the escape from work, family and city life took the rather more prosaic form of sporting activities or holiday-making.

For their part, menswear advertisers undoubtedly had an interest in emphasizing that sport and adventure need not preclude the wearing of comfortable, 'suitable' and elegant clothing. The London-based firm of J. C. Cording and Co., for example, offered its waterproof specialities for sportsmen, enticing potential customers with (unpriced) images of faultlessly attired gentlemen undertaking such exclusive activities as salmon fishing, riding and shooting.[85] Hope Brothers, 'complete football outfitters' based in Manchester, Liverpool and London, offered 'everything for the game at popular prices', and in 1908 advertised their 'New Association Jersey' (price 1s 11d) by using the image of a young man, sleeves rolled up, about to kick a football.[86] Even such very mild ruggedness, however, was overshadowed by images of sportswear that emphasized outdoor leisure, rather than strenuous action. An advertisement for Harrods' 'tennis, cricket and boating trousers' (ready-to-wear from 13s) used the image of a perfectly groomed man standing on a river punt, dressed spotlessly from the top of his straw hat to the bottom of his correctly turned-up trousers, the only sign of activity one rolled-up sleeve[87] (Figure 3).

Images of leisurely and relaxed outdoor activities were not limited to the more expensive sections of the market. In 1905 a Leeds-based 'tourist outfitters' advertised its 'indispensable' holiday suits with images of well-dressed men about to go shooting or rowing. In their case, the outfit was available made-to-measure for a very modest 25s.[88] Even when it was – rarely – acknowledged that a lifestyle of expensive leisure, sport and travel was not open to all, as in an advertisement for Catesby's cheap suits, an attempt was still made to show that all could achieve at least an approximation to it. A man was shown in the advertisement wearing one of Catesby's suits, while standing in front of an image of Blackpool: the potential customer was made to understand that even if a man could only afford a holiday in this popular working-class resort, rather than somewhere more exclusive, he could still enjoy the pleasures of looking elegant and smartly turned out[89] (Figure 4).

***

As historians are beginning to acknowledge, the purchase and use of a variety of consumer items, including clothing, were often of as great importance and absorbing interest to late Victorian and Edwardian men as they supposedly were to women. As Fred Burgess pointed out just before the First World War, if men

> saw a page, in which are illustrations of the latest cut in men's tailoring, or note a stylish waterproof or raincoat, or catch a glance at the latest thing in hats, the chances are they will be just as much interested as the lady ... who studies carefully the illustrations in a ladies' outfitting circular.[90]

Menswear advertisements both endorsed and encouraged men's acquisitive impulses, by associating the commodities for sale with images of desirable masculine lifestyles, and promising the possibility of success, ease and leisure, as well as the chance to escape the confines of home, workplace and the urban environment. It would be wrong to suggest that clothing advertisements reflected in a straightforward or complete way the diversity of contemporary male identities and aspirations, or, indeed, of male clothing styles. They do suggest, however, that the more hedonistic pleasures of consumption were important components of late Victorian and Edwardian masculinity, alongside the better-known and sterner qualities of moral, athletic, religious and imperial manliness.

Harrods Sporting Tailors.

SPECIALITIES FOR IMMEDIATE USE

BLANKET COAT

THIS Coat is a protection against chilling after tennis, cricket, and other sports, and an admirable over-garment for motoring, driving, and travelling. It retains the heat of the body, is light comfortable, roomy, and stylish. In shades of greys, greens, browns, also navy and white fleece blanket cloths. Body unlined, sleeves and shoulders lined satin.
Ready to wear in all sizes and fittings **45/-**

TENNIS CRICKET & BOATING TROUSERS

THE advantages embodied in these garments include straight cut tops, strap and buckle on each hip, affording a perfect fit and comfort to the wearer, five loops for belt or sash, bottoms permanently turned up. In white flannel, worsted, cream garbicord, and three shades of plain grey, thoroughly soap-shrunk. Thirty different fittings ready to wear.

13/- 16/- 18/6 21/-

HARRODS, LTD. (Richard Burbidge, Managing Director.) **LONDON, S.W.**

In answering this advertisement it is desirable that you mention THE BADMINTON MAGAZINE.

Figure 3 Harrods advertisement, *The Badminton Magazine*, July 1914.

Figure 4 Catesby & Sons advertisement, *Daily Mail*, 22 June 1904.

Acknowledgements
I would like to thank John Benson and Christopher Breward for their valuable comments and suggestions on this chapter.

Notes

[1] John Galsworthy, *The Man of Property* (William Heinemann, London, 1952, first published 1906), p. 7.

[2] On male consumption in late Victorian and Edwardian Britain, see Christopher Breward, *The Hidden Consumer: Masculinities, Fashion and City Life 1860–1914* (Manchester University Press, Manchester, 1999); Christopher Hosgood, '"Doing the shops at Christmas": women, men and the department store in England, c. 1880–1914', in G. Crossick and S. Jaumain (eds), *Cathedrals of Consumption: The European Department Store, 1850–1939* (Ashgate, Aldershot, 1999), pp. 97–115; Matthew Hilton, *Smoking in British Popular Culture 1800–2000: Perfect Pleasures* (Manchester University Press, Manchester, 2000). For a later period, see Frank Mort, *Cultures of Consumption: Masculinities and Social Space in Late Twentieth Century Britain* (Routledge, London, 1996); Jill Greenfield, Sean O'Connell and Chris Read, 'Gender, consumer culture and the middle-class male, 1918–39', in A. Kidd and D. Nicholls (eds), *Gender, Civic Culture and Consumerism: Middle-Class Identity in Britain, 1800–1940* (Manchester University Press, Manchester, 1999), pp. 183–97.

[3] Breward, *The Hidden Consumer*, p. 160.

[4] Lori Anne Loeb, *Consuming Angels: Advertising and Victorian Women* (Oxford University Press, Oxford, 1994). See also Thomas Richards, *The Commodity Culture of Victorian England: Advertising and Spectacle 1851–1914* (Verso, London, 1990), pp. 205–48.

[5] Apart from clothing and footwear, retailers advertised goods such as guns, bicycles, motorcycles, cars, sporting, travelling and camping equipment, as well as equipment necessary to pursue a variety of hobbies: gardening, body-building, photography, stamp or specimen collecting, and so on. Branded goods of all sorts were also advertised. Featuring particularly largely were food and drink, patent medicines, books and magazines, cigars and cigarettes, toiletries (particularly shaving equipment, soap and hair preparations), clocks and watches, bicycles, motorcycles and cars, sports equipment, and of course a whole range of items of clothing and footwear.

[6] *Progressive Advertising*, 28 February 1902. Jaeger specialized in 'sanitary' all-wool clothing for both men and women.

[7] John Benson, *The Rise of Consumer Society in Britain 1880–1980* (Longman, Harlow, 1994), pp. 27–8. See also William Leiss, Stephen Kline and Sut Jhally, *Social Communication in Advertising: Persons, Products and Images of Well-Being* (Routledge, London, 1990, first published 1986).

[8] Robert Roberts, *The Classic Slum: Salford Life in the First Quarter of the Century* (Penguin Books, Harmondsworth, 1974, first published 1971), p. 38. See also Jerome K. Jerome, *Three Men on the Bummel* (Oxford University Press, Oxford, 1998, first published 1900), pp. 274–6.

[9] *Progressive Advertising*, 24 January 1902. See also *ibid.*, 28 November 1902.

Although historians and other scholars have been more interested in investigating the ways in which advertising influenced, culturally and psychologically, the 'impulse' to buy, advertisements' role as sources of information, for example on the price, location and availability of particular commodities, should also not be underestimated.

[10] Breward, *The Hidden Consumer*, pp. 157–8.

[11] Retailers' advertisements appearing in the pages of the local press were able to draw on themes and images of significance and power within a geographically limited area. Christopher Breward, 'Fashion and the man: from suburb to city street. The spaces of masculine consumption, 1870–1914', *New Formations*, 'Issue on sexual geographies' 37 (1999), pp. 47–70; Laura Ugolini, 'Clothes and the modern man in 1930s Oxford', *Fashion Theory: The Journal of Dress, Body & Culture* 4/4 (2000), pp. 427–46.

[12] *The Wide World Magazine*, June 1913. The Captain's feature was obviously connected to the advertisements that appeared alongside it.

[13] *The London Tailor*, April 1909; *The Weekly Record of Fashion*, June 1886. See also *The Gentleman's Magazine of Fashion*, June 1892.

[14] Arnold Bennett, *The Old Wives' Tale* (Penguin Books, London, 1990, first published 1908), pp. 601–2. The concerns of the high-class tailoring trade press (fearful of the competition of 'show shops') and of novelists like Arnold Bennett (critical of what they saw as the development of a 'modern' homogenizing commercial culture) were of course not identical. However, all shared an emphasis on the association of aggressive advertising with untrustworthiness and low quality.

[15] *Ibid.*, p. 603.

[16] *The Weekly Record of Fashion*, March 1890.

[17] *The Tailor and Cutter*, 7 March 1889. See also 18 January 1900.

[18] Beverley Lemire, *Fashion's Favourite: The Cotton Trade and the Consumer in Britain, 1660–1800* (Oxford University Press, Oxford, 1991), pp. 56–61. See also Claire Walsh, 'The advertising and marketing of consumer goods in eighteenth-century London', in C. Wischermann and E. Shore (eds), *Advertising and the European City: Historical Perspectives* (Ashgate, Aldershot, 2000), pp. 79–95.

[19] See, for example, *The Tailor and Cutter*, 17 July 1902; 28 August 1913; Max Rittenberg, *Selling Schemes for Retailers* (George Routledge and Sons, London, 1911), pp. 47–8. For a useful discussion of retailers and advertising, see Michael J. Winstanley, *The Shopkeeper's World 1830–1914* (Manchester University Press, Manchester, 1983), pp. 58–61.

[20] Quoted in Terry R. Nevett, *Advertising in Britain: A History* (Heinemann, London, 1982), p. 86. Before the First World War, the market for men's clothes was still dominated by independent retailers, although their market share was slowly declining in the face of expansion on the part of multiples, co-operatives and department stores. See James B. Jefferys, *Retail Trading in Britain, 1850–1950* (Cambridge University Press, Cambridge, 1954), pp. 295–321.

[21] Reginald Pound, *Selfridge: A Biography* (Heinemann, London, 1960), p. 16.

[22] *Daily Mail*, 26 March 1909.

[23] Erika D. Rappaport, *Shopping for Pleasure: Women in the Making of*

London's West End (Princeton University Press, New Jersey, 2000), p. 171. See also pp. 142–77.

[24] *Daily Mail*, 26 March 1909.

[25] *The Graphic*, 5 October 1895. See also *ibid.*, 22 March 1890; *Illustrated London News*, 9 April 1898. For a discussion of Charles Baker & Co.'s 'magnificently appointed' branches in London's West End, see Breward, 'Fashion and the man', p. 66.

[26] *The Strand Magazine*, May 1912.

[27] In 1890 for example Taaffe & Caldwell, 'shirt tailors' based in Dublin, called upon potential customers to 'Save 30 per cent and buy your shirts direct from Ireland, the home of linen manufacture.' *The Graphic*, 15 November 1890.

[28] *The Strand Magazine*, June 1912.

[29] Gail Reekie, 'Impulsive women, predictable men: psychological constructions of sexual difference in sales literature to 1930', *Australian Historical Studies* 24/97 (1991), pp. 359–77; Hosgood, '"Doing the shops at Christmas"', pp. 104–6; Paul H. Nystrom, *The Economics of Retailing* (The Ronald Press, New York, 1920, first published 1915), p. 33.

[30] E. P. Thompson and Eileen Yeo, *The Unknown Mayhew: Selections from The Morning Chronicle 1849–50* (Penguin Books, Harmondsworth, 1973, first published 1971), p. 236.

[31] Siegfried Sassoon, *Memoirs of a Fox-Hunting Man* (Faber & Faber, London, 1989, first published 1928), pp. 114–17.

[32] Richards, *The Commodity Culture*, p. 53. It is interesting to note that most retailers' advertisements directed at women also focused on the goods for sale.

[33] *Publicity: A Practical Guide for the Retail Clothier and Outfitter to all the Latest Methods of Successful Advertising*, c. 1910, pp. 8–9.

[34] Geoffrey Crossick, 'From gentleman to the residuum: languages of social description in Victorian Britain', in P. J. Corfield (ed.), *Language, History and Class* (Basil Blackwell, Oxford, 1991), pp. 150–78, especially pp. 163–5. See also Andrew St George, *The Descent of Manners: Etiquette, Rules and the Victorians* (Chatto & Windus, London, 1993), pp. 37–44; Angus McLaren, *The Trials of Masculinity: Policing Sexual Boundaries 1870–1930* (University of Chicago Press, Chicago, 1997), pp. 89–110.

[35] Mrs Humphry, *Manners for Men* (James Bowden, London, 1897), pp. 1–4.

[36] David Trotter, *The English Novel in History 1895–1920* (Routledge, London, 1993), p. 57.

[37] Loeb, *Consuming Angels*, p. 179.

[38] Arthur Morrison, *A Child of the Jago* (Panther Books, London, 1971, first published 1896), pp. 90, 95. See also Colin Campbell, *The Romantic Ethic and the Spirit of Modern Consumerism* (Basil Blackwell, Oxford, 1987), pp. 88–95, for a thought-provoking discussion of the dreams of pleasure associated with the acquisition of consumer goods.

[39] *Illustrated London News*, 10 November 1894. See also *The Graphic*, 20 September 1890. The jumbling together of symbols makes the figure in reality absurd (why take a riding crop on a train journey?), but its meaning remains clear. For the use of a similar symbolism by the Wholesale Fur Manufacturing Co. at the cheaper end of the market for furs, see *The Strand Magazine*,

December 1897; *The Fortnightly Review*, February 1908. For a very interesting discussion of the relationship between fashion and stereotypes of class, see Breward, *The Hidden Consumer*, pp. 54–99.

[40] *The Graphic*, 12 November 1910, 8 October 1910.

[41] *Illustrated London News*, 12 March 1910, 16 April 1910, 30 April 1910. For an earlier advertisement (that followed the same conventions), see *The Graphic*, 8 April 1905.

[42] Thompson Bros. was a tailoring firm based on London's Oxford Street. *Illustrated London News*, 8 December 1900. See also *Daily Mail*, 17 May 1897; *Hobbies*, 7 December 1901; *News of the World*, 14 January 1900. Unsurprisingly, I have not found advertisements in the main pages of the national press for menswear retailers at the very cheapest end of the market: second-hand clothes and 'misfits' dealers. They are present, however, in the classified ads, which are outside the scope of the present enquiry.

[43] *Illustrated London News*, 16 April 1910. It is important to note that between the extremes of bespoke tailoring (where the garments were cut and made up to the customer's individual measurements) and ready-made clothing, there existed a grey area of garments for which the customer was measured, but that were then made up to the closest standard size, often, but by no means always, in a factory. For a revealing example of this grey area, see the shifts of the Leeds-based Factory Clothing Co., which in the mid-1890s veered between calling itself 'manufacturing clothiers' and 'bespoke tailors', while clearly selling the same merchandise. *Tit-Bits*, 6 April 1895, 13 July 1895, 19 October 1895, 21 November 1896. But see also Lewis's explicit merchandizing of cheap clothes suitable for working men. Asa Briggs, *Friends of the People: The Centenary History of Lewis's* (Batsford, London, 1956), pp. 131–2.

[44] W. Hamish Fraser, *The Coming of the Mass Market 1850–1914* (Macmillan, London, 1981), pp. 25–6, 62.

[45] *The Tailor and Cutter*, 6 July 1905. Interestingly, he apparently sold the suit to one of the labourers.

[46] On late Victorian and Edwardian 'sweating', see James A. Schmiechen, *Sweated Industries and Sweated Labor: The London Clothing Trades, 1860–1914* (Croom Helm, London, 1984).

[47] Beatrice Webb, 'The tailoring trade', in C. Booth (ed.), *Life and Labour of the People in London* (Macmillan & Co., London, 1893), vol. IV, p. 39.

[48] Webb, 'The tailoring trade', p. 66. See also Judith R. Walkowitz, *City of Dreadful Delight: Narratives of Sexual Danger in Late-Victorian London* (Virago, London, 1992), pp. 43–4; Peter Bailey, *Popular Culture and Performance in the Victorian City* (Cambridge University Press, Cambridge, 1998), pp. 66, 115, 121.

[49] *Publicity*, p. 35.

[50] R. K. Philp, *The Handy-Book of Shopkeeping* (Houlston and Sons, London, revised edition, 1892), p. 15.

[51] *The Strand Magazine*, June 1912. Burberrry's claimed outlets in London (Haymarket) and Paris.

[52] *News of the World*, 25 November 1900. Advertisement by J. & H. Ellis, London-based 'high-class tailors'.

[53] *C. B. Fry's Magazine*, March 1912. See also *The Sphere*, 25 March 1911.

[54] *C. B. Fry's Magazine*, April 1910. An advertisement for Cubitt and Co., London tailors.

[55] *The Wide World Magazine*, January 1913. Curzon Bros.' 21s suit, furthermore, was 'the most astonishing achievement of the century'. *News of the World*, 14 May 1905. By the early years of the twentieth century, the columns of the *News of the World* were full of advertisements for cheap 'made to measure' suits, all trying to outdo each other in claims of value and quality.

[56] *The Wide World Magazine*, August 1899.

[57] *The Young Man*, May 1889. By way of comparison, Sampson & Co. of Oxford Street, London, offered six surplice shirts, made to measure, for 45s or 51s. *The Fortnightly Review*, January 1898.

[58] Catesby & Sons, based on London's Tottenham Court Road, described itself as the 'department store for the people'. It sold a variety of goods, including menswear, but it was mostly noted for its cheap linoleum. *The Strand Magazine*, November 1907.

[59] *Tit-Bits*, 15 June 1912.

[60] *The Wide World Magazine*, December 1912, January 1913, November 1913, May 1913. For a further example of stress on notions of 'correct' clothing, see Humphry, *Manners for Men*, pp. 113–20.

[61] *The Young Man*, October 1889. *The Young Man* was a monthly magazine published by the Young Men's Christian Association, and costing 1d, later increased to 3d. W. H. Davenport Adams contributed a series of moralizing 'Letters to a Young Man on the conduct of life'.

[62] *The Strand Magazine*, April 1907. See also *News of the World*, 12 March 1905.

[63] *The Young Man*, April 1895. See also *ibid.*, July 1895.

[64] Richard Sennett, *The Fall of Public Man* (Cambridge University Press, Cambridge, 1974), pp. 153–69. Turning briefly back to Philip Bosinney's hat in John Galsworthy's *The Man of Property*, it was just such lack of attention to attire that the always-correct Forsytes found so suspicious.

[65] *The Young Man*, October 1889.

[66] Roland Marchand, *Advertising the American Dream: Making Way for Modernity, 1920–1940* (University of California Press, Berkeley, 1985), pp. 208–17.

[67] *The Wide World Magazine*, November 1912. Jacksons was a Stockport-based firm, which claimed branches in 'all large towns', and specialized in fixed-price shoes, raincoats and hats. Its prices were described as 'easily within reach of the man of moderate means'. See *The Strand Magazine*, April 1912, June 1912.

[68] *Tit-Bits*, 13 July 1912. See also *ibid.*, 29 June 1912, 6 July 1912.

[69] Interestingly, retailers also used 'comic' figures and content (in the national press at least) relatively rarely. But see, for example, the Phil May sketch used to advertise Samuel Bros.' 'Omne Tempus' raincoat, in *The Graphic*, 1 April 1905.

[70] John Tosh, *A Man's Place: Masculinity and the Middle-Class Home in Victorian England* (Yale University Press, New Haven, 1999), pp. 174–94.

[71] *C. B. Fry's Magazine,* June 1904. Quoted in John Lowerson, *Sport and the*

English Middle Classes 1870–1914 (Manchester University Press, Manchester, 1993), pp. 11–12.

[72] *The Wide World Magazine*, December 1912. The reference to officers is significant. The waterproofs cost a minimum of 55s. See also *The Sphere*, 24 November 1906.

[73] It is worth noting that contemporary commentators viewed this type of advertising as a response to ahistorical and essentialist 'hunting instincts' among (mostly young) men. See Walter Dill Scott, *The Psychology of Advertising* (Sir Isaac Pitman & Sons, London, 1909, first published 1908), pp. 64–6.

[74] *The Graphic*, 5 July 1890. Fifteen years after his mission to rescue David Livingstone (1871), Henry Stanley had led the Emin Pasha Relief Expedition. Richards, *The Commodity Culture*, pp. 121–46. Richards observes how in the hands of late nineteenth-century advertisers, commodities were made to serve as bulwarks of empire. *Ibid.*, pp. 119–67. See also Loeb, *Consuming Angels*, pp. 79–85.

[75] *News of the World*, 1 April 1900.

[76] Fred W. Burgess, *The Practical Retail Draper: A Complete Guide for the Drapery and Allied Trades* (Virtue and Co., London, 1912–14), vol. 3, p. 251.

[77] *The Badminton Magazine*, May 1896, August 1901; *C. B. Fry's Magazine*, April 1908.

[78] *The Badminton Magazine*, January 1896, May 1901; *C. B. Fry's Magazine*, January 1910.

[79] *C. B. Fry's Magazine*, June 1912; *Illustrated London News*, 28 July 1908.

[80] *The Badminton Magazine*, May 1906, April 1914; *C. B. Fry's Magazine*, September 1908, October 1912.

[81] *C. B. Fry's Magazine*, February 1905, March 1905, December 1912.

[82] *Daily Mail*, 12 October 1900; *C. B. Fry's Magazine*, January 1910.

[83] Graham Dawson, *Soldier Heroes: British Adventure, Empire and the Imagining of Masculinities* (Routledge, London, 1994), especially pp. 62–76. See also Christopher Breward, 'Sartorial spectacle: clothing and masculine identities in the imperial city, 1860–1914', in F. Driver and D. Gilbert (eds), *Imperial Cities: Landscape, Display and Identity* (Manchester University Press, Manchester, 1999), pp. 238–53.

[84] Erskine Childers, *The Riddle of the Sands* (Penguin Books, London, 1995, first published 1903), pp. 25, 88, 93, 118.

[85] *The Badminton Magazine*, February 1896, April 1896, August 1896. Lowerson, *Sport and the English Middle Classes*, pp. 29–63.

[86] *C. B. Fry's Magazine*, October 1908. Such 'energetic' images were not limited to sports popular among working-class men, as can be seen by the images of golfers swinging clubs, or cyclists pedalling against an often-idyllic backdrop.

[87] *The Badminton Magazine*, July 1914.

[88] *C. B. Fry's Magazine*, May 1905.

[89] *Daily Mail*, 22 June 1904. See also *News of the World*, 4 May 1913.

[90] Burgess, *The Practical Retail Draper*, vol. 4, p. 23.

II PATTERNS AND PROCESSES

CHAPTER 4
WOMEN, WORK, AND THE CONSUMER REVOLUTION: LIVERPOOL IN THE LATE EIGHTEENTH CENTURY
Sheryllynne Haggerty

Introduction

This chapter focuses on women working in late eighteenth-century Liverpool, and pays particular attention to those active within, or affected by, the developing consumer economy of that period. It uses a range of quantitative and qualitative sources, including trade directories, parish registers, newspapers, probate documents and apprentice registers. Such records offer a different perspective on retailing history from the more commonly used evidence left by individual traders and firms, and produce a broader contextualization of distribution and consumption.

Records of individual traders and businesses can provide very detailed information of one person's business and a more intricate view of daily life and business practice, but those that are extant are likely to be from larger and more successful enterprises. In contrast, nominal sources offer a sense of the broader business community, and facilitate analysis of change over time.[1] For example, by grouping occupations together, in bands such as textiles, crafts, or grocers and shopkeepers, we can assess changes in Liverpool's working community across the period. The relative growth or decline of each sector can also be analysed by gender.[2] The Liverpool trade directories, mostly compiled by J. Gore, are very useful in this respect, as they are one of the few sources available in which women are listed on their own terms.[3] Parish registers and census records usually listed women with reference to their relationship to men, for example as 'wife of' or 'widow', whereas in directories they were more often entered by occupation. A quantitative analysis of the directories makes possible an assessment of the contribution of women to the formal economy. This methodology not only allows the contribution of both men and women at all levels of society to be discussed, it also moves away from a focus on the personal business histories of the 'giants' of the consumer revolution, such as Josiah Wedgwood. It must be stressed, however, that the figures below still underestimate the importance of women in the economy, since many women were not entered in the directories. These included domestic servants, as well as many (but not all) of the women who worked alongside their husbands, and others who, for various reasons, did not deem themselves, or were not deemed by others, to be worthy of an entry in the directory.

In order to conduct such a quantitative analysis, a database was constructed.[4] All women listed in *Gore's Directories* (*Gore's*) in the decennial sample years were entered, as were records from the parish registers and local newspapers.[5] A database not only facilitates 'number crunching', it also assists linkage and case studies. A variety of searches and queries can be performed, for example by name, gender, street or occupation. This means that disparate records can be traced regarding the same individuals, or families.[6] These can be connected and a case study of their lives reconstructed. However, eighteenth-century record keeping was often of a low standard, and this, combined with heavy in- and through-migration in Liverpool, meant that many people were not mentioned in the official records. In addition, the fact that sampling by its very nature only captures some people meant that linkage was severely hindered.[7] However, even in the case of women, notoriously under recorded, a certain amount of linkage has been possible.

The first section of this chapter will consider Liverpool's role within an Atlantic consumer society, before moving on to briefly discuss the occupational structure of both men and women. The bulk of the discussion then will focus on women's work and the changes produced by, or associated with, the consumer revolution. It will argue that despite the many problems faced by female entrepreneurs, women in Liverpool were an important factor in the distribution of consumer goods within the city.

Liverpool and the Atlantic consumer society

Britain's first commercial wet dock was opened in Liverpool in 1715. This was in response to the increasing trade of the port and its concomitant shipping needs. Leading merchants, whose trade was improving and who had influence on the town council, pushed for this important and pioneering project.[8] Soon, however, this first dock became known as the 'Old Dock'; as trade increased, so did the port infrastructure, and further docks were built throughout the century, reaching a total of 28 acres of dock space by 1796. Tonnage entering the port was 14,600 tons in 1709, 29,200 in 1751 and a massive 450,000 tons in 1800.[9] Seaborne trade was encouraged and facilitated by the development of inland transport infrastructure, including the Bridgewater Canal (completed in 1767) and the Trent and Mersey Canal (1777).[10] Liverpool's exports included rock salt, coal, English linen, glass, metal goods, and increasingly from the 1750s, earthenware and other manufactured items. Imports included hides and linen from Ireland, Baltic timber, sugar and rum from the West Indies, tobacco from America and wines from the European continent.[11] From small beginnings in the seventeenth century, Liverpool had become a major player in the late eighteenth-century Atlantic economy.

The rising prosperity of the port encouraged immigration into Liverpool, the population of which grew at an enormous rate during the eighteenth century. From a small populace of around 7000 in 1708, the town grew to over 34,000 by 1773 and to over 77,000 by 1801.[12] These people, until the end of the eighteenth century at least, could find employment within a wide manufacturing base. *Gore's*, printed from 1766 onwards, shows a great diversity of trades practised by men and women alike, including pottery, watch and clockmaking, metal making, shipbuilding, carpentry, sailmaking, ropemaking, textiles and milling. However, the laws of comparative advantage prevailed; as the Lancashire hinterland concentrated on producing textiles and Staffordshire increased earthenware production, Liverpool found that it could not compete in these areas; gradually the emphasis turned towards its strength – the port and commerce.

The rise of Liverpool as a major international port during the eighteenth century was part of a wider movement of people, ideas, ships and goods. Historians increasingly argue that a consumer economy was at the centre of the growing transatlantic trade. For example, Timothy Breen states that the spread of 'baubles' led to 'the birth of an Anglo-American "consumer society"';[13] the same Staffordshire pottery and Manchester textiles that were purchased in London and Liverpool could also be found in Philadelphia and Charleston.[14] The distribution of such goods was so wide that it allowed a common language of resistance to form in colonial responses to the Stamp Act of 1765 and the Townshend Act of 1767.[15] In England, entrepreneurs such as Josiah Wedgwood were able to exploit the widespread desire for new consumer items.[16]

Carole Shammas has shown that new consumer goods, especially food items, were available throughout all sections of society on both sides of the Atlantic.[17] She argues that by the end of the eighteenth century, tea, tobacco and sugar had become items of mass consumption, and estimates that the English 'working class' spent around 10 per cent of its budget on these commodities, especially tea and sugar.[18] Labourers and other poor people in cities such as Liverpool found that a breakfast of bread and butter, accompanied by sugared tea, was both easy and cheap to prepare. It saved on fuel costs and time, in addition to providing a quick and invigorating sugar rush. Furthermore, these were goods commonly imported through Liverpool, and were presumably easily available for distribution by grocers and shopkeepers around the city. These goods, as well as textiles and pottery, were broken down into smaller and smaller parcels as they reached further down the distribution process, making small shops a vital link in the provision of these goods to the poor.

Hoh Cheung and Lorna Mui have stressed the importance of small shops in the eighteenth-century urban economy. They state that 'such shops performed indispensable services without which a take-off into sustained growth would hardly have been possible.'[19] It is arguable that shops were especially important in fast-growing urban environments such as Liverpool, where self-sufficiency in any form must have been virtually impossible. Roger Wells' assertion that by the 1790s 'up to one hundred percent of urban inhabitants, were dependant on the market' may be an exaggeration, but there is no doubt that eighteenth-century town dwellers became increasingly reliant on small local shops and the credit they offered.[20] Mui and Mui suggest that back-street retailers would have stocked imported goods such as currants, raisins, pepper, rice and figs, as well as mustard, candles, soap, starch and many kinds of flour and bread. Small shops, they argue, were an essential link in the chain between wholesalers, principal shops and consumers, providing cheap versions of fashionable manufactured items, as well as foodstuffs, to the poorer sections of society.[21] Mui and Mui stress the importance of women in this section of the distribution chain. Women whose husbands or other family members worked outside the home could staff the small back street-shops, while at the same time caring for household and children. For women with children and no access to capital, the home may indeed have been the only place where they could afford to set up shop.[22]

In Liverpool, a number of circumstances affected women's opportunities to work within this consumer economy, many of which took the form of entrepreneurial, rather than paid employment. A particular problem common to port cities was the high percentage of men working as sailors, combined with the effects of press gangs in wartime, which left women to fend for themselves for long periods of time. In a study of London's East End, Michael Power has found that a third of the male labour force consisted of mariners of all ranks, with around 63 per cent of these being absent at any one time. When at home, these mariners were usually unemployed and often spent their wages very quickly.[23]

This is the context in which women working in Liverpool must be placed. They were urban women; but they were also working within the special environment of a fast-growing port, which might have presented them with particular problems or opportunities, just at the time when the country's economy as a whole was changing. As we shall see, women made a significant contribution to the economy of Liverpool. They were involved in the distribution of transatlantic consumer goods, which were both wanted and needed by a growing population.

Women and work in Liverpool

Before examining in detail the occupations of women in Liverpool, it is necessary to consider them in relation to the occupational structure of the city as a whole. When looking at occupational profiles, parish records are usually considered a reasonably reliable source, and are used here to study the male occupational structure, highlighted in Table 1.[24]

The table shows the persistent importance of 'Transport' (which includes mariners) and of 'Miscellaneous Crafts' as the main employment sectors for men. There was a rise in the number of 'Labourers' over the period (many of them presumably employed in the labour-intensive dock building programmes undertaken by the city), but a decline in the 'Textiles and Clothing' sector. The reduction in employment within the 'Textiles' sector reflects the enormous growth of cotton and linen production elsewhere in Lancashire. By 1811 Liverpool had the distinctive occupational structure of a port – very different from that of a manufacturing town. In 1811, for example, 94 per cent of Manchester's population was involved in 'Trade, Handicrafts and Manufacture', compared to 37 per cent in Liverpool, and 40 per cent in Hull, another port city.[25] This relatively small manufacturing base would therefore appear to be a common characteristic of a port economy. This was certainly the case in Liverpool, with transport being the second largest source of employment for men, and labouring becoming the third.

A cursory glance through the eighteenth-century trade directories shows that although women were involved in all types of crafts and occupations throughout the city, their occupational structure was very different from that of the men. However, this was also to change significantly during the period, and Table 2 illustrates this change.[26] Note the sharp rise in the number of women entered with an occupation in the directories. This was partly a reflection of the growing popularity of the directories, and partly of the general population increase. People entered in the directories rose from

TABLE 1 *Adult male occupations by year*

Occupation	1766 (n)	%*	1786 (n)	%	1805 (n)	%
Textiles and Clothing	35	12.6	19	6.2	10	2.7
Grocers and Shopkeepers	4	1.4	5	1.6	7	1.9
Food and Drink	12	4.3	13	4.2	12	3.3
Merchants, Brokers And Dealers	25	9.0	15	4.9	12	3.3
Professional, Administration And Education	9	3.2	18	5.9	27	7.3
Domestic Service, Taverns And Coffee Houses	6	2.2	1	0.3	2	0.5
Transport (including Mariners)	71	25.5	85	27.8	87	23.6
Miscellaneous Crafts	97	34.9	126	41.2	163	44.3
Labourers (including Agriculture)	19	6.8	23	7.8	48	13.0
Total	278	100	306	100	368	100

*Percentage of all male heads of households.
Source: Liverpool Parish Burial Registers.[27]

around 7 per cent of the population in 1773–4 to over 11.5 per cent in 1805.[28] It must be kept in mind therefore that the trends discussed below are relative; the absolute number of women listed in all categories rose over the period. Another *caveat*; the listings in *Gore's* appear to be a mixture of business and personal addresses of adults, rather than of businesses *per se*. The figures quoted below, therefore, refer to the number of persons involved in an activity, rather than the actual number of businesses.

The most striking trends can be observed in the 'Food and Drink' and 'Textiles and Clothing' categories, almost rising and falling conversely. Also significant are the rises in 'Grocers and Shopkeepers' and 'Merchants, Dealers and Brokers'. These areas were of vital importance to the consumer revolution, and will be discussed in detail below. Suffice to say that, despite Liverpool being the main port of the textile heartland of Lancashire, employment in the 'Textiles and Clothing' sector dropped dramatically, while the numbers of those involved in the provision of food and drink for the rising population, grew. Although women were involved in 'Miscellaneous Crafts', it was

TABLE 2 *Adult female occupations by year*

Occupation	1766 (n)	%*	1774 (n)	%	1787 (n)	%	1796 (n)	%	1805 (n)	%
Textiles and Clothing	33	50.0	65	31.6	55	15.9	104	14.5	103	12.3
Grocers and Shopkeepers	8	12.1	52	25.2	46	13.3	104	14.5	139	16.6
Food and Drink	6	9.1	46	22.3	179	51.9	284	39.6	363	43.3
Merchants, Brokers and Dealers	2	3.0	13	6.3	24	7.0	94	13.1	85	10.1
Professional, Administration and Education	3	4.5	10	4.9	17	4.9	85	11.9	73	8.7
Domestic Service, Taverns and Coffee Houses	6	9.1	1	0.5	6	1.7	2	0.3	31	3.7
Transport (including Mariners)	0	0.0	2	1.0	5	1.4	3	0.4	10	1.2
Miscellaneous Crafts	8	12.1	16	7.8	11	3.2	28	3.9	27	3.2
Labourers (including Agriculture)	0	0.0	1	0.5	2	0.6	13	1.8	7	0.8
Total	66	100.0	206	100.0	345	100.0	717	100.0	838	100.0

*Percentage of all women entered in *Gore's* with an occupation. Many more were simply entered as 'Mrs' or 'Miss', without an occupation.
Source: *Gore's Directories*.[29]

never a significant source of employment for them, and actually declined in importance over the period. This could be partly due to the general shift in emphasis in Liverpool from manufacture to trade, as well as to wider factors regarding apprenticeship and access to skilled trades more generally.[30] The small rise in the 'Professional, Administration and Education' category hides two movements, and is slightly misleading. First, women were pushed out of older professional occupations such as midwifery, and denied access to newer occupations, such as bookkeeper or clerk.[31] Second, women were increasingly moving into teaching. Of 73 women listed in this category in 1805, 52 were teachers, including those running five out of the six 'Ladies Boarding Schools' in the city.[32]

The category of 'Domestic Servants, Taverns and Coffee Houses' also hides conflicting movements. There was an increase in women working within the service sector as household servants, none of whom was entered in the directories.[33] At the same time, many women turned to running boarding and lodging houses. While there were no boarding houses recorded in 1796, women ran 17 of the 32 listed in 1805.[34] This may have been a response to being pushed out of working in taverns and coffee houses (as well as frequenting them), as these increasingly became male-orientated business spaces.[35] For instance, Ann Fishwick was running St George's Coffee House between at least 1766 and 1769, and Mary Fleetwood ran the Exchange Coffee House from at least 1766 to 1774, perhaps longer. Ann Fishwick eventually became a grocer, whilst by 1787 Mary Fleetwood was listed together with her sister Elizabeth in the millinery business.[36] Changing notions of what was suitable employment for women may also have affected their decision to shift trades.[37]

'Transport' was an insignificant occupation for women in Liverpool, although some, like Alice Liptrot, provided carrier transport between Liverpool and nearby cities.[38] This is in sharp contrast to men, for whom transport (which included mariners) provided around 23.5 per cent of employment in 1805.

Women, work and the consumer revolution in Liverpool

Having surveyed the broad patterns, this section considers key areas of female occupation in Liverpool, highlighted in Figure 1: 'Textiles and Clothing', 'Grocers and Shopkeepers', 'Food and Drink and Merchants' and 'Dealers and Brokers'.

As a whole, Figure 1 demonstrates that women managed to adapt to changing conditions in the port's economy. However, we must first deal with the sector that suffered the most serious decline in real terms. The growth of comparative advantage, and the increasing importance of the port itself to the economy, precipitated a serious decline in

women working in 'Textiles and Clothing'. This was especially
marked considering that elsewhere in the North-west females were in
demand for such work, due to their cheapness and supposed
dexterity.[39] Not only was there no large textile industry in Liverpool,
but significantly, women were generally deterred from entering the
more prestigious occupations of quality dressmaking, staymaking and
men's tailoring. *Gore's* of 1796 lists only three female staymakers,
compared to 26 male. One of these exceptions was Mrs Binks, who
was advertising as a stay and corset manufacturer in 1805, when she
announced her return from the capital with the leading fashions for
that year.[40]

In 1805 Liverpool women constituted 69 per cent and 100 per cent
of the millinery and mantua-making trades respectively.[41] However,
the number of women listed purely as milliners declined over the
period, while the number of mantua-makers increased. In 1766 there
were 24 female milliners and no mantua-makers listed. In 1805 these
numbers had changed to 18 and 18 respectively. Milliners combined
the functions of producers and retailers. Their stock was usually
wide-ranging, including hats, gloves, aprons, ruffles and hoops, and
their status may have been boosted by being able to advise their
customers on the 'correct' pattern, colour or style of clothing. Robert
Campbell, writing about the nature of different sources of
employment in the eighteenth century, stated that a milliner needed to
be a 'perfect Connoisseur in Dress & Fashion'.[42]

However, running a business in the millinery trade required capital,
and so was mostly restricted to the middle ranks of society. Between
£100 and £1000 would have been required, and at least £500 to set up
in a 'genteel' manner, very important in attracting the 'right'
clientele.[43] The decline in women milliners may have been due to the
increasing difficulty of raising the capital necessary to run a successful
shop, while mantua-making could be done from the home.[44] Castle
Street was the 'place to be seen' in Liverpool at this time.[45]
Significantly, while there were seven female milliners in Castle Street
in 1766, there were only two in 1787, and none after that. This could
have been due to financial pressures, or may have represented a
movement to other, newer streets. In 1805 there were milliners in
various areas of the city. Some, such as Sarah Karr and Ann Dewhurst,
both running millinery shops in 1774, may have been lesser
establishments. Both were situated in Pool Lane, which was near the
market and the butchers' shambles. Others had shops on busy main
streets, where they could enjoy a long career. For example, Elizabeth
Green ran a millinery shop at 16 Dale Street between 1766 and 1787.
Dale Street had a mixture of shops such as tailors, hosiers, warehouses
and merchants. It is possible therefore, that Elizabeth was running a

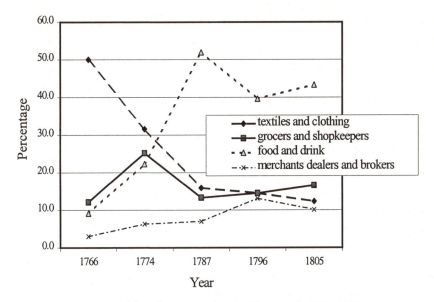

Figure 1 Key areas of female occupation in Liverpool 1766–1805.
Source: Gore's Directories.

'respectable' and profitable enterprise. Unfortunately there are no
records that allow us to estimate the scale of these businesses, or their
reasons for moving.

In contrast to the relative decline of 'Textiles and Clothing' was the
'Food and Drink' category, which in various ways was affected by, and
was part of, Liverpool's growing consumer economy. This sector rose
from 9.1 per cent of women's employment (six women) in 1766 to
43.3 per cent (363 women) in 1805, and included victuallers as well as
brewers and other food providers. Furthermore, women were a large
percentage of the total workforce employed in this sector, accounting
for 42 per cent of all victuallers in 1805.[46] This may have been due to
the fact that they could use their traditional skills in acquiring and
making food, and could fit this employment around their other duties.
A comparison with Birmingham confirms the importance of
victuallers to the urban economy; lists of business activity in both 1777
and 1830 show that their numbers were double those of shopkeepers
and dealers in groceries.[47] In the case of Liverpool, the growth of port
activity would not only have meant that many sailors and poor
labourers had to be catered for, but also that ships had to be
provisioned. Even women operating on a small scale could provide
victuals for ships. Ann Leadbetter provided fowls worth £4 13s and
Sarah Crutchley sold herbs worth £2 19s to the ship *Ingram* in 1784.[48]
It could be a lucrative occupation for some. One victualler, Elizabeth

Maddocks, had an estate worth between £2000 and £5000 when she died in 1796.[49]

As a percentage of women's occupations, 'Grocers and Shopkeepers' rose from 12.1 per cent in 1766 to 16.6 per cent in 1805. This may not appear to be a significant rise, but it should be seen in the context of the many problems women had to overcome. These included the need for increasing capital outlay, to which they had less access than men, and changes in weights and measures, which were often discussed in the male arenas of market administration or coffee houses.[50] There were 332 persons listed as purely grocers and general shopkeepers in *Gore's* for 1805, 38 per cent of whom were women. Grocery was considered the prestigious end of the retail market, and customers were likely to be drawn from the middle ranks of society. Grocers often ran wholesale as well as retail establishments, and mostly sold imported goods such as sugar, tea, coffee, currants and spices.

'Shopkeepers' include those who specialized in items such as stationery or ironmongery, but many shops were smaller general shops run by and for the poorer classes. Sometimes these had formal premises, but many may have just been part of a room at the back of a house. Shops on main roads were more select, and their clientele would have included merchants, professionals and manufacturers. General shopkeepers sold imported items, but also carried a variety of dry goods; these might include candles, wax, cotton, pots, pans and soap. They usually operated on a smaller scale than grocers and were purely retailers. In the later eighteenth century, women in Liverpool were running grocery and general shops throughout the city. Some of these were located behind the dock areas, where many of the poor would have lived. Elizabeth Hankey, for example, ran a grocery shop at 27 Mersey Street, near the old dock, over the period 1796 to 1805. However, there were also many businesses elsewhere around the city. Hannah Queen was running a general shop in Dale Street in 1796, while Elizabeth Ward had a shop in the less salubrious Stanley Street.[51] In the 'working-class' streets, and by the docks, the shops may have been of the 'meaner' sort, but they were still an important part of a local, regional and Atlantic distribution system.[52] Even the poor drank tea with sugar. Once a luxury, by the 1780s 'tea was the drink of the common British people'.[53] Sugar was almost a pre-requisite accompaniment, and as prices fell, similar goods acquired the status of 'necessities' rather than 'luxuries'.

The rise in the 'Merchant, Dealer and Broker' category may not look spectacular, but it hides a variety of important factors. In 1766 there were only two women in *Gore's* described as 'Merchants, Dealers or Brokers', while by 1805, 85 (10.1 per cent of all women with an occupation) listed themselves as such.[54] Some women described themselves in *Gore's* as dealers or traders in specific commodities, such as tea, flour, earthenware, cheese or liquor. For example, there were 15 tea dealers listed in Liverpool in 1805, eight of whom were women. This growth is in contrast to the percentage of men occupied within this area, which declined from 9.0 per cent to 3.3 per cent of all male employment.[55] This trend is probably a function of two factors; the higher capitalization required for the (overwhelmingly male) merchant sector, and women's entry into the lower status dealing areas.[56] Although they handled smaller quantities than men, women were not afraid to deal directly with merchants, wholesalers and shippers. In 1774, for example, Elizabeth Fleetwood was importing linen from Drogheda and Belfast.[57] Ann and Mary Hayes provided Iron Hoops worth £56 16s 2d for the cargo of the *Earl of Liverpool* in 1797.[58] Credit availability may have affected women's ability to engage in trade, but certainly did not entirely deter them.[59] However, most women were effectively debarred from importing directly from the Americas and Africa, due to the large-scale and long-term nature of credit in these areas of trade.

Somewhere below the more substantial dealers were the hucksters and higglers. These were often poorer women catering for the poorer sections of the community, outside the formal marketplaces and, possibly, nearer the margin of legality. Forestalling (buying up stock in order to make it scarce and push up the price) was a common crime. While it has not been possible to assess whether Liverpool women were more likely than men to be prosecuted for these crimes, Wendy Thwaites found that in her Oxfordshire sample of 1712, out of 24 people prosecuted for forestalling, 21 were women.[60] Women also encountered problems over regulations concerning weights and measures, and there were examples of this in Liverpool. Elizabeth Brown, for example, was convicted of selling bread deficient in weight in 1795, and Mary Edge was convicted for selling bread without a mark denoting its quality in the same quarter sessions.[61] However, Pamela Sharpe suggests that the risks entailed in breaking the law were considered worthwhile, because women 'could make equal gains with men' when they were acting as dealers or distributors, and working for profits, not wages.[62]

Occupations such as huckstering were often taken up and dropped as and when it was necessary to supplement the family income. However, times of necessity could also be the hardest for finding work. For example, Thwaites suggests that in good years such as 1766, female licensees might account for 11.8 per cent of total licenses, rather than the average 3.2 per cent. This would indicate that women were only allowed to participate in the formal economy when there was enough work for everyone, and that they were pushed into irregular and illegal trading in leaner times. She argues that there was only a token number of women within the formal arena, and that these were often widows carrying on their husbands' businesses. She states that women were rarely influential and never involved in the regulation of the marketplace.[63] Huckstering did not appear to be a long-term occupation in Liverpool. None of the women listed as hucksters was found in more than one directory.

Conclusion

This chapter has considered the employment of women in a commercial environment, complementing previous writing on women's involvement in agriculture and textiles. The use of quantitative sources such as directories has made possible an assessment of women's contribution to the formal economy. Using a mixture of quantitative and qualitative sources has also allowed a human aspect to be added to the economic discussion. Furthermore, it has shown how wider trends applied to the particular demography and economy of Liverpool.

Liverpool women were involved in the new consumer trades at many levels. They sold dry goods such as clothing and pottery, and were involved in the distribution and sale of goods such as tea, sugar and tobacco. Even though some of these businesses may have been carried out on a very small scale, Mui and Mui have argued that so-called 'petty retailers' were very important in the distribution of foods such as bread or flour, tea, sugar and various dried fruits and spices to the lower classes, and this would certainly appear to be the case in Liverpool.[64]

The chapter has argued that the decline in the textile sector was probably a function of comparative advantage at the regional level, while the distribution of food rose as a source of employment in order to feed the rising population. Women in Liverpool were also able to deal directly with wholesalers and importers and, on occasion, to import on their own account. A legal, social and business framework that worked to the benefit of their male counterparts may have inhibited Liverpool women's activities, as they no doubt did elsewhere. However, through determination or necessity, women could still perform vital functions within the formal economy. We cannot, from this evidence, say whether women were pushed out of textiles and resorted to food and drink, or whether they were pulled into the new areas by hopes of higher income and independence. We cannot impute motive; further qualitative research will be required to ascertain these essential factors and motivations. What we can say is that women became a very important factor in the growth of Liverpool itself, and in the distribution and sale of consumer goods at the local level, thereby becoming part of a transatlantic network of distributors.

Acknowledgements
I would like to thank Dr Graeme J. Milne and Dr Diane Ascot for their help and comments on drafts of this chapter.

Appendix A
Sources and methodology
Gore's Directories were the main source used to establish women's employment patterns during the period. These trade directories listed the names, addresses and occupations of those who *wanted to be so listed*. Where an occupation was given, the entries appeared to be for business addresses, which would appear correct inasmuch as the directory was meant as a guide for prospective customers (with regard to men, multiple addresses were sometimes given, but this never happened in the case of women). One hundred per cent of women listed for the years 1766, 1774, 1787, 1796 and 1805 were entered on to the database. Early editions were compact, and the entries quite sparse. However, in the course of the eighteenth century the fashion for these types of publications grew, and while there were around 1150 entries in 1766, the number grew to over 9000 by 1805. More importantly, the range of entries also changed, including an increasingly diverse number of occupations, although some were still not considered worthy of inclusion. Mariners were not entered, nor were domestic servants, a major source of employment for women. Furthermore, this source did not list any informal economic activity. Housewives, and those women who assisted their husbands in their trades, may have been omitted. The directories are not therefore simply a reflection of the growth in trade in Liverpool, but also of the recording of it. However, they are an invaluable source that lists the work women did in their own right, rather than in connection with men. The classification of occupations into categories is listed in Appendix B. In the chapter, where a figure is given for an occupation, this is the number of those listed purely or primarily with that occupation. Where no female first name or prefix was given for a person listed in the directory, the gender was taken to be male. As a consequence, although the numbers quoted for women are the minimum, they are also robust.

In order to provide a comparison with male employment in Liverpool, samples of the Burial Registers were taken. One hundred per cent samples of the following Burial Registers were taken: St George's – 1766, 1782 and 1805; St Nicholas' – 1766, 1786 and 1805 and St Paul's – 1769, 1782 and 1805. Where records for a particular year were not extant, the nearest one was taken. The details of the (male) head of household or of the relative of the person who had been buried were taken. Burials were used because they covered a wide span of ages. Baptisms would have skewed the data towards younger males, and Marriage Registers are not reliable in Liverpool because many people came from the surrounding parishes to be married in the city.[65] Some of the richer members of the city's population may have left the parish on retirement, but this would have been a small number, and should not significantly affect the results given here. The numbers (n) given in Table 1 do not include female heads of households where given, i.e. as spinster or widow, or those listed as 'Mrs'. It is intended, as part of ongoing research, to include later a sample from another large Anglican register, St Peter's. There are also some small non-Anglican registers extant for the same period. However, these are relatively small in number, patchy, and do not consistently provide information of use for this project. They were therefore omitted from the sample. The registers already sampled include addresses from all over the city, and a comprehensive range of occupations; it is therefore probable that further sampling will not significantly change the results presented here.

Decennial samples of the local newspapers were also taken, and other sources were used where available and appropriate. However, in the context of this paper they were mainly used to highlight and colour the quantitative discussion, rather than as substantial sources in their own right. The newspapers sampled were *Williamson's Liverpool Advertiser*, 1766, 1774 and 1787; *Billinge's Gazeteer*, 1795; *Billinge's Liverpool Advertiser and Marine Intelligencer*, 1796; *Gore's General Advertiser*, 1805; *Liverpool Chronicle*, 1805.

Appendix B
List of occupations included in each sector of employment (male and female)

Textiles and Clothing
Bonnet Manufacturer, Calenderer, Clear Starcher, Collarmaker, Cordwainer, Cotton Spinner, Drapers of all descriptions, Dressmaker, Embroiderer, Flax Dresser, Glover, Gown Glazer, Haberdasher, Hatter, Heelmaker, Hosier, Mantua Maker, Milliner, Muslin Darner, Seamstress, Shoemaker, Silkworker, Slopshop, Staymaker, Stocking Grafter, Weaver.

Grocers and Shopkeepers
Bookseller, China Shop, Glass Shop, Greengrocer, Grocer, Ironmonger, Navigation Shop, Seed Shop, Shopkeeper, Staffordshire

Ware Shop, Stationer, Tea Shop, Tobacconist, Toy Shop.

Food and Drink
Baker, Brewer, Butcher, Cheesemonger, Confectioner, Cook, Cowkeeper, Eating House, Fishmonger, Fruiterer, Maker and Seller of Sweets, Milk House, Poulterer, Victualler.

Merchants, Dealers and Brokers
Brokers of all description, Changekeeper, Chapman, Dealers of all descriptions, Factor, Flour Seller, Higgler, Huckster, Linen Repository, Maltman, Merchants of all descriptions, Pawnbroker, Tinker, Upholder, Warehouse Keeper.

Professional, Administration and Education
Apothecary, Architect, Armed Service Personnel, Attorney, Bookkeeper, Circulating Library, Clerk, Comedian, Doctor, Druggist, Holder of Public Office, Keeper of Leeches, Land Surveyor, Matron, Midwife, Minister of Religion, Musician, Organist, Painter, Public Officers of all kinds, Register Office for Servants, Schools and Teachers of all descriptions, Surgeon, Undertaker, Writing Master.

Domestic Service, Taverns and Coffee Houses
Boarding and Lodging House, Coffee House, Hostler, Inn and Tavern Keeper.

Transport (including Mariners)
Boatman, Boathouse Manager, Carrier, Carter, Coachman, Coach and Horse Hirer, Horse and Stable Keeper, Mariner, Pilot, Porter, Sailor, Tidesman, Waterman.

Miscellaneous Crafts
Barber, Boatbuilder, Blockmaker, Bricklayer, Brushmaker, Cabinetmaker, Chairmaker, Clockmaker, Coachmaker, Combmaker, Cooper, Cork Cutter, Currier, Engraver, Farrier, Glassmaker, Glazier, Gluemaker, Gunsmith, Hairdresser, Instrument Maker, Iron Water Manufacturer, Joiner, Mason, Metal Workers of all descriptions, Miller, Painter, Paper Box Maker, Pearl Ash Maker, Perfumer, Peruke Maker, Pipemaker, Plaisterer, Plumber, Pot Ash Manufacturer, Potter, Printer, Rigger, Roper, Sadler, Shipwright, Sailmaker, Sawyer, Skinner, Slater, Tallow Chandler, Tanner, Tobacco Manufacturer, Turner, Umbrella Maker, Upholsterer, Watchmaker, Well Sinker, Wheelwright.

Labourers (including Agriculture)
Chimney Sweep, Farmer, Fisherman, Gardener, Groom, Husbandman,

Labourer, Mangler, Soldier, Washer, Watchman, Yeoman.

Notes

[1] Nominal sources are those that list only brief personal details, such as parish records, directories or tax lists.

[2] See Appendix A for a discussion of the sources and sampling method, and Appendix B for a list of the occupations included in each category.

[3] Trade directories were often compiled using different parameters; in some cases, for example, only heads of household or only those deemed 'worthy' by the compiler were included. In Liverpool, people were invited to propose themselves for entry. There is no evidence to suggest that entries were rejected, and the wide range of occupations entered would imply that they were not. For a discussion of the rise of trade directories, see Penelope Corfield, '"Giving directions to the town": the early town directories', *Urban History Yearbook* 11 (1984), pp. 22–35. For their use in other studies, see Edward P. Duggan, 'Industrialization and the development of urban business communities: research problems, sources and techniques', *Local Historian* 11/8 (1975), pp. 461–2; Roger Scola, 'Food markets and shops in Manchester, 1770–1870', *Journal of Historical Geography* 1/2 (1975), p. 156.

[4] The database amounted to over 21,000 records at the time of presenting the paper on which this chapter is based. I am indebted to Paul Laxton, Department of Geography, University of Liverpool, for the generous use of his computerized editions of the 1796 and 1805 *Gore's Directories*. The database is still under construction and forms part of my doctoral thesis. Sheryllynne Haggerty, 'Trade and trading communities in the late eighteenth-century Atlantic Liverpool and Philadelphia', unpublished PhD thesis, University of Liverpool (2002).

[5] The years sampled were 1766, 1774, 1787, 1796 and 1805.

[6] For more on quantitative history and the uses of databases, see Roderick Floud, *An Introduction to Quantitative Methods for Historians* (Methuen, London, 1973); Evan Maudsley and Thomas Munck, *Computing for Historians: An Introductory Guide* (Manchester University Press, Manchester, 1993).

[7] For a discussion of the problems of linkage in Liverpool, see Fiona Lewis, 'The demographic and occupational structure of Liverpool: a study of the parish registers, 1660–1750', unpublished PhD thesis, University of Liverpool (1993), chapter 5.

[8] For further information regarding the influence of the merchants over the council and the rise of the port, see Michael J. Power, 'Councillors and commerce in Liverpool, 1650–1750', *Urban History* 24/3 (1997), pp. 301–23.

[9] Sheila Marriner, *The Economic and Social Development of Merseyside, 1750–1960* (Croom Helm, London, 1982), p. 31. For a detailed view of the construction of the docks, see Adrian Jarvis, *The Liverpool Dock Engineers* (Alan Sutton, Stroud, 1996).

[10] For further information on the transport infrastructure, see Marriner, *The Economic and Social Development*, pp. 14–23; John Langton, 'Liverpool and its hinterland in the late eighteenth century', in B. L. Anderson and P. J. M. Stoney (eds), *Commerce, Industry and Transport: Studies in Economic Change in*

Merseyside (Liverpool University Press, Liverpool, 1983), pp. 1–25.

[11] T. C. Barker, 'Lancashire coal, Cheshire salt and the rise of Liverpool', *Transactions of the Historic Society of Lancashire and Cheshire* 103 (1951), pp. 83–101; Francis E. Hyde, 'The growth of trade 1700–1950', in W. Smith (ed.), *Scientific Survey of Merseyside* (University Press of Liverpool, Liverpool, 1953), pp. 148–63.

[12] Richard Lawton, 'Genesis of population', in Smith (ed.), *Scientific Survey*, pp. 120–31; John Langton and Paul Laxton, 'Parish registers and urban structure: the example of late eighteenth century Liverpool', *Urban History Yearbook* 5 (1978), pp. 74–84; Paul Laxton, 'Liverpool in 1801: a manuscript return for the first national Census of population', *Transactions of the Historic Society of Lancashire and Cheshire* 130 (1981), pp. 73–113; Michael J. Power, 'The growth of Liverpool', in J. Belchem (ed.), *Popular Politics, Riot and Labour: Essays in Liverpool History 1790–1940* (Liverpool University Press, Liverpool, 1992), pp. 21–37.

[13] Timothy H. Breen, 'Baubles of Britain: the American and consumer revolutions of the eighteenth century', *Past and Present* 119 (1988), p. 77. He argues that consumer goods made it possible for the colonists in America to 'imagine' themselves as a nation, p. 104. These 'baubles', or manufactured goods, were often seen as unnecessary by contemporary American thinkers, such as Benjamin Franklin.

[14] Timothy H. Breen, 'An empire of goods: the Anglicization of colonial America, 1690–1776', *Journal of British Studies* 25/4 (1986), pp. 467–99; Ian K. Steele, 'Empire of migrants and consumers: some current approaches to the history of colonial Virginia', *Virginia Magazine of History and Biography* 99/4 (1991), pp. 489–512.

[15] Breen, 'Baubles of Britain'. The Stamp Act, which taxed items in the American colonies such as commercial and legal documents and pamphlets, was enacted in order to recover the costs of the seven-year war, but was seen by the colonists as the imposition of taxation without the benefits of representation.

[16] See Neil McKendrick, John Brewer and John H. Plumb, *The Birth of a Consumer Society: The Commercialisation of Eighteenth Century England* (Indiana University Press, London, 1982), for discussions of the rising 'consumer society'.

[17] Carole Shammas, *The Pre-Industrial Consumer in England and America* (Clarendon Press, Oxford, 1990).

[18] Carole Shammas, 'The eighteenth-century diet and economic change', *Explorations in Economic History* 21/3 (1984), p. 266. For the adoption of tea, coffee, chocolate, sugar and tobacco into European diet and culture, see Woodruff D. Smith, 'From coffee house to parlour: the consumption of coffee, tea and sugar in north-western Europe in the seventeenth and eighteenth centuries', in J. Goodman, P. E. Lovejoy and A. Sherratt (eds), *Consuming Habits: Drugs in History and Anthropology* (Routledge, London, 1995), pp. 148–64; Jordan Goodman, 'Excitantia: or, how Enlightenment Europe took to soft drugs', in Goodman, Lovejoy and Sherratt (eds), *Consuming Habits*, pp. 126–47.

[19] Hoh Cheung Mui and Lorna H. Mui, *Shops and Shopkeeping in Eighteenth*

Century England (Routledge, London, 1989), p. 6.

[20] Roger Wells, *Wretched Faces: Famine in Wartime England, 1793–1801* (Alan Sutton, Gloucester, 1988), p. 21.

[21] Mui and Mui, *Shops and Shopkeeping*, p. 71.

[22] *Ibid.*, p. 188.

[23] Michael J. Power, 'The East London working community in the seventeenth century', in P. Corfield and D. Keene (eds), *Work in Towns* (Leicester University Press, Leicester, 1990), pp. 106–9.

[24] The parish records were used because sampling them was a more manageable task than the directories. They also provided a good control sample, as the directories are not comprehensive in coverage. My thesis does, however, include direct comparisons of men and women listed in the directories as members of the trading community.

[25] BPP Census Reports, *Abstract of the Answers and Returns – 1801* (reprinted Cass, London, 1968). For a comparison with Hull, see Gordon Jackson, *Hull in the Eighteenth Century* (Oxford University Press, Oxford, 1972).

[26] All the figures and names quoted in this section and the next are based on the author's directories' database unless otherwise noted.

[27] Parish Burial Registers: St Nicholas'– 1766 (283 NIC 1/5), 1786 (283 NIC 1/6), 1805 (283 NIC 1/8); St George's – 1766, 1782, 1805 (283 GEO 1/1); St Paul's – 1769, 1786, 1805 (283 PAU 1/1); Liverpool Record Office, Liverpool.

[28] Entries in *Gore's Directory* for 1774 (2500) and 1805 (9000) compared to population figures for 1773 (34,000) and 1801 (77,000) respectively.

[29] *Gore's Directories*, 1766, 1774, 1787, 1796 (MIC.513), 1805 (DA690.L8.K1.1805), Sidney Jones Library, University of Liverpool, Liverpool.

[30] Regarding the changing gender divisions of labour, see Maxine Berg, *The Age of Manufactures* (Basil Blackwell, Oxford, 1985), chapters 6 and 7; Bridget Hill, *Women, Work and Sexual Politics in Eighteenth Century England* (Basil Blackwell, Oxford, 1989); Deborah Valenze, *The First Industrial Woman* (Oxford University Press, New York, 1995); Pamela Sharpe, *Adapting to Capitalism: Working Women in the English Economy 1700–1850* (MacMillan Press, London, 1996).

[31] Leonore Davidoff and Catherine Hall, *Family Fortunes: Men and Women of the English Middle Class, 1780–1850* (Hutchinson, London, 1987), p. 309. Davidoff and Hall suggest that professionalization, which often seemed to exclude women, also occurred in some craft-based trades; for example, wheelwrights and millwrights were the forerunners of engineers.

[32] For a further discussion regarding education as a female occupation, see Susan Skedd, 'Women teachers and the expansion of schooling in England, c. 1760–1820', in H. Barker and E. Chalus (eds), *Gender in Eighteenth Century England* (Longman, London, 1997), pp. 101–25.

[33] It would appear that *Gore's* was typical of most directories in excluding servants. See Peter Lindert, 'English occupations 1670–1811', *Journal of Economic History* 40/4 (1980), pp. 685–712; Hill, *Women Work and Sexual Politics*, chapter 8; Valenze, *The First Industrial Woman*, chapter 9.

[34] See also Olwen Hufton, 'Women without men: widows and spinsters in Britain and France in the eighteenth century', *Journal of Family History* 9/4

(1984), pp. 355–76. Hufton argues that women often worked together in various small businesses. This acted as protection and allowed them to share living costs.

[35] John Pelzer and Linda Pelzer, 'The coffee houses of Augustan London', *History Today* 32 (1982), pp. 40–7; Smith, 'From coffee house to parlour', pp. 154–7; James Walvin, *Fruits of Empire: Exotic Produce and British Taste, 1660–1800* (MacMillan Press, London, 1997), p. 42.

[36] See also A. H. Arkle, 'The early coffee houses of Liverpool', *Transactions of the Historic Society of Lancashire and Cheshire* 64 (1912), p. 7.

[37] Davidoff and Hall, *Family Fortunes*, especially chapter 6.

[38] *Liverpool Chronicle*, 7 August 1805.

[39] As previously mentioned, this decline was in real terms. The actual number of women recorded in *Gore's* as engaged in this area rose over the period, but declined as a percentage of entries. See Table 2. Weaving continued in Liverpool as a male occupation, but spinning was rarely mentioned.

[40] *Liverpool Chronicle*, 7 August 1805.

[41] In Colchester, women controlled 84 per cent of the making and retailing of women's clothes, suggesting that women always dominated this sector. See Shani D'Cruze, 'To acquaint the ladies: women traders in Colchester c. 1750–1800', *Local Historian* 17/3 (1986), p. 159.

[42] Robert Campbell, *The London Tradesman* (printed by T. Gardner, London, 1757, first printed 1747), p. 207.

[43] Ivy Pinchbeck, *Women Workers and the Industrial Revolution* (Routledge, London, 1930), p. 287.

[44] For more about credit arrangements in the Liverpool area, see Bruce L. Anderson, 'Aspects of capital and credit in Lancashire during the eighteenth century', unpublished MA thesis, University of Liverpool (1966); Bruce L. Anderson, 'Provincial aspects of the financial revolution of the eighteenth century', *Business History* 11/1 (1969), pp. 11–22; Bruce L. Anderson, 'Money and the structure of credit in the eighteenth century', *Business History* 12/2 (1970), pp. 85–101. For the law regarding women's property, see Susan Staves, *Married Women's Separate Property in England, 1660–1833* (Harvard University Press, Cambridge MA, 1990).

[45] Langton and Laxton, 'Parish registers', p. 81.

[46] Women accounted for 301 of the 718 victuallers.

[47] Duggan, 'Industrialization', pp. 461–2.

[48] Tuohy Ships Papers, 380 TUO 4/10, Liverpool Record Office.

[49] Will of Elizabeth Maddocks, WCW Maddocks, 26/6/1796, Preston Record Office, Preston.

[50] Changes in weights and measures were mostly discussed in the male sphere of the inn or the coffee house, which often left women uninformed. Wendy Thwaites, 'Women in the market place: Oxfordshire c. 1690–1800', *Midland History* 9 (1984), p. 34.

[51] I. C. Taylor, 'The court and cellar dwelling: the eighteenth century origin of the Liverpool slum', *Transactions of the Historic Society of Lancashire and Cheshire* 122 (1970), pp. 75–6.

[52] I have used the term street rather than area or district because spatial

organization was not very advanced for most of this period in Liverpool. See Colin Pooley, 'The residential segregation of migrant communities in mid-Victorian Liverpool', *Transactions of the Institute of British Geographers*, New Series 4/2 (1979), pp. 258–77.

[53] Walvin, *Fruits of Empire*, p. 15.

[54] 'Huxsters and higglers' were included in the Merchants, Dealers and Brokers category because their role was considered more that of a dealer (distributor) than a provider of food.

[55] It should be stressed, however, that the male figures are derived from the parish records rather than the directories, and so are not directly comparable.

[56] Ralph Davis, *A Commercial Revolution: English Overseas Trade in the Seventeenth and Eighteenth Centuries* (The Historical Association, London, 1967), p. 14.

[57] *Williamson's Liverpool Advertiser*, 20 May 1774.

[58] Leyland and Bullins Ships Papers, AE52/2, HSBC Archives, London. Other women were involved in providing food for the crew as well as working on the outfitting of the ship itself.

[59] Many women also held bank accounts. At Heywood's Bank in Liverpool, women held 27 per cent of accounts between 1788 and 1797. They did not hold as much money as men, nor for as long, but they were not deterred from entering the 'male' business environment of the bank. Heywood's Bank Ledger 1788–1797, Hey 0199–0001, Barclays Archives, Manchester.

[60] Thwaites, 'Women in the market place', p. 30.

[61] *Billinge's Gazeteer*, 19 October 1795.

[62] Sharpe, *Adapting to Capitalism*, p. 17.

[63] Thwaites, 'Women in the market place', pp. 26–7.

[64] Mui and Mui, *Shops and Shopkeeping*.

[65] For a further discussion regarding the parish registers in Liverpool, and population trends generally, see Lewis, 'Demographic and occupational structure'.

CHAPTER 5
REGIONAL VARIATIONS IN THE DEVELOPMENT
OF MULTIPLE RETAILING IN ENGLAND, 1890–1939
Andrew Alexander, Gareth Shaw and Deborah Hodson

Introduction: the regional dimension

Existing studies of the evolution of retail patterns have been by and large intra-regional in nature, focusing as they have on variations within particular regions, sub-regions or individual settlements. Studies on Tyneside, parts of the West Riding of Yorkshire, South-west England, the Potteries and Norfolk are all clear examples of such intra-regional perspectives.[1] In spite of their different aims, approaches and periods of study, they are suggestive of a complex, and at times conflicting, picture of retail development. As such they indirectly highlight the significance of regional variations in the patterns of retail growth. In addition to these studies there is a rather limited literature that attempts a wider, inter-regional view of retailing. For example, Martin Phillips used census data to explore county level variations in retail provision for selected trades in the nineteenth century.[2] On a less rigorous basis, Henry Smith sought to provide a contemporary view of levels of retail provision for England in the 1930s.[3] Both studies show strong geographical patterns of retail provision that serve to highlight regional variations, which were identifiable in both the nineteenth and twentieth centuries.

Peter Scott, in his pioneering work on the geography of retailing, claimed that 'even in Britain there are significant regional variations that result from the evolution of multiple shop trading and consumer preference.'[4] He also argued, from a somewhat limited study of multiple retailers and their branch shops, that over time such variations would become less pronounced, but nevertheless still persist for various reasons. Closer study of Scott's ideas and explanations reveal that they were largely based on more detailed research by

127

Margaret Hall, John Knapp and Christopher Winsten, which had sought to explain variations in retail patterns in Britain, the USA and Canada in 1950.[5] This was a wide-ranging comparative study that had as its main focus levels of retail provision and productivity. Both studies highlighted variations in provision and argued that such variations could be explained by three main causal variables, namely: 'levels of per capita income', 'variations in population density', and 'rates of population growth'. More importantly, they presented these key variables as different but interrelated explanatory models. Hall, Knapp and Winsten found that such variables were more robust than inter-regional patterns in explaining variations between different countries.[6]

Space does not permit a full discussion of these causal models, but we can highlight some of their key features. Firstly, all of the models explained the growth of large-scale multiples as some function of changes in consumer demand, as measured by per capita income, variations in consumer density and population growth. Secondly, strong emphasis was given to the interactions between demand variables and supply ones, again to explain the differential growth of large multiples. Supply side variables such as the 'price of management', the 'flexibility of capital' and the 'cost of labour' were all highlighted. In a further attempt to explain the growth and pattern of chain stores, they added a model based on 'age of settlement'. Here they conceded that other effects were also at work, namely, 'that chains have tended to start in areas where their founders were already shopkeeping and then spread'.[7]

Hall, Knapp and Winsten's study highlights the need to explore the relationship between structural and spatial change within the industry. As argued elsewhere,[8] the structural-spatial nexus, the reflexive relationship between retail structure and organization and the geography of retail activity, is significant in determining the nature of retail competition – and hence change – at two inter-related levels. Firstly, at the level of 'inter-type' competition; for instance, competition between independent and multiple retailers. Secondly, at the firm level; here we might consider the pathways to growth of individual multiple firms in the light of changing structural, internal organizational and spatial tendencies. While the case for a closer integration of structural and spatial elements is neither new nor fleeting,[9] it has received surprisingly limited attention in much of the retail history literature. Two consequences are worthy of brief mention: retailers' spatial strategies have on occasion been analysed in isolation from the very competitive conditions that demanded their establishment; and concerns have been raised that the emergence of innovative retail institutions, such as the multiple retailers, has been confused with questions of their rate of diffusion and overall significance.[10]

What can we learn from these different and fragmented perspectives on the regional dimension of retailing? One obvious point is that variations in retail patterns, as measured by levels of retail provision, have some longevity, being identifiable throughout the nineteenth and twentieth centuries. Indeed, contrary to Scott's argument,[11] they have shown little sign of becoming less pronounced over time.[12] Furthermore, the rise of large-scale multiples represents a significant factor in variations in regional patterns of retailing. Finally, our levels of knowledge on the scale and significance of regional variations is somewhat limited. Past studies provide hints of variations and possible explanatory frameworks, but few concrete answers have emerged.

This chapter seeks to improve our understanding of regional variations in the pace and nature of retail change. Part of a wider project to explore the locational strategies of British multiple retailers between 1850 and 1939, the chapter focuses on the development of multiple retailing in three English regions between 1890 and 1939. The methodology employed is outlined below. The ensuing analysis and discussion considers regional variations in retailing in the light of previous work that suggests that multiple retailers pursued policies of 'disruptive' competition on many fronts.[13] The scale and significance of regional variations in multiple retail development is explored firstly through an analysis of the grocery and provisions trade at three time periods across our three regions. A firm-level approach is then adopted, focusing on the variety store trade. This highlights the importance of regional variations in retail provision on individual firms' locational strategies.

Definitions, methods and sources

A common obstacle faced by the student of retail history is the confusion that exists in the definition and classification of retail types. This is no different in the case of multiple retailing. Organizations with a minimum of two,[14] five,[15] and ten or more[16] retail outlets have variously been defined as multiples. James Jefferys' definition of the multiple as 'a firm, other than a Co-operative society, possessing ten or more retail establishments',[17] has been one of the most widely adopted. It is based in part, he claimed, on an economic justification 'in that in most trades significant economies of scale were not present until a firm operated from at least ten branches'. However, no conclusive empirical evidence can be found for claims that significant economies of scale begin to function when the retailer's business exceeds nine stores. Indeed, other studies have suggested that greater savings in operating expenses could be achieved in the expansion between six and ten branches.[18]

Our study definition broadly corresponds with the lower limits to economies of scale that have been identified, considering those organizations with five or more retail establishments to be multiple retailers. This permits the inclusion of those firms operating small chains of establishments at a local and regional scale, but with fewer than ten outlets, as well as those larger retailers operating at a national scale. Analysis of the project database reveals a significant number of the former type of company in our chosen study trades. These retailers were of unequivocal importance to the retail structure in the areas where they traded.[19]

Alternative attempts have been made to provide a definition of the multiple store based on the degree of centralization of the management function, but these are no less problematic. Richard Longstreth, for instance, in his study of retail change in Los Angeles between 1920 and 1950, concluded: 'A true chain operation had centralised management that included accounting, advertising, purchasing of stock, price and policy setting, and warehousing.'[20] He considered that a clear distinction needed to be drawn between the 'multiple store' and the 'branch shop'. However, a cursory glance at the retail trade press in inter-war Britain highlights the difficulties inherent in drawing such distinctions. If the issue in branch shop management was the balance between efficiency and individuality, then the methods used to achieve this balance would appear to have differed markedly. Hence, in the 'Branch Store Management' feature of *Grocery*, the headline of an interview with the general manager of the Birmingham-based grocery firm Wrenson's proclaimed: 'Each branch a Separate Unit. We rely on the Manager's Judgment.'[21] The article continued: 'Every branch is virtually a master grocer and his shop is a separate unit run on lines which he considers make for success in his particular district.' By way of contrast, in a later issue the same feature revealed the seemingly alternative approach of Thompson's Red Stamp Stores, a similar sized chain, (over 100 branches), originating in Gateshead. In this case standardization throughout the entire organization was considered to make for equal success for all branches. Consequently, 'all are Head Office controlled, as in our experience successful branch store management relies entirely upon thoroughly training all employees into our ways and seeing that they keep to them in practice.'[22] Indeed, more detailed consideration of 17 case studies presented in the Branch Store Management feature of *Grocery* between 1936 and 1939 reveals little real evidence of the individualization of branches beyond some attempts to personalize service and to develop specialized window displays. In one case, branch managers were empowered to manage staffing.[23]

Shop location data presented in this chapter is derived from the large-scale database of fixed-shop retail provision in England between 1850 and 1939 compiled as part of the wider project.[24] The structure of the main 'Outlets' table of the database and its content is illustrated in Table 1. Store location data, drawn from the trade directories, is linked to population data taken from the population census.[25] The location of each outlet has been identified and assigned to its appropriate settlement. This has been a considerable task, given the inconsistency with which fixed-shop locations were listed in the original trade directory sources. Each location has subsequently been assigned to its appropriate census enumeration district (Rural District, Urban District, Metropolitan Borough and County Borough. More than 500 districts are listed in the database), and given their respective population total.[26]

The 'Outlets' table is itself linked to a catalogue of selected materials from the trade press, retailer archives and government and trade association records. A comprehensive picture of multiple retailing activity can thus be generated from the database at a variety of spatial and organizational scales. The classified trades sections of more than 230 Kelly's county directories have been used to derive the locational data incorporated in the database. In the case of four cities, Bristol, Birmingham, Hull and York, the cross-checking of county and town directories revealed the former to be insufficiently comprehensive as a source for our purposes. In these instances the county directory was augmented with the classified trades listings from the relevant Kelly's town directories.

The database records individual shop entries for the multiple and the independent retailers listed. Co-operative stores are excluded as these are insufficiently reported in the directories. Nonetheless, we of course recognize their significance to national, regional and local retail structures and acknowledge that co-operative retailing displayed a complex picture of intra- and inter-regional variations during the study period that also requires further study.[27] The database includes three retail trades: the grocery and provisions, menswear and variety store trades. This choice incorporates important consumer goods trades in which multiple retail firms quickly developed a significant market share. In addition, the particular character of each of our chosen trades, including the composition of its retail types, the presence or otherwise of price control, and the locational requirements of its retailers, means that significant contrasts also exist between them.

The database incorporates a total of more than 343,000 individual shop entries, and covers three regions: South-west England (Cornwall, Devonshire, Dorsetshire, Somersetshire, Wiltshire, Gloucestershire), the West Midlands (Staffordshire, Shropshire, Warwickshire,

TABLE 1 *An extract from the 'outlets' table of the retail trades database**

Id	Date	Reg	Gr	Trade	Company	St no	Street	District	Town/City	Mple?	Population
3048	1914	SW	G	G&TD	HOME & COLONIAL	33	FORE STREET		TIVERTON	Yes	10205
3049	1914	SW	G	G&TD	HOME & COLONIAL	5	UNION STREET		TORQUAY	Yes	38771
3050	1914	SW	G	G&TD	HOME & COLONIAL	5	CHAPEL STREET		EXMOUTH	Yes	11962
3051	1914	SW	G	G&TD	HOME & COLONIAL	97	UNION STREET	EAST STONEHOUSE	PLYMOUTH	Yes	207456
3052	1914	SW	G	G&TD	HOME & COLONIAL	80	HIGH STREET		BIDEFORD	Yes	9078
3053	1914	SW	G	G&TD	HOME & COLONIAL	3	BANK STREET		NEWTON ABBOT	Yes	13711
3054	1914	SW	G	G&TD	HOME & COLONIAL	31	OLD TOWN STREET		PLYMOUTH	Yes	207456
3055	1914	SW	G	G&TD	HOOKE JAMES		TEMPLE STREET		SIDMOUTH	No	5612
3056	1914	SW	G	G&TD	HOOPER MRS. E.	19	WEST EXE SOUTH		TIVERTON	No	10205
3057	1914	SW	G	G&TD	HOOPER GEORGE	28	HIGH STREET		CREDITON	No	3640
3058	1914	SW	G	G&TD	HOOPER GEORGE	10	HIGH STREET		BUDLEIGH SALTERTON	No	2170
3059	1914	SW	G	G&TD	HOOPER J.				ZEAL MONACHORUM	No	10919

* The column 'Gr' refers to the trade group, in this case grocery (G). Retailers listed are 'Grocers and Tea Dealers' (G&TD).
Source: retail trades database.

Worcestershire) and the North-east of England (Durham, Northumberland, North Riding and East Riding of Yorkshire). Shop locations are typically recorded at four-yearly intervals in each of the regions, thus permitting a comprehensive assessment of retail change. The regions included in the database permit a comparison of the pace and nature of retail change in areas at the core and at the periphery of industrializing Britain.[28] Furthermore, inclusion of the West Midlands and the North-east as core regions illustrates the changing historical geography of the resource-based economy of industrializing Britain. Only after the mid-nineteenth century did the North-east (along with South Wales) 'take a fuller part in the resource-based economy, showing their own distinctive patterns of growth and cultural change'.[29] Yorkshire, Lancashire and the West Midlands had emerged as distinctive areas of social and economic innovation earlier.[30] Differences within core and peripheral regions, as well as differences between such regions, might also help explain regional variations in the patterns and processes of the retail industry. For instance, our analysis below highlights the greater importance of the North-east of England over the West Midlands as a spawning ground for multiple retailers during the first part of the twentieth century. However, robust explanatory cause and effect relationships are much harder to identify.

In this chapter we restrict our attention to the grocery and provisions trade and the variety store trade. The grocery and provisions trade accounts for most entries in our database, over 228,000 retail outlet entries for the entire project period (1850 to 1939). The variety store trade is the smallest, with some 1907 entries. The database is used here only to provide direct measures of multiple retail provision, but its composition facilitates more complex analyses. At the trade level, we utilize population census data and trade directory data on the grocery and provisions sector to explore basic measures of per capita multiple retail development by region and county. Trade directory data is also employed to explore regional variations in intra-type competition through a comparison of the importance of local and regional multiples in our core regions. Finally, a combination of the directory, retailers' archive material and population data stored in the database, together with published company histories, is utilized to explore elements of retail locational activities at the firm level in the variety store trade.

National multiple retailing and the significance of inter-type competition

Figure 1 illustrates the rapid growth in market share of selected large-scale retail types in the period 1900 to 1939.[31] As shown, such

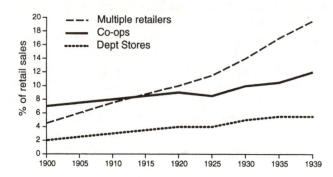

Figure 1 Estimated maximum shares of retail sales by large-scale retailers, 1900–1939.
Source: James B. Jefferys, *Retail Trading in Britain 1850–1950* (Cambridge University Press, Cambridge, 1954).

retailers accounted for an increasing proportion of total retail sales, with the multiples key among them. Jefferys estimated that large-scale retailers' share in the national trade was in the order of 13 per cent of sales at the beginning of the twentieth century. Twenty-five years later it was as high as 24 per cent, and by 1939 it represented as much as 37 per cent of total retail sales.[32] However, as he noted, such averaging of sales penetration across trades masks important sectoral trends, and in trades such as footwear, menswear, grocery and provisions, the dairy trade and chemists, the impact of large-scale retailers was becoming more considerable. In the case of the grocery and provisions trade, which is the focus of later sections of this chapter, he estimated that multiple retailers alone accounted for as much as 14 per cent of total sales by 1915, rising to 25 per cent by 1939.[33]

Jefferys observed two distinct phases in the rise of the multiples. The first, between 1870 and the mid-1890s, saw multiples developing chiefly in the footwear, grocery, meat and household stores trades. The second phase, between the 1890s and 1914, was, he suggested, characterized by the rapid and continuous spread of multiple retailing in these trades, and the successful extension of multiple shop retailing to the menswear, chemists' goods and variety store trades among others. Despite this apparently rapid and continuous spread of multiple retailing, Jefferys said surprisingly little about the geography of multiple shop retailing and inter-type competition. In the case of the grocery and provisions trade, for instance, he considered that reliable figures were not available before 1919. This date saw the issuing of the permits for the sale of government-controlled butter that afforded Jefferys the opportunity of comparison with data from 1949, relating to permits for the sale of sugar. From his brief comparison, he concluded that two main trends were evident. Firstly, that the shifts in the proportion of total number of branches located in different regions were not very great between these dates, and that with the exception of Durham, Northumberland and Wales, they largely corresponded with a southward shift in population. We return to this finding later. Secondly, that in both 1919 and 1949 branches of multiple shop organizations were thicker on the ground in the North of England and in Scotland, a fact that he attributed to the smaller size of units in the latter areas.[34]

More recently, the nature of the spatial competition between the independent and the multiple retailer has been given detailed consideration. In the context of 1930s Britain, for instance, Andrew Alexander, John Benson and Gareth Shaw have argued that multiple retailers contested and reshaped retail space in three critical and interrelated ways: through competition in the realms of locational space, store space and perceptual space – that is, the consumer's mind space.[35] They considered that in all three realms the larger multiples generated 'disruptive competition' in the retail system. In their consideration of locational competition, for instance, Alexander, Benson and Shaw noted that by tapping into both the growing investment market in the distributive trades and the property development market, many multiples were in a position to generate finance for branch network development and redevelopment on a scale that was disruptive to the existing retail order.[36] Spatial competition became a central battleground in the retail trade press, which reveals the deep-seated despair of independents unable to agree as to how to react.[37]

In a broader ranging discussion, Shaw, Alexander, Benson and Hodson have also considered the interactions between retailer competition, conflict and regulation.[38] Exploring failed attempts to secure anti-large-scale retailer legislation in inter-war Britain, they argued that this period saw the emergence of large, heavily capitalized retail corporations, important among which were the multiples. Their emergence started to fracture the continuum of retail businesses along which independent firms believed they 'could pass and grow into yet larger enterprises, given hard work and a modicum of luck'.[39] State regulation of big business was seen by some as the only way ahead for the smaller retail firms. The failure to gain such regulation illustrates not only the intensity of inter-type competition, but also its complexity. In particular, the failure of the 'Balfour Bill' of 1937 highlights the diversity of retailers existing in the independent trade and, arguably just as important, the deep divisions in the way in which this 'group' of retailers perceived themselves.[40]

While its intensity and ubiquity was arguably at a higher level during the inter-war period, such inter-type competition was not new, of course. Harold Dyos's study of the growth of Camberwell provides a revealing illustration of the consequences of its earlier manifestation.[41] In his evocative description of the changing character of Rye Lane, he noted:

> It was from this date (1893) that Rye Lane began to be transformed by the appearance of a number of the multiple stores which were then being established in various parts of London and its suburbs. The Victorian Tea Company had had a brief existence at No 55 before 1884, but it was the appearance of Lipton's Ltd, provisions dealers, at No 98 (formerly a private dwelling house) in 1891 which marked the real beginning of this trend. Salmon and Gluckstein Ltd, tobacconists, opened next door to Lipton's in 1893. In 1894, Nos 8–10, which had been occupied by two different shoemakers since the middle 1880s, were absorbed into E. H. Rabbits' expanding empire. The following year a Dun & Company, hatters, opened a shop at 106, where an oyster merchant had stood before; and the Singer Sewing Machine Company Ltd opened one of their branches on the former premises of a dispensing chemist.[42]

Clearly, inter-type competition could result in important changes to retail structure, and thus to possible consumption patterns, in individual localities. However, at present we have insufficient information to determine how representative such descriptions are of change in the wider marketplace both in this period and in others. Comparisons of broadly contemporaneous regional and local studies can be made, of course, but these present problems regarding the consistency of definitions, data sources and interpretation.

Regional patterns of retailing: variations over time and space
In this part of the chapter we make a first attempt to redress the present lack of firm conclusions concerning regional patterns of retailing, using our retail trades database. We start by highlighting some of the basic features of the regional retail patterns for our three study regions, before going on to consider the role played by settlement structure in affecting such patterns. Figures 2, 3 and 4 illustrate in fairly basic terms the levels of provision of multiple grocers and provision dealers for the periods c. 1890, c. 1914 and c. 1933.[43] As previously mentioned, the regions were selected to be representative of two types of environment: core, industrial regions (the North-east and the West Midlands of England) and a peripheral region (the South-west of England). There are parallels here with

Smith's analysis of the structure of British retailing during the inter-war period. He argued that in order to fully understand structural patterns it was 'necessary to compare the ratio of shops to population in different parts of the country'.[44] Smith also used Kelly's trade directories as a data source. However, his analysis was limited in that, apart from a sample of nine large cities, his data was only available at a county level. This made it impossible for Smith to explore the relationship between settlement structure and retail patterns. In contrast, our study is not limited in this way, as our database has been constructed at the settlement level.

Figure 2 shows a common level of provision across all three regions at the county level, by the end of what Jefferys identified as the first phase of multiple retail development. In terms of our three regions, the rapid growth of grocery and provisions multiples up to c. 1890 had not produced markedly different patterns of provision. By the end of the second phase of the expansion of multiples, c. 1914, inter-regional differences started to become evident, as the core regions increased their level of multiple retailer provision (Figure 3). There were also strong patterns of intra-regional variations, especially in the North-east and South-west. In both cases there were distinct sub-regions (counties) that showed much higher per capita rates of multiple shop provision, particularly in the North-east region. By contrast, the West Midlands still displayed a uniform pattern of provision, although overall levels had risen since the 1890s. Finally, by the end of the 1930s, variations between the three regions had become much more marked and complex (Figure 4). The North-east had two distinct levels of provision between the industrial north of the region and its southern counties. Interestingly, such differences had emerged by c. 1914, and appear to have remained largely consistent in the ensuing twenty years. The West Midlands region showed even more internal differentiation, with three levels of provision.

From this basic discussion it becomes clear that before 1890 levels of provision of multiple grocery and provisions stores showed little regional variation between core and periphery. It was only by the end of the second phase of growth that regional differentiation occurred. Such variations persisted over time, and if anything became more complex during the inter-war period.

As we have shown, both Smith and Hall, Knapp and Winsten attempted to explain regional variations in retail patterns as a function of settlement structure. [45] Hall, Knapp and Winsten outlined four 'a priori' causal frameworks based on three comprehensive national studies. One of these frameworks highlighted the role of so-called 'density variables', as shown in Figure 5, which stresses the importance of inter-settlement distances, the ratio of urban to rural population and

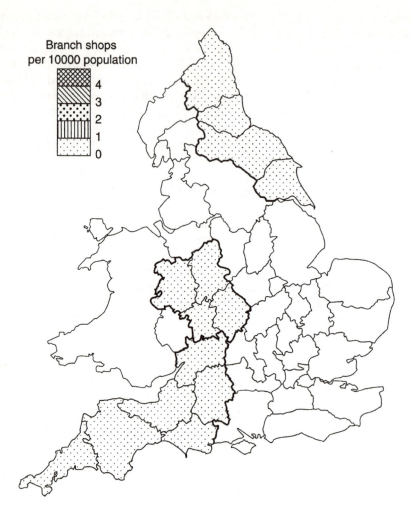

Figure 2 Multiple grocery and provisions branch shops by county, 1888-1894.
Source: Retail trades database.

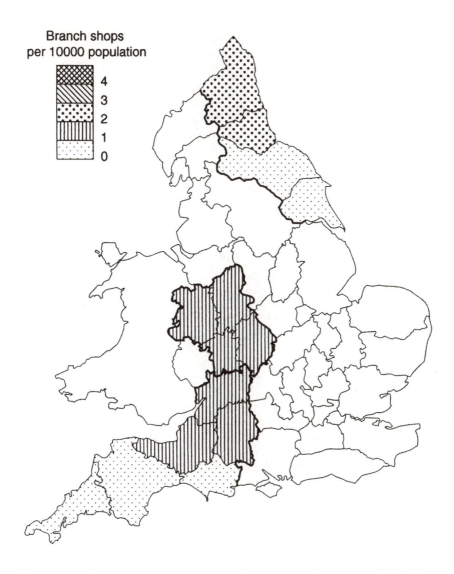

Figure 3 Multiple grocery and provisions branch shops by county, 1910-1914.
Source: Retail trades database.

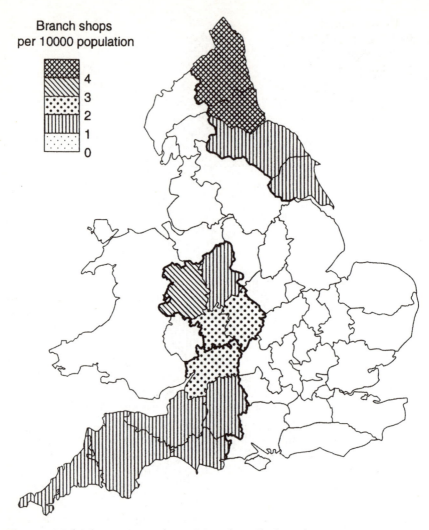

Figure 4 Multiple grocery and provisions branch shops by county, 1930-1934. *Source*: Retail trades database.

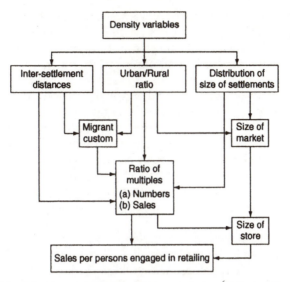

Figure 5 Model of density variables and impacts on multiple retailers.
Source: Modified from Margaret Hall, John Knapp and Christopher Winsten, *Distribution in Great Britain and North America: A Study in Structure and Productivity* (Oxford University Press, London, 1961).

the settlement hierarchy. Such a framework may, in part, help us to understand some of the processes occurring within our three regions. For example, the North-east was characterized by a high density of fairly small industrial settlements of fewer than 10,000 people. The spread of multiples within these smaller settlements was as follows: in c. 1890 some 13 settlements had multiple stores, by c. 1913 this had grown to 23 and to 31 by c. 1933. If we compare this to South-west England, which was also characterized by small settlements, we see a very different rate of spread by multiple retailers. Over the same time period the number of small settlements with multiples were 5, 44, and 110 respectively. One possible explanation is that in the South-west greater inter-settlement distances forced multiples to locate in a larger number of smaller settlements in order to reach consumers. In addition, it could also be that in South-west England these smaller settlements were the most common within the regional settlement hierarchy, providing the main infrastructure for multiple retailers.

It would appear that settlement structure provides one explanatory variable, but it is only partial and the whole picture is certainly far more complex. Three other factors are considered in this chapter. The first concerns the nature of core and periphery regions. This relates both to economic conditions and, in turn, to settlement patterns. For example, core regions acted as important spawning grounds of multiple retailing. Often these were based around large cities, such as London and Birmingham, or key industrial ports, like Glasgow, Liverpool and Newcastle.[46] In contrast, peripheral regions like the South-west only received retail innovations much later, when other locations had been captured. A second variable concerns the relationship between national and regional multiples and their varying growth patterns. Again this relates to regional structure and economic opportunities and highlights the difference between core and peripheral regions. We briefly consider this next. The last variable is concerned with the process of firm level growth and the management of the retail firm, and is explored in the penultimate section of the chapter. Of course, all of these factors are strongly interrelated, but at this stage of our research it is appropriate to outline their individual influences.

Finally, in this section we highlight important variations in the extent of regional multiple retailer development.[47] As with the independent retailer, from which this group usually originated, attempts to identify and classify such firms are problematic, because of the differences in the way such retailers perceived and represented themselves. According to an editorial in a 1938 edition of the short-lived *Chain and Multiple Store* journal, a 'peculiar form of class distinction in retail distribution' compounded the problem. This, it claimed, saw even large multiples attempting to pose as individual traders, while enjoying the benefits of multiple distributive outlets.[48] The reason for such 'subterfuge', it presumed, was a 'fear ... that they will lose caste with a "family minded" public'.[49] Similarly, while it is possible to identify conservatively run small-scale family-managed multiples, hindered in their expansion plans by a shortage of capital (as Jefferys suggested[50]), local and regional multiples could equally bear considerable similarity to the larger nationally recognized multiples, both in their marketing and financial strategies.

A comparison between core and peripheral regions serves to illustrate inter-regional variations in the emergence of regional multiples. With the possible exception of Bristol, 'none of the towns in the South West played a significant role in fostering the growth of the early multiples ... being increasingly overshadowed by the new centres of industrial and urban growth of the nineteenth and early twentieth century.'[51] These industrial towns were in the North and Midlands, and it was there that many of the major firms had their roots. Indeed, Peter Mathias considered that the multiples 'owe their life completely to the new urban society spawned by the process of industrialisation ... '.[52] Our inter-regional comparison broadly supports Mathias's contention, but it also highlights important variations between core industrial areas. Table 2 reveals the increasing importance of regional multiple firms in the North-east during our study period, such that by the 1930s a far higher ratio of the branches of regional multiples to overall multiples was recorded than in the West Midlands area. As we have noted, explanation may come in part from differences in regional economic development and settlement structures, but we will need to undertake more detailed research of the recently completed database in order to reveal the fuller picture.

The process of multiple retailer growth: locational strategy and organizational structure

In this final section of our chapter we explore inter-regional variations at the firm level. We do so through a comparative analysis of the geographical development of Marks & Spencer and F. W. Woolworth, two leading retailers in the UK variety store trade. In her essay on European consumption regimes between 1930 and 1970, Victoria de Grazia remarked in relation to variety store retailing that:

> One-price marketing responded to two major gaps in the distribution cycle that the department store, with its tendency to remain in the major commercial cities and to move to an upscale clientele, had not addressed: one gap was the outlying urban areas and towns under 100,000 people; the other was the gap between quality and price that was satisfied by offering a range of non branded convenience goods at low fixed price.[53]

This, she considered, explained the potency of the variety store's challenge to the values and identity embedded in earlier forms of commerce, and hence the clamour for the regulation of the variety store chains that surfaced across much of Europe. Unlike the situation in many other European states, no such legislation emerged in Britain, and variety store trading grew rapidly during the early decades of the twentieth century. It is estimated, for instance, to have accounted for as much as 7 per cent of turnover in inter-war England.[54] Nonetheless, its geography was far from uniform. Figure 6 illustrates the geographical expansion of Marks & Spencer and F. W. Woolworth in our study regions.[55] In relation to Marks & Spencer several trends are clear. Firstly, a comparison of the North-east (core) and South-west (periphery) highlights a delay in the development of this innovative retail type in the periphery. Marks opened his first stall in the Kirkgate market of Leeds in 1884, and within ten years had a small chain of stalls in markets stretching across Yorkshire, Derbyshire and Lancashire. Following his partnership with Spencer in 1894, the company began to look further afield for new locations. A new phase

TABLE 2 *Regional and national multiple branch provision in the 'core'*

Date	Region	Branches of national multiples	Branches of regional multiples
1891–94	North-east	24	98
	West Midlands	61	95
1912–14	North-east	259	390
	West Midlands	254	253
1932–34	North-east	437	1133
	West Midlands	568	360

Source: Retail trades database.

of expansion saw initial developments further south, in Cardiff, Birmingham, Bath and London, the latter having three shops by 1900.[56] But more concentrated development was undertaken in the North-east during this phase, particularly in the largely working-class and industrial towns of Teesside and Tyneside, such as Middlesborough, Sunderland, Newcastle and Stockton. As J. H. Bird and M. E. Witherwick noted, 'presumably their entrepreneurial attentions had been drawn to the North East by the fact that it was able to satisfy the basic requirements for the successful operation of the penny bazaar formula, namely the availability of covered market halls located in well-established urban centres having large working-class populations.'[57] A hiatus then ensued before development was resumed in the North and East Riding regions, with openings in towns including York and Darlington as well as smaller towns such as Bishop Auckland and, latterly, Durham.[58] By way of contrast, it was not until 1911–14, and thus comparatively late, that more significant inroads were made into the South-west and West Midlands. This was despite the early development of initial market presence in both regions. In the South-west, for instance, market-hall bazaars (Bath), shops (Cheltenham) and arcade branches (Bristol) were all present by 1902.

Secondly, we note that the process of expansion was largely similar in all instances, with initial representation being restricted to the larger towns before a gradual diffusion down the urban hierarchy to smaller centres. No stores were opened in towns in our study region with a population of less than 10,000, and in 85 per cent of cases the population at the date of opening was in excess of 20,000. The hierarchical diffusion pattern,[59] commonly identified in typologies of retailers' locational strategies, and previously identified in the expansion of Marks & Spencer into the South-west,[60] is thus confirmed by our consideration of the additional regions. This is the expected result, given that such a strategy (and its resulting pattern of development) is commonly associated with more mature firms, and typifies a need to locate in towns or catchment areas of suitable population size or functional characteristics. However, we cannot find additional evidence of spatial (contagious) diffusion beyond that previously identified in the case of Marks & Spencer's expansion into the South-west.[61] This type of locational strategy (and hence diffusion profile) is frequently associated with the initial stages of network development, when financial and logistical limitations are often most evident, and also with non-comparison goods retailers. Absence of such a profile in our North-east and West Midlands regions suggests the primacy of the hierarchical diffusion strategy to Marks & Spencer, and it would appear that the particular settlement geography of South-west England accounts for the elements of spatial diffusion identified therein.

Thirdly, it is interesting to note that it is in the South-west that most instances occurred of openings in towns with fewer than 20,000 people. This resulted in a higher density of development in this region than in the other two. Bearing in mind the comparative ubiquity of smaller towns in the settlement hierarchy of the South-west, two additional factors can be suggested to account for this. The first of these is that many of the openings in the South-west, like those in the West Midlands, occurred in what Simon Marks, then Chairman of the company, termed the 'formative period' of growth. In this period (which spans 1918–1926), the company increasingly turned its attention from the solidly working-class markets of the industrial North to upper working-class and middle-class markets, particularly in the South. As is well known, this locational switching was related to wider strategic shifts that saw the penny price abandoned and a new five shilling price point adopted, and the penny bazaar shop format replaced with larger outlets that were increasingly acquired freehold, and termed 'super stores' by the company.[62] More concentrated 'super store' branch development occurred in the period between 1927 and 1939, funded by new capital raised from the company's public issue and from private loans. The number of stores increased from 126 in 1927 to 234 by 1939. In the South, where the existing branch network was less dense than in northern England, emphasis was placed on developing in new market areas considered appropriate for this new strategy. By way of contrast, in the North the process of redevelopment was more far-reaching, with, for example, only one-fifth of branch locations in the North-east region trading throughout our study period from their date of opening. The remainder saw either store relocation or redevelopment. As Goronwy Rees noted:

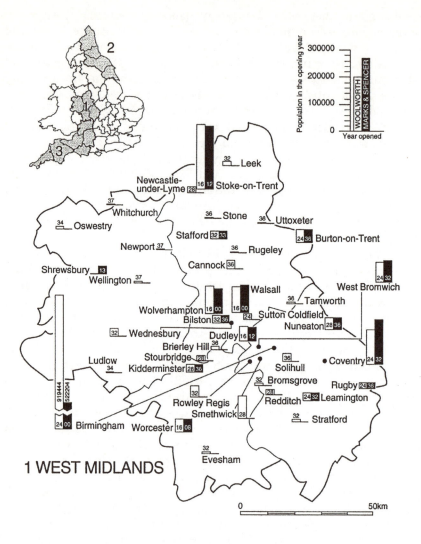

Figure 6 The opening of Marks & Spencer and Woolworth stores in the West Midlands, North-east and South-west regions.
Source: Retail trades database.

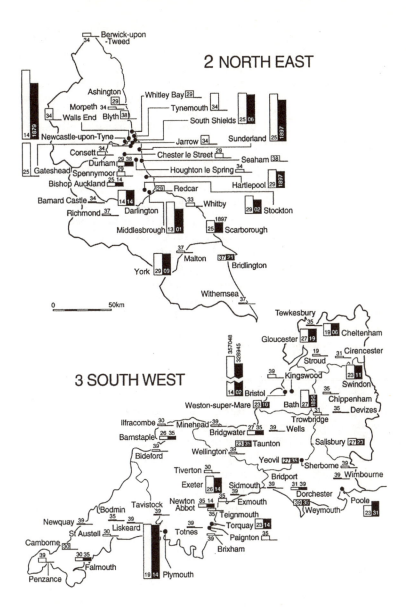

The old stores rarely had a frontage of more than 20 feet and most had a depth of under 75 feet. The new store opened at Darlington in 1922 had a frontage of 20 feet and a depth of 94 feet ... The new store in Darlington also showed changes in design and layout. The old one, which was closed in 1921, had the familiar layout of the Penny Bazaars ... The new store was a shop with a double glass window; the horseshoe counter was replaced by two long wall counters; the fascia was a plain 'Marks and Spencer' against a white background, and the lighting was greatly improved.[63]

Secondly, the South-west's seaside resort towns provided a specialized market, the size of which, of course, grew considerably during the summer season.[64] This specialized market made them more profitable as sites for multiple store location, despite often small indigenous populations.[65] Yet, away from the region's resorts, variety store branch development was not especially dense compared to other comparison goods trades. It was not until the latter half of the 1930s, with the rapid expansion of Woolworth's chain, that national variety store multiples began to diffuse down the urban hierarchy of the region in a more comprehensive manner. This was to provide a more thorough challenge to the values and identity of earlier forms of commerce.[66]

The rapid development of Woolworth's variety stores in the UK after 1909 also represented a significant and growing challenge to Marks & Spencer. Having assumed control of the company by 1917, Simon Marks noted: 'I was free to face up to its problems. Woolworth's had been making extraordinary progress and were rapidly developing throughout the country. They had become a household word, a great commercial institution.'[67] The rapidity of growth of the Woolworth chain and the extent of the competition it created for Marks & Spencer in the regions can be ascertained from Figure 6. The denser pattern of development of Woolworth stores is immediately apparent. Like Marks & Spencer, Woolworth's expanded in a largely hierarchical manner, targeting many of the largest urban centres first, and using stores in these towns as regional or sub-regional offices, providing administrative support to newly established branches opened as part of their aggressive development strategy.[68]

However, branches diffused far further down the urban hierarchy than in the case of Marks & Spencer. A minimum viable settlement population figure would appear to have been between 3000 and 4000 in each of our regions (Barnard Castle, Durham, population at date of opening: 3884; Newport, Shropshire, population at date of opening: 3437; Wimborne Minster, Dorset, population at date of opening: 3895). Clearly, the rapid and apparently successful proliferation of Woolworth's branches informed Simon Marks's decision to shift the company's strategy. This shift was to lay the foundation for one of Britain's great retail success stories of much of the latter half of the twentieth century.

Conclusion

Preliminary analysis of our large-scale retail database highlights the significance of regional variations in the pattern and process of multiple retailing in three English regions between 1890 and 1939 at two inter-related levels. At the trade level, we have highlighted significant and enduring variations in the levels of grocery branch shop provision between the regions. By 1914 marked variations existed in per capita provision between core and peripheral regions, despite the apparently rapid and continuous spread of multiple retailing. Core regions displayed higher levels of development, which endured to the end of our study period, contrary to earlier suggestions that such differences should become less pronounced over time. Similarly, our analysis of competition and change in variety store retailing confirms the pertinence of inter-regional analysis at the level of the firm. Such firm level studies can provide detailed evidence of the link between locational and other corporate strategies, as well as institutional and environmental change. These links are highly complex, but worthy of further study by those interested in the historical geography of retailing.

The economic significance of such variations was revealed by reference to inter-type spatial competition. Multiples often generated disruptive competition, particularly in terms of competition for store locations. This was clearly played out at a regional as well as a local level. However, consideration also needs to be given to the social and political ramifications of the inter-regional variations identified. The products of this 'retail revolution' were not equally distributed across the nation, and were of more than just economic importance to those people to whom they were accessible.[69] We need to understand better the ramifications of inter- and intra-regional variations in multiple retailing for all those in the circuit of consumption.[70]

Finally, explaining variations in the pattern and process of multiple retailing is clearly a complex task, requiring the consideration of a range of connected variables relating to structural, firm-level, organizational and spatial factors, among others. However, in this exploratory analysis we have illustrated the potential of a series of different approaches from the retail studies and geography literature. Further and more detailed attention now needs to be given to the testing of these approaches. We consider that our recently completed database of the retail trades is well equipped for this task.

Acknowledgements
The authors would like to acknowledge the generous support of the
Leverhulme Trust in funding the research for this chapter.

Notes

[1] David Thorpe and T. C. Rhodes, 'The shopping centres of Tyneside urban
region and large scale grocery retailing', *Economic Geography* 42 (1966), pp.
52–73; Martin T. Wild and Gareth Shaw, 'Population distribution and retail
provision: the case of the Halifax-Calder valley area of West Yorkshire during
the second half of the nineteenth century', *Journal of Historical Geography* 1/2
(1975), pp. 193–210; Andrew Alexander, 'The evolution of multiple retailing
in Britain 1870–1950: a geographical analysis', unpublished PhD thesis,
University of Exeter (1994); Andrew Alexander and Gareth Shaw, 'Retail
trading 1850–1939', in R. Kain and W. Ravenhill (eds), *Historical Atlas of
South West England* (University of Exeter, Exeter, 1999), pp. 462–71; Jon
Stobart and Alan Hallsworth, 'Change and stability, structure and agency in
retailing: the case of Stoke-on-Trent', *The International Review of Retail,
Distribution and Consumer Research* 9/2 (1999), pp. 203–21; Annie McAuley
Brownfield-Pope, 'Keeping abreast on "the road to nowhere": overcoming
geographical disadvantage in Norfolk retailing, c. 1880–1935', unpublished
paper presented at the 'Petty Traders and Captains of Commerce. Retailing
and Distribution, 1500–2000' conference, University of Wolverhampton, 13–
14 September 2000.

[2] Martin P. Phillips, 'Market exchange and social relations: the practices of
food circulation in and to the three towns of Plymouth, Devonport and
Stonehouse 1800–c.1870', unpublished PhD thesis, University of Exeter
(1992).

[3] Henry Smith, *Retail Distribution* (Oxford University Press, London, 1948,
first published 1937).

[4] Peter Scott, *Geography and Retailing* (Hutchinson, London, 1970), p. 49.

[5] Margaret Hall, John Knapp and Christopher Winsten, *Distribution in
Great Britain and North America: A Study in Structure and Productivity*
(Oxford University Press, London, 1961).

[6] *Ibid.*

[7] *Ibid.*, p. 138.

[8] Gareth Shaw, Andrew Alexander, John Benson and John Jones, 'Structural
and spatial trends in British retailing: the importance of firm-level studies',
Business History 40/4 (1998), pp. 79–93.

[9] See, for instance, Phil Kivell and Gareth Shaw, 'The study of retail
location', in J. Dawson (ed.), *Retail Geography* (Croom Helm, London, 1980),
pp. 95–155; Leigh Sparks, 'Spatial-structural relations in retail corporate
growth: a case study of the Kwik Save Group PLC', *Service Industries Journal*
10/1 (1990), pp. 25–84; Stephen Brown, *Retail Location: A Micro-scale
Perspective* (Avebury Press, Aldershot, 1992).

[10] Michael J. Winstanley, *The Shopkeeper's World 1830–1914* (Manchester
University Press, Manchester, 1983).

[11] Scott, *Geography and Retailing*.

[12] See Gareth Shaw and Andrew Alexander, 'Retail development and the changing shopping hierarchy in the late twentieth century', in Kain and Ravenhill (eds), *Historical Atlas*, pp. 476–81.

[13] Andrew Alexander, John Benson and Gareth Shaw, 'Action and reaction: competition and the multiple retailer in 1930s Britain', *The International Review of Retail, Distribution and Consumer Research* 9/3 (1999), pp. 245–59. For an explanation of the notion of 'disruptive competition', see Joseph Schumpeter, *Business Cycles* (Wiley, New York, 1939). See also Perry Bliss, 'Schumpeter, the "big" disturbance and retailing', *Social Forces* 39/1 (1960), pp. 72–6.

[14] David Alexander, *Retailing in England During the Industrial Revolution* (The Athlone Press, London, 1970).

[15] International Chamber of Commerce, *Trial Census of Distribution in Six Towns* (1937); Alexander, 'The evolution of multiple retailing'.

[16] James B. Jefferys, *Retail Trading in Britain 1850–1950* (Cambridge University Press, Cambridge, 1954).

[17] *Ibid.*, p. 465.

[18] R. Bellamy, 'Size and success in retail distribution', *Oxford University Institute of Statistics Bulletin* 8/10 (1946), pp. 324–39. See also Paul Nystrom, *Economics of Retailing* (Ronald Press, New York, 1930, first published c. 1917).

[19] Alexander, 'The evolution of multiple retailing'.

[20] Richard Longstreth, *City Center to Regional Mall: Architecture, the Automobile and Retailing in Los Angeles, 1920–1950* (MIT Press, London, 1998), p. 110.

[21] H. Carlin, 'Each branch a separate unit', *Grocery*, September 1936, p. 204.

[22] J. T. Thompson, 'Inspectors run my branches', *Grocery*, November 1936, p. 341.

[23] 'Branch store management' feature, *Grocery*, 1936–9.

[24] Fixed-shop retail provision includes stalls in market halls and arcades as well as retail stores.

[25] A four-yearly sample of Kelly's county directories has been employed. In some instances, wider intervals are necessary due to the absence of suitable directories.

[26] The changing status of certain districts and the redrawing of some district boundaries further complicate this process.

[27] Martin Purvis, 'Co-operative retailing in Britain', in J. Benson and G. Shaw (eds), *The Evolution of Retail Systems c. 1800–1914* (Leicester University Press, Leicester, 1992), pp. 107–34; Martin Purvis, 'Crossing urban deserts: consumers, competitors and the protracted birth of metropolitan co-operative retailing', *The International Review of Retail, Distribution and Consumer Research* 9/3 (1999), pp. 225–43.

[28] Core and periphery are defined here broadly along the lines adopted in resource-based interpretations of Britain's industrialization. Hence, the North-east and West Midlands of England are considered to be in the core, the South-west of England in the periphery. However, we acknowledge that in their discussion of the spatial patterns of industrialization, John Langton and Robert Morris consider that Britain was and remained in large part a

metropolitan economy. Consequently, they observe a tension between a metropolitan-periphery structure and a resource-based core-periphery structure. See John Langton and Robert J. Morris, 'Introduction', in J. Langton and R. J. Morris (eds), *Atlas of Industrializing Britain* (Methuen, London, 1986), pp. xxvii–xxviii. The changing retail structure of London during the study period certainly warrants closer attention, but it is beyond the scope of this project.

[29] *Ibid.*, p. xxvii.

[30] *Ibid.*

[31] Data presented in Figure 1 is drawn from Jefferys, *Retail Trading in Britain*. It reflects his definition of a multiple retailer.

[32] *Ibid.*, pp. 73–4.

[33] *Ibid.*; see also W. Hamish Fraser, *The Coming of the Mass Market 1850–1914* (Macmillan, London, 1981); Smith, *Retail Distribution*.

[34] Jefferys, *Retail Trading in Britain*, p. 155.

[35] For a discussion of these terms, see Alexander, Benson and Shaw, 'Action and reaction'.

[36] Alexander, Benson and Shaw, 'Action and reaction'; see also James B. Jefferys, 'Trends in business organization in Great Britain since 1856, with special reference to the financial structure of companies, the mechanisms of investment, and the relations between the shareholders and the company', unpublished PhD thesis, London School of Economics (1938); Peter Scott, *The Property Masters: A History of the British Commercial Property Sector* (E. & F. N. Spon, London, 1996).

[37] Alexander, Benson and Shaw, 'Action and reaction'.

[38] Gareth Shaw, Andrew Alexander, John Benson and Deborah Hodson, 'The evolving culture of retailer regulation and the failure of the 'Balfour Bill' in interwar Britain', *Environment and Planning A* 32 (2000), pp. 1977–89.

[39] *Ibid.*, p. 1986.

[40] See John Benson, *The Penny Capitalists: A Study of Nineteenth Century Working-Class Entrepreneurs* (Gill & Macmillan, Dublin, 1983); Winstanley, *The Shopkeeper's World*; Shaw, Alexander, Benson and Hodson, 'The evolving culture of retailer regulation'.

[41] Harold Dyos, *Victorian Suburb: A Study of the Growth of Camberwell* (Leicester University Press, Leicester, 1966).

[42] *Ibid.*, pp. 151–2.

[43] At the time of writing some data for Hull and environs was unavailable. Data from this area has therefore been omitted from all maps presented in this chapter, in order to achieve consistency.

[44] Smith, *Retail Distribution*, p. 39.

[45] Hall, Knapp and Winsten, *Distribution in Great Britain and North America*.

[46] See Gareth Shaw, 'The evolution and impact of large-scale retailing in Britain', in Benson and Shaw (eds), *The Evolution of Retail Systems*, pp. 135–65; Alexander, 'The evolution of multiple retailing'.

[47] Multiples were accorded the designation 'regional' if they were found to trade in only one of our study regions and could not be otherwise identified through the use of available published and archival sources. Published sources include specialized directories of multiple retailing.

[48] Anon., 'Why this snobbery?', *Chain and Multiple Store*, 13 August 1938, p. 565.

[49] *Ibid.*

[50] Jefferys, *Retail Trading in Britain.*

[51] Andrew Alexander, 'Spatial trends in the development of multiple retailing in Great Britain', *Revue Belge de Géographie* 1/4 (1997), p. 12.

[52] Peter Mathias, *Retailing Revolution: A History of Multiple Retailing in the Food Trades Based Upon the Allied Suppliers Group of Companies* (Longmans, London, 1967), pp. 38–9.

[53] Victoria de Grazia, 'Changing consumption regimes in Europe, 1930–1970', in S. Strasser, C. McGovern and M. Judt (eds), *Getting and Spending: European and American Consumer Societies in the Twentieth Century* (Cambridge University Press, Cambridge, 1998), p. 75.

[54] Giuseppe Lucrezio, *I Magazzini a Prezzo Unico in Europa e in America* (Città di Castello, 1943), quoted in de Grazia, 'Changing consumption regimes', p. 75.

[55] The data presented in this part of the chapter are restricted to a comparison of the diffusion of the retailers in our study regions. As such the chapter focuses only on branch openings, rather than transfers and closures.

[56] Asa Briggs, *Marks & Spencer 1884–1984* (Octopus Books, London, 1984); Goronwy Rees, *St Michael: A History of Marks & Spencer* (Weidenfeld & Nicolson, London, 1969).

[57] J. H. Bird and M. E. Witherwick, 'Marks & Spencer: the geography of an image', *Geography* 71/4 (1986), p. 309.

[58] Due to the limitations of our four-yearly sample of Kelly's county directories, it is possible that in some cases actual dates of openings were slightly earlier than those illustrated. Nonetheless, the patterns of openings illustrated are considered accurate.

[59] There is a long tradition of diffusion studies in geography. For a discussion of the application of the hierarchical and spatial (contagious) diffusion concepts to retail studies, see Risto Laulajainen, *Spatial Strategies in Retailing* (D. Reidel Publishing, Dordrech, 1987).

[60] Alexander, 'The evolution of multiple retailing'; Shaw, Alexander, Benson and Jones, 'Structural and spatial trends'.

[61] *Ibid.*

[62] Rees, *St Michael.*

[63] *Ibid.*, p. 60.

[64] See, for instance, Gareth Shaw and Alan Williams, 'From bathing hut to theme park: tourism development in South West England', *The Journal of Regional and Local Studies* 11/1 and 2 (1991), pp. 16–32.

[65] The trading potential of such markets was enhanced by social changes that saw an estimated three million enjoy the 'privilege' of a week's paid holiday by the 1930s. It is calculated that 11 million benefited from the 'Holidays with Pay Act' of 1939. For a discussion of this, see Brian T. Robson, 'The years between', in R. A. Dodgshon and R. A. Butlin (eds), *An Historical Geography of England and Wales* (Academic Press, London, 1990), pp. 545–78.

[66] de Grazia, 'Changing consumption regimes'.

[67] Quoted in Rees, *St Michael*, p. 60.

[68] Shaw, Alexander, Benson and Jones, 'Structural and spatial trends'.

[69] See, for instance, de Grazia, 'Changing consumption regimes'; Frank Mort and Peter Thompson, 'Retailing, commercial culture and masculinity in 1950s Britain: the case of Montague Burton the "Tailor of Taste"', *History Workshop Journal* 38 (1994), pp. 106–27.

[70] For a discussion of the concept of a circuit of consumption, see Peter Jackson and Nigel Thrift, 'Geographies of consumption', in D. Miller (ed.), *Acknowledging Consumption: A Review of New Studies* (Routledge, London, 1995), pp. 204–37.

CHAPTER 6
CITY CENTRE RETAILING IN LATE NINETEENTH- AND EARLY TWENTIETH-CENTURY STOKE-ON-TRENT: STRUCTURES AND PROCESSES
Jon Stobart

Introduction

The relationship between city centres and retailing has been perhaps the most enduring feature of urban structures in Britain over the last hundred years or more. Despite the fact that city centres fulfil a wide variety of business, recreation, religious and cultural functions, retailing forms both the popular image of the city centre and the touchstone of its viability and vitality.[1] Unlike most North American central business districts (CBDs), British city centres have, until the last decade or so at least, maintained their primacy in retail hierarchies and in general remain the focus of the majority of shopping experiences. That said, the once axiomatic link between city centre and retail activity has been broken by the successive waves of edge- and out-of-town retail development fuelled by rising standards of living and, especially, growing car ownership.[2] Popular attitudes to this shift in the geography of British retailing are, at best, ambiguous, but recent government policy has sought to protect and maintain the existing retail hierarchies and structures.[3] This has focused attention on the city centre as a spatially defined area for which boundaries can and must be drawn if planning policies are to be meaningfully formulated and rigorously applied. Recent work has highlighted factors such as the type and range of activities and facilities, the intensity of land use and financial turnover,[4] but it is important to recognize that the city centre has a temporal as well as spatial dimension, a point recently emphasized by Nicholas Alexander.[5]

The historical development of the city centre is of much more than academic interest, as it provides the structure in which modern agencies – planners, developers, property agents and so on – will operate.[6] These historical geographical processes are, at one and the

155

same time, widely accepted and under-researched, especially in the British context; Gareth Shaw's work being the basis of much of our understanding of the spatial processes.[7] The clustering of shops onto the central streets of towns and cities dates back at least to the seventeenth century, but the notion of a primary concentration of the city's retailing into what might be termed a CBD is generally seen as a nineteenth-century phenomenon.[8] In brief, population growth, rising standards of living and changing socio-cultural attitudes brought increased consumer spending. Some was dispersed to the emerging suburban shopping centres, but greater mobility and changes in the organization of retail provision focused higher order retailing onto a spatially expanding and financially dominant city centre.[9]

Within this process of city centre formation, much has been made of the role of department stores and multiple retailers. They are seen as having fundamentally changed the ways in which goods were perceived and desired, bought and sold, and were therefore both a driving force in retail change and the spatial linchpins around which these changes were structured.[10] Department stores swept away numerous smaller stores through site amalgamations, whilst multiples, needing the highly accessible sites in the city centres, helped to push independent stores to the spatial and often financial margins of urban retailing.[11] Ultimately, these pressures brought about a rationalization of retail outlets that saw the number of shops per capita fall markedly from its 1914 peak.[12]

Given this key role, it is unsurprising that present day planners and city centre managers are so concerned with the decentralization of such retailers. Even so, the universal importance of department stores and multiples in the emergence and structuring of city centres is not yet fully established by empirical research. The notion of a spatial and hierarchical diffusion of such innovatory forms of shopping from London, through the major cities, to small market towns is persuasive, but remains an under-researched process.[13] Most studies have focused on individual firms or stores, and the only systematic analysis of the processes underlying the changing geography of city centre retailing remains Shaw's work on Hull.[14] Clearly, many of these ideas of retail change are inappropriate for the majority of small towns, and there is evidence that they are of limited relevance to some larger places as well.[15] Indeed, the different socio-economic structures of nineteenth- and early twentieth-century cities, and the diverse spatial structure of their central areas, would appear to make some significant variations inevitable. In Hull, for example, two secondary centres are defined in terms of their isolation from the city centre by the docks.[16] Clearly, local geography mattered.

This chapter explores the role of the multiple retailers and department stores in structuring the city centre of the Potteries in the period 1872 to 1932. The towns of the North Staffordshire Potteries – Tunstall, Burslem, Hanley, Stoke, Fenton, Longton and Newcastle-under-Lyme – grew rapidly in the nineteenth century and increasingly coalesced into a single conurbation. This process was formally recognized in 1910, when all but Newcastle were united in the County Borough (and later city) of Stoke-on-Trent. To analyse the retail structure of the conurbation and especially the city centre, I draw on data from *Kelly's Directories*. Whilst these are not unproblematic sources – there are difficulties in terms of their coverage, the classification of occupations and the double-counting of entries – trade directories are the most widely available and reliable source for the study of retail geography during this period.[17] In essence, these data suggest that multiples and department stores were slow to emerge in the Potteries and were less significant in shaping the structure and geography of the city centre than is generally believed. I will argue that this has much to do with the local economy and the geographical structure of the Potteries, and that we must be more sensitive to such factors when seeking to understand city centre retail development.

Hanley as the city centre: department stores and multiples

Hierarchies of retail centres or business districts can be identified in many towns by the middle decades of the nineteenth century.[18] The city centre usually formed the primary retail centre, defined in terms of the number, range and quality of its outlets. Secondary and other lesser centres – identified by their relatively lower concentration of outlets – were located off-centre or in suburban locations. In the Potteries, Hanley town centre had emerged as the primary retailing location for the whole conurbation by the third quarter of the nineteenth century, accounting for about one in seven traders.[19] With the increasingly integrated nature of the Potteries space economy, the central areas of the smaller towns can be seen as constituting secondary centres within the conurbation's retail hierarchy. In terms of the number of outlets, the persistent strength of these centres meant that Hanley never achieved true dominance of the retail hierarchy. It is reasonable to suppose that a dominant central area should be at least three or four times more powerful than any two nearby secondary centres combined.[20] At best, the number of retail and service outlets in Hanley exceeded that in its two nearest rivals by around 13 per cent and was never more than about twice the size of the largest secondary centre (Table 1). Moreover, this overall lack of domination was reflected in the muted development of those two key features of city centres, multiples and department stores, seen by contemporaries as

TABLE 1 *Number of retail and service outlets in central Hanley and secondary centres 1872–1932*

	1872	1892	1912	1932
Central Hanley	486	802	1012	1005
Secondary 1	258	400	458	488
Secondary 2	226	333	434	461
Two largest secondary centres combined*	484	733	892	949
Secondary 3	152	330	417	433
Secondary 4	150	308	339	419
Secondary 5	147	204	207	286
Other secondary centres combined**	449	842	963	1138

*The two largest secondary centres 1872–1912 were Newcastle-under-Lyme and Longton; in 1932 they were Newcastle-under-Lyme and Burslem.
**The other secondary centres in 1872–1912 comprised Burslem, Stoke and Tunstall; in 1932 they were Longton, Stoke and Tunstall.
Source: *Kelly's Directory for Staffordshire.*

touchstones of retail modernity.

When compared with other towns and cities in the Midlands, the emergence of department stores in Hanley appears to have been slow and incomplete. Most provincial department stores grew gradually from small origins, the business branching out into new areas of retailing and the premises expanding by plot amalgamation.[21] In Coventry, Wolverhampton, Walsall and Leamington, for example, there appears to have been a steady, if by no means certain, progression from multi-fronted shop to part- and then to full department store (Table 2).[22] However, although Hanley contained a significant number of multi-fronted shops from an early date – more than any of the other sample towns around 1870 – only four had grown beyond this by c. 1910. The oldest and most developed of these was M. Huntbach and Co. Ltd. First listed as a linen draper in 1872, Michael Huntbach gradually expanded his business and by 1912 the company appeared as 'drapers, hosiers, costumiers, milliners and outfitters, cabinet, furniture and carpet warehousemen, ladies' and children's footwear'.[23] The other three were trading from around 1890: McIlroy Bros. and Teetons Ltd were essentially very large-scale drapers, whilst Bratt and Dyke also offered millinery and some furniture, bedding and carpets. Such success stories were the exception everywhere, but they were particularly rare in Hanley. Just one of the fifteen multi-fronted shops appearing in 1912 occupied more than two fronts, and only three were still trading 20 years later. At the turn of the century, a correspondent to the local newspaper complained that

TABLE 2 *Large-scale retailing and department stores in selected Midlands towns, c. 1870–c. 1910*

	Multi-front* shops		Part-department stores		Full department stores	
	c. 1870	c. 1910	c. 1870	c. 1910	c. 1870	c. 1910
Potteries towns						
Hanley	6	15	1	3	0	1
Longton	2	4	0	1	0	0
Newcastle	1	2	0	1	0	1
Other Midland towns						
Coventry	1	28	0	6	0	2
Leamington	3	15	1	6	0	3
Walsall	1	24	0	3	0	5
Wolverhampton	5	7	1	5	3	2

*Multi-front shops were those with more than one street address.
Source: *Kelly's Directory for Staffordshire*; Shaw, 'The evolution and impact of large-scale retailing', Table 8.2.

Coventry lacked the attractive modern department stores of more fashionable Birmingham or Leamington, its tradesmen having 'for the most part been to sleep for the last twenty years'.[24] Hanley, it seems, was still further off the pace.

The relative 'under-development' of modern city centre shopping in the Potteries was also seen in multiple retailing. There were only three national multiples with branches in the town by 1892 – Home and Colonial, James Nelson and Sons Ltd, and Freeman, Hardy and Willis – compared with six in Coventry and eight in Wolverhampton, both of which had comparable populations to the Potteries (Table 3). The following 20 years saw the addition of over 200 outlets to Hanley's retail and service provision, amongst them several multiples, which brought the conurbation closer to the level of provision seen in other Midlands towns. Growth took place across the full range of shop types, including grocers and butchers, drapers and shoe dealers, newsagents and chemists, reflecting a general growth in the range of shops found in Hanley. Subsequent development, though, was slower and more uneven. The overall number of outlets in central Hanley actually fell slightly between 1912 and 1932, and it dropped behind other towns in the development of multiple retailing. An impressive number of fashionable multiples selling clothing and shoes opened branches in the town, among them Montague Burton, Fifty Shilling Tailors, Dunn and Co., Stewarts Ltd and Timpson's. However, this growth took place as part of an overall expansion and centralization of clothes and shoe retailing in Hanley and the Potteries as a whole.

TABLE 3 *Multiple retailing in selected Midlands towns, 1892–1932*

	Food 1892	1912	1932	Clothes/Shoes 1892	1912	1932	Other 1892	1912	1932	Total 1892	1912	1932
Potteries towns												
Hanley	2	5	4	1	4	12	0	4	4	3	13	20
Newcastle	1	5	5	1	1	2	0	2	5	2	8	12
Burslem	1	3	3	1	2	2	0	2	3	2	7	8
Longton	1	4	4	0	0	3	0	2	4	1	6	11
Stoke	0	3	3	0	1	4	0	3	5	0	7	12
Tunstall	2	3	5	1	1	2	0	2	2	3	6	9
Other Midlands towns												
Coventry	2	6	8	2	5	10	2	6	12	6	17	30
Leamington	1	6	7	1	1	5	2	4	9	4	11	21
Walsall	1	6	5	1	3	9	1	5	9	3	14	23
Wolverhampton	4	7	8	2	7	11	2	7	10	8	21	29

Source: Kelly's Directory for Staffordshire; Kelly's Directory for Warwickshire.

Between 1912 and 1932, the number of independent tailors, shoe dealers and drapers rose in the town centre (from 85 to 97), but remained constant in the suburbs.[25]

Multiple retailing in this sector thus seems to have mirrored growth in, and focusing of demand, rather than a modernization of Hanley's retailing. Certainly, it was not matched by developments in other sectors. There was no growth in multiples retailing food, hardware or fancy goods. By 1932, Hanley had a third fewer multiples than maligned Coventry and lacked branches of several important national retailers, including W. H. Newman, H. Samuel, and Marks & Spencer.[26] Its retailing was, therefore, more reliant upon 'old-fashioned' independent retailers than appears to have been the case elsewhere.

Intra-urban competition

Two questions arise from this analysis. One concerns the spatial development of the city centre: with the key players being relatively weak, what forces structured the geography of the conurbation's central shopping area? Such issues will be dealt with in the next section. First we must consider some of the reasons for the lack of department stores and multiples in Hanley.

One problem faced by Hanley as multiple retailing spread across the country was its geographical location – some distance from London and set apart from the major industrial centres of the Midlands and the North, where many multiples had their origins.[27] Such spatial considerations may explain the earlier appearance in Coventry, Leamington, Walsall and Wolverhampton of Foster Brothers Clothing Company (a Birmingham firm) or Sketchley's dyers and dry cleaners (originally from Coventry), but Hanley was hardly isolated. By the 1930s it had branches of Stewarts Clothiers of Middlesbrough, Crook and Sons of Manchester and the Halford Cycle Company of Birmingham. In any case, many multiple retailers were operating at a national rather than regional scale by this date.[28] Moreover, the strong demographic expansion seen in the Potteries – the population rose from around 160,000 in 1871 to c. 250,000 in 1911 and over 300,000 by 1931[29] – meant that there was a growing mass market for both department stores and multiples in the conurbation.

However, while the population easily exceeded any formal or informal thresholds required by retailers, it was dispersed between seven towns and almost 20 smaller settlements. These places became increasingly close in spatial, functional and political terms – a process officially recognized in 1910 with the creation of the county borough of Stoke-on-Trent – but the towns retained strong individual identities in a manner and extent not seen in other industrial coalescences.[30] This dispersal of population was one of the major reasons for Hanley (then and now) lacking the status of a dominant city centre.[31] Contemporary analysis of Stoke-on-Trent's retail trade observed that 'residential areas are not widely dispersed, so that the shops, even in the central streets ... can participate in the steady trade resulting from family custom'.[32] However, while Hanley's retailers gained custom through spatial proximity to residential areas, they lost out to secondary centres that offered a surprising range of higher order goods and services. For the majority of their everyday needs, many people shopped in their local town centre rather than travel to the city centre.

The strongest of these secondary centres was Newcastle-under-Lyme. This contained a significant concentration and range of shops, including several multiples and by 1912 one full and one part-department store (Tables 2 and 3). Many of the multiples were food and footwear retailers (for example, Home and Colonial, Maypole Dairies and Freeman, Hardy and Willis), which Shaw suggests were increasingly common in the suburbs,[33] but Boots, Halford Cycle Company, Woolworth and Montague Burton also had shops in Newcastle by 1932. The larger of its department stores, T. W. Carryer and Co., began as pawnbrokers and clothiers before 1872, but were trading as 'house furnishers and cabinet makers, pawnbroker, clothier, boot and shoe factors, and jewellers' by 1912. James Myott and Sons were styled simply as drapers, but were another old-established company and occupied substantial premises on the corner of High Street and Ironmarket in the centre of the town. Of the other secondary centres, only Longton contained a part-department store: William Martin, a draper with one very large store and three smaller shops in Longton as well as branches in Burslem, Stoke and Fenton. However, all towns contained a handful of multi-fronted clothes shops and all had a significant number of multiples. As with Newcastle, many were grocers, butchers or footwear dealers, but W. H. Smith, Boots and the Singer Sewing Machine Company were present in several by 1912, and Woolworth, Montague Burton, Halford's, Stewart's and the Provident Clothing Company had joined them twenty years later.[34]

The retail provision in these towns was not simply a reflection of basic shopping facilities suburbanizing as population growth shifted away from the city centre.[35] These secondary centres were 'more virile than those usually existing around big cities'.[36] They formed important competition to the retailers in Hanley and were significant counter-attractions to multiple retailers wishing to establish stores in this growing conurbation. Indeed, it is notable that, while the central streets of Coventry, Walsall and Wolverhampton contained several branches of many national multiples, with the exception of food retailers Hanley invariably had just one. Writing of the late nineteenth century, Arnold Bennett noted that 'people would not go to [Hanley] for their bread or groceries, but they would go for their cakes.'[37] However, it is clear that luxuries as well as necessities could and frequently were bought more locally. Whilst Hanley was by far the strongest retail centre and was probably strengthening its dominance, intra-urban competition served to restrict 'modern' retail development in the city centre to a level some way below that seen in comparable towns. How did this affect its spatial structure?

The geography of city centre retailing

The general problems in defining and delimiting the city centre have been dealt with in detail elsewhere.[38] What are of greater concern to us here are the processes of change taking place within Hanley's so-called CBD. At a broad scale, the most obvious trend was the physical expansion of this area of concentrated commercial activity as shops spread from their initial focus around the market to the surrounding streets.[39] Although it offers only a crude measure of this highly complex process, Figure 1 highlights two significant features of this expansion. The first is the ribbon nature of development, with much development taking place along the main routes to the city centre. From there, growth sometimes continued to follow the arterial road (as with Broad Street) and sometimes branched out along side streets (for example, Church Street, leading off High Street). Alongside this sprawl was an infilling of space within the central area itself. Thus, the number of traders and professionals on the major thoroughfares grew during the period; in the case of Piccadilly, Stafford Street and Parliament Row, from a combined total of 131 in 1872 to 160 by 1932. More importantly, retailers and professionals progressively colonized the secondary streets of the city centre. For example, Percy Street and Pall Mall contained only a handful of traders in 1872, but over 45 between them in 1932.

This expansion and intensification brought with it a significant shift in the locus of the city centre (Figure 1, section D). In 1872 Market Square was the hub of commercial activity, with High Street, Market Street, Parliament Row and Piccadilly forming the main axes of development. Over the succeeding decades, the focus of the core area moved to the south and west to progressively encompass the streets between Piccadilly and Parliament Row. By 1932 Market Square formed the northern boundary of the core and High Street and Market Street were increasingly characterized by lower order functions. Such fundamental changes in the geography of the city centre are ignored in most spatial models, which assume a stable equilibrium or end-point, which, in the case of the Potteries at least, appears never to have been achieved.[40] Indeed, by 1932, there appears to have been something of a

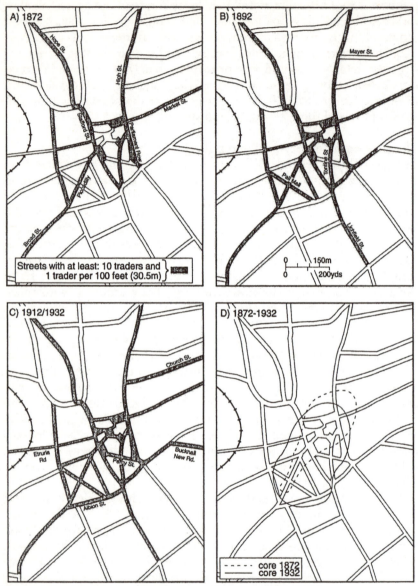

Figure 1 Spatial change of Hanley's retail centre, 1872–1932.
Source: Kelly's Directory for Staffordshire.

retreat from the bottom of Piccadilly and a corresponding concentration around the junction with Stafford Street and on Upper Market Square. Certainly, the structure of Hanley's retail core has again been altered considerably in recent decades. The building of the Potteries Shopping Centre in 1988 served to accelerate the refocusing of commercial activity back on to Market Square, leaving Piccadilly and the surrounding streets to slide into the so-called 'frame' – the marginal areas within a central business district characterized by lower order functions and less intensive land use.[41]

Within these general changes in the structure of the city centre were more complex series of processes affecting specific types of retailing and professional services. Throughout the study period, food retailing remained a feature of almost all city centre streets, but its relative importance on the main shopping thoroughfares declined steadily. In part, this reflected the refocusing of such activities onto the growing suburbs.[42] However, there was also a more local shift. Food retailing was the dominant feature of much of the ribbon development spreading out from the city centre, initially along established shopping streets such as High Street, Broad Street and Hope Street, but later along previously residential streets, including Church Street and Mayer Street or newly built routes such as Bucknall New Road. The selling of clothes also spread along these ribbons, but more fundamentally remained concentrated in the centre of the town. This was seen, in 1872, in the clustering of drapers around Market Square and down Piccadilly. However, such patterns were by no means stable. By 1892, the main concentration was shifting away from Market Square and onto Stafford Street, Tontine Street and Percy Street, although there was a pronounced mixing in the retail character of these streets. Analysis of the sequencing of shop types suggests that the localized and stable clusters of functions recorded by Stephen Brown for Belfast were rare in Hanley even by 1932.[43] Along Piccadilly, for example, only five pairs of shops sold goods of a similar nature to each other and just once were there three cognate shops in a row.

This intermixing also affected very specialized dealers, such as jewellers and gramophone and musical instrument sellers. Many of these were again found in or around Market Square or down Piccadilly, but they were far from being clustered into specialist districts, as models of the CBD would suggest.[44] The only activities that did display such spatial concentration were not shops, but professional services, especially solicitors and accountants. Moreover, their distribution remained remarkably stable through the years. In 1872 they were already concentrated to the south of the main shopping streets on Cheapside and Albion Street; by 1892, and despite a doubling in their numbers, three-quarters were still found on these two streets. As these professions expanded further in the early twentieth century some took offices on neighbouring Pall Mall, but the clustering remained both impressive and unique in the city centre.

The role of department stores and multiples

Shaw suggests that in Hull multiples played a leading role in the suburbanization of shopping around the turn of the century.[45] In the Potteries, only a handful of multiples had branches in the suburbs. Most were located in the secondary centres and in the city centre, where they were especially numerous along Piccadilly, Stafford Street and Parliament Row/Upper Market Square – reflecting their status as the principal shopping streets (Figure 2). In general, the location of multiples and, by implication, the locational strategies of the multiple retail companies were conservative. In the case of higher order and especially clothes retailing, it matched the general trend towards centralization (see above). Multiples appear to have sought sites that were already well-established within the spatial structure of the city centre and that were most accessible and visible to their potential customers. They did correspondingly less to develop new locations at the fringes of or away from the main thoroughfares. There were no multiples on the up-and-coming Percy Street and Pall Mall, and only one on Tontine Street. The emergence of these as shopping streets was driven instead by the location there of independent outlets.

In this sense, the multiples reinforced the prevailing trends in the retail geography of the city centre and did so in a powerful way. The clustering of Dunn, Burton, Stewarts, Fifty Shilling Tailor and Barratt at the junction of Piccadilly and Stafford Street must have further promoted this area as a prime retail location. That said, there is little evidence that localized competition for retail space was especially intense just here. The rate of turnover in businesses was no greater on Piccadilly than on the other main streets and there were still several frontages not listed as commercial businesses as late as 1932. One reason for this might be that, even here, the concentration of multiples was quite low: only six of 68 businesses or nine of 56 frontages were multiples. Also significant was the fact that individual retailers, both independents and multiples, were clearly not wedded to particular sites; nor were they always moving into the more obviously favoured locations. Of the four multiples on Piccadilly in 1912, only Boots remained 20 years later. Singer had moved to Tontine Square, Cash Clothing Company had gone to Upper Market Square and Marks & Spencer had apparently ceased trading (although they later reappeared on Upper Market Square). Equally, some incoming multiples chose to locate in apparently more marginal areas, as with City Tailoring on High Street.

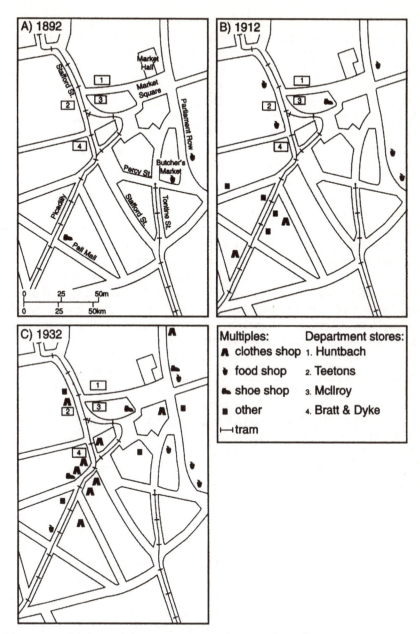

Figure 2 Multiples and department stores in central Hanley, 1892-1932.
Source: *Kelly's Directory for Staffordshire.*

Such dispersal served to reduce pressure on key locations, but can be interpreted in a number of different ways. It might simply reflect a lack of choice in available premises. More probably, it was a result of the varying needs of different retailers: the markets were an important attraction to food retailers and certain multiples may have chosen locations convenient for their working-class clientele. Alternatively, though, it could be an indication that there was no clear and generally accepted notion as to where the best locations might be found. Then, as now, retailers were often making locational decisions based on a very incomplete knowledge of the area. In 1938, it was already recognized that the complex geography of the district posed 'peculiar problems from the viewpoint of [national] retailing organisations'. Today, confusion abounds among national property agents in London over the location, identity and strength of the city's shopping centre.[46]

The geography and development of Hanley's full and part-department stores was rather different, but their overall impact was much the same, being a force for continuity rather than change. All four stores were located together towards the top of Stafford Street and Lamb Street. From an early date, they occupied highly accessible locations on major thoroughfares close to the market. The premises of each were initially fairly modest, but all grew progressively to occupy a total of 12 fronts in 1892 and over 24 by 1912 (Table 4). Two stores, McIlroy and Bratt and Dyke, had very large corner premises by the latter date. This expansion inevitably meant a reduction in frontages available to other retailers, and naturally encouraged the physical spread of the city centre as retailers sought 'edge of centre' locations.[47] However, it was in its timing and spatial clustering that department store development was most telling.

When establishing their stores in the late nineteenth century, the original proprietors clearly sought the best sites available, and their location towards the market reflects Hanley's retail geography as it stood in the 1870s and 1880s. Once expansion was underway, these stores were effectively locked in space. Some minor reorientation was possible, but only Bratt and Dyke moved to an entirely new address and then only to the premises immediately next door. This spatial lock-in meant that the department stores formed important constants in the structure of the city centre, but it also meant that they could be marginalized by broader shifts in Hanley's retail space. That this did not occur is a reflection of the economic and social influence of these stores. However, it is notable that they formed the effective north-western boundary of the core shopping area rather than lying at its very core. Crook and Halford's had shops beyond them on Stafford Street, but the shops on Hope Street and Bryant Street further to the north sold mostly the lower order goods characteristic of the 'frame'.[48]

TABLE 4 *The expansion of department store premises in Hanley, 1872–1932*

	1872	1892	1912	1932
Huntbach	2 Lamb St	2–8 Lamb St	Lamb St	Lamb St
McIlroy Bros	–	7–13 Lamb St	Lamb St & Fountain Square	Lamb St & Stafford St
Bratt and Dyke	–	49–51 Stafford St	53–55 Stafford St & 1–17 Trinity St	53–55 Stafford St & 1–17 Trinity St
Teetons	–	75–77 Stafford St	69–77 Stafford St	69–73 Stafford St

Source: Kelly's Directory for Staffordshire.

Other influences on the geography of the city centre

It would appear that, while both were important elements of the retail geography of the city centre, department stores and multiples had a much greater impact on the shopping habits of their customers, the working lives of their employees, and the fortunes and behaviour of other retailers.[49] Other forces were clearly important in shaping the spatial structure of central Hanley and other towns and cities. Not least, of course, were local variations in property values and rents arising from competition, availability and land ownership patterns. These ideas have been explored in the past,[50] and it is not the intention of this paper to investigate them in any detail here. However, four other influences – less fully considered in the literature – are highlighted as worthy of further research.

The first concerns the distribution of population within the Potteries and in Hanley in particular. The modular structure of the conurbation clearly served to limit the suburbanization of shopping, but also, as was argued earlier, the development of a powerful city centre.[51] Population growth in the suburbs effectively took the form of infilling between towns, and was often met by enhanced provision in one of the pre-existing secondary shopping centres. Nonetheless, rapid demographic growth was a strong underlying factor in the continued numerical growth of traders in central Hanley, at least through to the 1930s. More locally, the distribution of population growth within Hanley encouraged ribbon development along roads linking the expanding residential areas to the city centre. Thus we see the growth of retailing south-west down Broad Street and Snow Hill towards Shelton; north up Hope Street towards Cobridge, and east along Bucknall New Road and Mayer Street towards Northwood (see Figure 1).

Local residents might walk to the shops, but adequate transport links were required for Hanley to operate effectively as a shopping centre for the entire conurbation. These form a second main influence on city centre structure. Rail transport to Hanley was made difficult by its position on the top of a steep incline. This limited rail links to a loop line connecting to the main Birmingham to Manchester line at Stoke.[52] Although some shoppers from Tunstall and Burslem especially might arrive in Hanley via the station on Trinity Street, this was relatively unimportant in shaping the town's retail geography. Far more significant were the trams that from the 1880s ran from Stoke and Shelton through the centre of town along Piccadilly and Stafford Street to Cobridge, Burslem and Tunstall, and from Longton and Fenton to a terminus at the corner of Percy Street and Tontine Street (Figure 2). Only Newcastle was not directly linked to the centre of Hanley (there was later a connecting service), something that no doubt helps to explain the well-developed nature of its shopping infrastructure. Elsewhere, 'the electric trams ... simply carried to [Hanley] the cream and much of the milk of [Burlem's] trade.'[53] Within the city centre, it was the streets directly served by the trams that were also the most important and/or growing shopping thoroughfares (compare Figures 1 and 2). Shops along these routes would have benefited not just from the ease of access afforded by the trams, but also from their extra visibility and the easy and direct advertising they afforded. For obvious reasons, Market Square was not directly served by trams. Significantly, though, there was no link up High Street until well into the twentieth century – a factor that must have limited its potential for development in relation to the streets south of the market.

While it alone might not make or break a shopping street, the custom brought by the trams appears to have been a big influence on the relative success of different parts of the city centre. That said, the trams were only a means to an end: people needed a reason to travel, and so key destinations form a third spatial influence on the geography of the city centre. Journeys to the food markets remained significant well into the twentieth century, especially for the working classes. Market Square and the butchers' market between Tontine Street and Parliament Row were therefore important constants in shopping patterns, and served as anchor points in the changing structure of the city centre. Although Market Square maintained many of its higher order functions, including banks and building societies, clothes retailing and even a travel agent, the market itself became primarily a source of food, and the surrounding streets – especially those to the north and east – were also increasingly characterized by lower order food retailing. Furthermore, like the department stores, the market was locked in space; not least by the Doric-columned market house erected in 1831 and still the focus of the thrice-weekly market a hundred years later. With the higher order functions locating in the streets to the south, the market and Market Square more generally came to form the northern boundary of the core shopping area. This shift to the south was, in part, caused by the proliferation of high-order professional services along Cheapside, Albion Street and later Pall Mall; a strong clustering largely explained by the presence of the town hall on the corner of Albion Street and Bagnall Street (Figure 3). Although most municipal functions passed to the city council that met in Stoke from October 1910,[54] the local administrative functions and the impressive physical presence of the town hall were, if anything, a more important focus for accountants, solicitors and other professionals in the early twentieth than they had been in the late nineteenth century. The town hall was thus another key anchor point within the city centre, forming the effective southern boundary to the core area. Its influence on the reorientation of this core was further strengthened by the presence of Victoria Hall immediately to the south, and the public library, Theatre Royal and Hanley Museum on Pall Mall. Together these formed the principal cultural capital of Hanley.[55] They not only formed important city centre functions in their own right, but also served as foci for further commercial development in the surrounding streets.[56]

Not all non-commercial land uses were so conducive to such development, however, and central Hanley was characterized by a large number of factories, churches and schools that formed the last main structural influence on the city centre.[57] The close intermixing of industry and housing was a characteristic feature of the Potteries landscape, but there was also a juxtapositioning of potworks, commerce and retailing. This was most notable in the streets surrounding the core areas and influenced the geography of retailing in two main ways. Firstly, the potworks (and the churches and schools) limited the amount of land available for commercial use. Secondly, the image and environmental degradation caused by manufacturing industry acted as a negative locational factor, especially for higher order activities. This process was most obvious on High Street: beyond Church Street there was relatively little street frontage available for shops, while the cluster of earthenware works and brickworks at the north end of the street, incorporating some 20 bottle kilns in 1900, must have discouraged retailing from the immediate vicinity. It is perhaps unsurprising that the core shopping area expanded to the south of the market, along streets largely free of such activities. Constraint as well as choice clearly conditioned the development of the city centre.

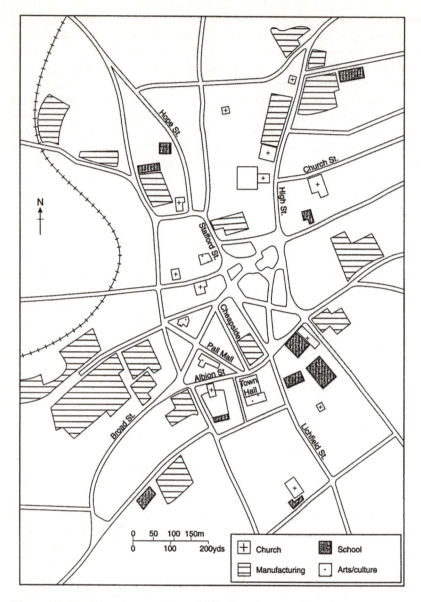

Figure 3 Industrial and non-commercial land use in central Hanley, 1900.
Source: Ordnance Survey map, 1900.

Conclusion

Present day concerns over the fate of our city centres has prompted renewed interest in their formation and structure. Indeed, a fuller understanding of the growth and geography of the city centre is essential in formulating and implementing policies to manage their use and plan for their future. And yet each city centre is different in its historical development and (hence) its current organization. The built and business environments reflect past 'layers of investment' that, in turn, shape current decisions about and processes of investment and economic (re)development.[58] The peculiar geography of the Potteries inevitably made the historic processes of growth and change that it experienced different, even unique. However, the analysis presented here highlights that we should not assume that even the most basic and widely accepted trends in retail location and city centre structure were universal in their operation, timing or outcome.

At a city-wide scale, it is clear that the development of multiples and department stores – both touchstones of retail modernity – did not follow the same trajectory in all places. Some towns, such as Leamington or Chester, became fashionable and important shopping centres despite their modest size. Many industrial towns, Coventry, Walsall and Wolverhampton included, developed a wide range of shops, including several big department stores and a large number of national and regional multiples. In Hanley, however, there were relatively few multiples and only limited development of department stores. This reflected the presence of strong secondary shopping centres within the conurbation and was an important factor in Hanley's persistent weakness as a regional retail centre. Traditional development models of urban retailing that juxtapose the hegemony of a dominant city centre with the emergence and growth of suburban retailing may, therefore, need revision. Certainly, we have to be aware of the long-term implications of local economic and political circumstances for urban retail development.

Similar problems arise with our models of the spatial structure and development of the city centre. Broad notions of core and frame are clearly useful, at least as descriptive terms, but care is needed about how they are delimited in space and time. Instead of a stable equilibrium, the analysis of Hanley suggests that both core and frame were in constant flux. The latter expanded throughout the period and continues to do so today, especially if we accept current definitions that look to include Festival Park as part of this area, despite its location some three-quarters of a mile from the established centre of town. The core shopping area, meanwhile, shifted significantly to the south in the early twentieth century before returning more recently to its old focus on Market Square.

Within this process, it is possible to identify forces for stability and others encouraging change, but any notion of a final stable state is absent. Multiples and department stores were essentially stabilizing influences; their conservative locational policies serving to reinforce the status quo. Multiples, in Hanley at least, tended to locate in well-established areas, strengthening their centrality and attraction to other retailers. Department stores, while forcing some movement to the edge of town or suburbs, were locked in space and thus formed important anchor points within the city's core retail area. Similar stability was offered by other spatially fixed institutions, most notably the market. New infrastructure, be it commercial, cultural or social, could serve to radically restructure the city centre. This is clearest in the way that improved transport facilities helped to pull the core area into previously under-developed areas: accessibility and visibility brought obvious benefits to retailers and professionals alike. However, the positive impact of Hanley's cultural infrastructure shows the possibility for active intervention by civic authorities in the 'natural' development of the city centre. Victorian city fathers were as alive to the potential of civic boosterism as any city or borough council today.[59]

In sum, then, the structure of city centre retailing has been and continues to be shaped by a complex interaction of geographical, economic, political and cultural processes. Towns and cities experienced these processes in unique combinations and the spatial and developmental outcomes were themselves unique. There is a danger, of course, of descending into particularism, but it is essential that we remain mindful of the historical geographical distinctiveness of different places,[60] and that we ensure our theories of retail structure and change are sensitive to local circumstances.

Notes

[1] Clifford Guy, 'Controlling new retail spaces: the impress of planning policies in Western Europe', *Urban Studies* 35/5 (1998), p. 954. See also Clifford Guy, *The Retail Development Process: Location, Property and Planning* (Routledge, London, 1994).

[2] See, for example, Geoff Walker, 'Retailing development: in town or out of town?', in C. Greed (ed.), *Investigating Town Planning: Changing Perspectives and Agendas* (Longmans, London, 1996), pp. 155–80; Phil Rushton, *Out of Town Shopping: The Future of Retailing* (British Library, London, 1999).

[3] Clifford Guy, 'High Street retailing in off-centre retail parks – a review of the effectiveness of land use planning policies', *Town Planning Review* 69/3 (1998), pp. 291–313.

[4] A recent (unpublished) survey by CASA/URBED (1999) on behalf of the DETR suggested seven defining characteristics of the city centre: type of activities and facilities; diversity of use; intensity of use; pedestrian

accessibility; absence of resident population; visitor attractions and financial turnover.

[5] Nicholas Alexander, 'Objects in the rearview mirror may appear closer than they are', *The International Review of Retail, Distribution and Consumer Research* 7/4 (1997), pp. 383–403.

[6] Jon Stobart and Alan Hallsworth, 'Change and stability, structure and agency in retailing: the case of Stoke-on-Trent', *The International Review of Retail, Distribution and Consumer Research* 9/2 (1999), pp. 203–21. See also Peter Larkham, 'Constraints of urban history and form upon redevelopment', *Geography* 80/2 (1995), pp. 111–24.

[7] Gareth Shaw, 'Processes and patterns in the geography of retail change, with special reference to Kingston upon Hull, 1880–1950', University of Hull, Occasional Papers in Geography, 24 (1978). See also Gareth Shaw, 'The role of retailing in the urban economy', in J. Johnson and C. Pooley (eds), *The Structure of Nineteenth-Century Cities* (Croom Helm, London, 1982), pp. 171–94; Gareth Shaw, 'The evolution and impact of large-scale retailing in Britain', in J. Benson and G. Shaw (eds), *The Evolution of Retail Systems c. 1800–1914* (Leicester University Press, Leicester, 1992), pp. 135–65.

[8] For a useful summary of these long-term processes, see Harold Carter, *An Introduction to Urban Historical Geography* (Edward Arnold, London, 1983), pp. 150–69. A more detailed discussion of nineteenth-century trends is found in Shaw, 'The role of retailing in the urban economy', pp. 177–92; David Alexander, *Retailing in England During the Industrial Revolution* (Athlone Press, London, 1970).

[9] Harold Carter and Roy Lewis, *An Urban Geography of England and Wales in the Nineteenth Century* (Edward Arnold, London, 1990), pp. 93–4, but see also Jon Stobart, 'Patterns of urban retailing: suburbanisation, centralisation and hierarchies in the Potteries conurbation, 1872–1932', *Journal of Regional and Local Studies* 18/1 (1998), pp. 11–26.

[10] James B. Jefferys, *Retail Trading in Britain, 1850–1950* (Cambridge University Press, Cambridge, 1954); Gareth Shaw, 'The European scene: Britain and Germany', in Benson and Shaw (eds), *The Evolution of Retail Systems*, pp. 23–32; Geoffrey Crossick and Serge Jaumain, 'The world of the department store: distribution, culture and social change', in G. Crossick and S. Jaumain (eds), *Cathedrals of Consumption: The European Department Store, 1850–1939* (Ashgate, Aldershot, 1999), pp. 1–45.

[11] Shaw, 'The role of retailing in the urban economy', pp. 185–8; Shaw, 'The evolution and impact of large-scale retailing', pp. 139–46 and 159–64. For details of individual trades, see Jefferys, *Retail Trading in Britain*, sections V–XIX.

[12] Shaw, 'Processes and patterns', p. 29.

[13] Risto Laulajainen, 'Chain store expansion in national space', *Geografiska Annaler B* 70/3 (1988), pp. 292–9; David Benninson, Ian Clarke and John Pal, 'Locational decision making in retailing: an explanatory framework for analysis', *The International Review of Retail, Distribution and Consumer Research* 5/1 (1995), pp. 1–20; Andrew Alexander, 'Strategy and strategists: evidence from an early retail revolution in Britain', *The International Review of Retail, Distribution and Consumer Research* 7/1 (1997), pp. 61–78.

[14] Shaw, 'Processes and patterns', but see the recent work by Andrew Alexander, Gareth Shaw and others on the regional and national development of multiple retailing, for example in chapter 5 in this collection.

[15] Stobart, 'Patterns of urban retailing'.

[16] Shaw, 'Processes and patterns', p. 184.

[17] Shaw, 'The role of retailing in the urban economy', pp. 189–92; Stephen Brown, 'The complex model of city centre retailing: an historical application', *Transactions of the Institute of British Geographers* 12/1 (1986), p. 7; Craig Young and Stephen Allen, 'Retail patterns in nineteenth-century Chester', *Journal of Regional and Local Studies* 16/1 (1996), p. 2.

[18] For example, nineteenth-century retail hierarchies have been identified in Hull by Shaw, 'Processes and patterns'; and in Chester by Young and Allen, 'Retail patterns in nineteenth-century Chester'. For a general discussion of intra-urban retail hierarchies, see Brian J. Berry, *Geography of Market Centers and Retail Distribution* (Prentice Hall, Englewood Cliffs, 1967).

[19] Stobart, 'Patterns of urban retailing', p. 18.

[20] Stobart and Hallsworth, 'Change and stability', p. 206.

[21] Shaw, 'The evolution and impact of large-scale retailing', pp. 140–6.

[22] James Jefferys defined a full department store as 'a large retail store with 4 or more separate departments under one roof, each selling different classes of goods of which one is women's and children's wear'. A part-department store was a 'large firm that had more than one retail department but would not appear to have reached the status of a full department store'. Jefferys, *Retail Trading in Britain*, p. 326.

[23] *Kelly's Directory for Staffordshire* (Kelly's Directories, London, 1912), p. 212.

[24] Alfred Lowe, *History and Antiquities of the City of Coventry* (the author, Coventry, 1903–4), p. 92.

[25] Stobart, 'Patterns of urban retailing', p. 19.

[26] Marks & Spencer, found on Piccadilly in 1912 and 1916, had apparently gone by 1928. It was not listed again until 1936, by which time it had moved to its present location in Upper Market Street. See *Kelly's Directory of Staffordshire*.

[27] Peter Mathias, *Retailing Revolution: A History of Multiple Retailing in the Food Trades Based Upon the Allied Suppliers Group of Companies* (Longmans, London, 1967), pp. 38–9; Shaw, 'The evolution and impact of large-scale retailing', pp. 153–4.

[28] Alexander, 'Strategy and strategists', pp. 63–74.

[29] For more details on population growth in the Potteries, see Anthony D. M. Phillips, 'The growth of the conurbation', in A. D. M. Phillips (ed.), *The Potteries: Continuity and Change in a Staffordshire Conurbation* (Alan Sutton, Stroud, 1993), pp. 109–14.

[30] See John Briggs, 'Urban institutions and administration'; Michael Greenslade, 'The Potteries: a question of regional identity', both in Phillips (ed.), *The Potteries*, pp. 130–44 and 164–73.

[31] Stobart and Hallsworth, 'Change and stability', pp. 212–13.

[32] *Chain and Multiple Store*, 28 May 1938. See also Stobart, 'Patterns of urban retailing', pp. 19–20.

[33] Shaw, 'Processes and patterns', pp. 77–9.

[34] The presence of Burton's in these towns reflects definite company policy of network infilling. See Alexander, 'Strategy and strategists', p. 70.

[35] See Stobart, 'Patterns of urban retailing', pp. 19–22.

[36] *Chain and Multiple Store*, 28 May 1938.

[37] Arnold Bennett, *The Old Wives' Tale* (Everyman, London, 1935; first published 1908), p. 508.

[38] Brown, 'The complex model of city centre retailing', p. 6; Young and Allen, 'Retail patterns in nineteenth-century Chester', pp. 2–3; Stobart, 'Patterns of urban retailing', pp. 12–13.

[39] A similar process is seen in Hull and Chester, although the initial focus was not always the marketplace. See Shaw, 'Processes and patterns'; Young and Allen, 'Retail patterns in nineteenth-century Chester'.

[40] See Brown, 'The complex model of city centre retailing', pp. 4–6 and 11–16.

[41] The core-frame model was developed by Edgar Horwood and Ronald Boyce, *Studies of the CBD and Urban Freeway Development* (University of Washington Press, Seattle, 1959). It is discussed, *inter alia*, in Harold Carter, *The Study of Urban Geography* (Edward Arnold, London, 1995, first published 1972), pp. 163–7.

[42] Stobart, 'Patterns of urban retailing', pp. 14–17.

[43] Brown, 'The complex model of city centre retailing', pp. 11–14.

[44] See Ross Davies, 'Structural models of retail distribution: analogies with settlement and land use theories', *Transactions of the Institute of British Geographers* 57/3 (1972), pp. 59–82.

[45] Shaw, 'Processes and patterns', pp. 77–9.

[46] *Chain and Multiple Store*, 28 May 1938; Stobart and Hallsworth, 'Change and stability', pp. 215–19.

[47] Stobart, 'Patterns of urban retailing', p. 17.

[48] Brown, 'The complex model of city centre retailing', p. 11.

[49] Shaw, 'The evolution and impact of large-scale retailing', pp. 159–64. See also Crossick and Jaumain, 'The world of the department store', pp. 9–24.

[50] See, for example, Wayne Davies, John Giggs and David Herbert, 'Directories, rate books and the commercial structure of towns', *Geography* 53/1 (1968), pp. 41–54; Carter and Lewis, *An Urban Geography of England and Wales*, pp. 102–9; Young and Allen, 'Retail patterns in nineteenth-century Chester', pp. 3–6.

[51] See also Stobart, 'Patterns of urban retailing', pp. 19–22.

[52] Brian Turton, 'The Potteries in the interwar period', in Phillips (ed.), *The Potteries*, pp. 150–5.

[53] Bennett, *The Old Wives' Tale*, p. 508.

[54] Briggs, 'Urban institutions and administration', especially p. 143.

[55] Jon Stobart and Chris Thomas, 'Cultural capital and competition in the Five Towns', unpublished paper presented at the Urban History Group Meeting, University of Bristol, April 2000. Copy available from the author.

[56] Such facilities appear in the CASA/URBED defining characteristics under the heading, 'Visitor attractions'.

[57] Employment in 'non-town centre' uses, such as manufacturing, is

highlighted by CASA/URBED as a negative element in defining city centres.

[58] Doreen Massey, *Spatial Divisions of Labour* (Macmillan, London, 1995, first published 1984).

[59] Stobart and Thomas, 'Cultural capital and competition in the Five Towns'. See also Gerry Kearns and Chris Philo (eds), *Selling Places: The City as Cultural Capital, Past and Present* (Pergamon, Oxford, 1993).

[60] See, *inter alia*, Massey, *Spatial Divisions of Labour*; Nigel Thrift, *Spatial Formations* (Sage, London, 1996).

III PROPERTY, POLITICS AND COMMUNITIES

CHAPTER 7
RETAIL PROPERTY OWNERSHIP IN EDWARDIAN ENGLAND
Michael Winstanley

The emergence of a consumer society in Britain from the late eighteenth century has been associated with the rise of retailing from fixed premises.[1] Historians have explored these shops' changing spatial diffusion, architectural styles, the types of businesses operating within them and the ways in which their proprietors and staff interacted with customers. Yet apart from Peter Scott's pioneering study, *The Property Masters*, which explored the emergence of large-scale commercial developers and speculators in the twentieth century, there has been no systematic attempt to find out who owned these premises.[2] The potential significance of changes in patterns of ownership and tenancies, sources of capital, parties' responsibilities for undertaking investment, and the factors that influenced the timing, nature and appropriateness of that investment, are all issues that have characterized historical debates about industrial and agricultural development but have rarely been addressed in retail history. This chapter, therefore, is a preliminary attempt to answer the simple question, 'Who owned shops?' in three English provincial towns, exploiting an as yet little-used source, the Inland Revenue's District Valuation of *c.* 1909–14. It describes the background and nature of the source, assesses the extent of owner-occupancy in the retail sector, considers the various individuals and organizations involved in each of these towns and suggests ways in which further study could be developed.

I

The accepted view of the period prior to the First World War is that urban property was held 'for the most part, in small parcels by a multitude of small and medium-sized owners'. Avner Offer estimates, on the basis of Inland Revenue returns, that there were probably more than a million such proprietors by 1909, each of them owning on average seven or eight units, most of them letting their properties at rack-rent.[3] Shopkeepers have traditionally been regarded as part of this propertied petite bourgeoisie, owning not just their own business premises but acting as small landlords of rented housing stock in the locality.[4] This impression of retail owner-occupiers has been strengthened by well-documented examples of department store proprietors who redesigned their emporiums from the late nineteenth century in order to meet, and shape, consumer demand.[5] As we shall see, however, such men were not typical of either property owners or shopkeepers during this period.

The decades leading up to 1914 were traumatic for private shopkeepers and urban property owners alike. Revolutions in retailing, symbolized by the growth of the co-operative movement, national multiples and flamboyant department stores, seemingly threatened to undermine the viability of the individual proprietor.[6] Equally, if not more threatening, was the dramatic erosion of the financial returns on urban property in the 1900s. The final decades of Victoria's reign were characterized by low interest rates, rising real wages and house-building booms, especially in the mid-to-late 1890s.[7] After 1903 there was an unprecedented collapse in both house building and property values, symptomatic of a precipitous decline in the appeal of property as a secure and profitable long-term haven for funds. Property values depreciated by up to 40 per cent and transactions fell from a peak of £394 million in 1899 to a low of just £223 million in 1912.[8] Although we have no separate index of retail property values, the scale, nature and profitability of investment in shop premises could not have remained unaffected by this reversal. In part, the decline reflected increasing returns from other more liquid forms of investment, but it was primarily caused by falling profit margins in the property sector itself. Rising mortgage interest charges and building costs, combined with the stagnant earnings of tenants and an escalation in local authority rates from the late 1890s, squeezed margins for owners and shopkeepers alike. The rise in rates impacted particularly severely on shop premises, since they were already heavily taxed in comparison to residential and industrial properties.[9] Not surprisingly, shopkeepers were ardent supporters of retrenchment in local government throughout the Edwardian period and their pressure, combined with that of other ratepayer organisations, helped to ensure that the years leading up to 1914 were characterized by massive cuts in municipal capital expenditure on transport, water, power, roads and central 'improvement' schemes.[10]

Developments in national politics also increasingly challenged the perceived advantages and privileges of property ownership.[11] Although the state had long resorted to real estate as a reliable basis for local and national taxation, a new element entered the debate in the Edwardian period, as fundamental questions were asked about the appropriate level and distribution of the tax burden. The 'People's Budget' of 1909 eventually committed the Liberal government to implement a new land tax.[12] It was this fiscal initiative that led to the compilation of the survey that forms the basis of this study.

The Inland Revenue's District Valuation Survey was undertaken as a preliminary to the implementation of the most contentious element of the then Chancellor of the Exchequer Lloyd George's budget proposals, the Incremental Value Duty. This was to be levied on increases in site values, and consequently required that values for sites and for the buildings or structures be ascertained, in order to provide base figures for subsequent calculations. A national survey of every property in Britain was undertaken. The project has been likened to a 'New Domesday' and represents the 'the largest data bank in British history', containing individual descriptions of some 13.5 million hereditaments (or separately rated properties).[13]

The surviving records comprise three distinct, but related, classes of documents. The so-called 'Domesday Books' were drawn up on the basis of the 1909 rate books and are now held in county record offices. These specify the names and address of owners, occupiers, classifications of properties by use, and various valuations for each property including gross annual value, rateable value, gross value, and the estimated values of sites and buildings. Large-scale maps identifying each hereditament by number were also compiled, enabling individual premises to be located accurately within each tax district. Working copies that have survived are retained in county record offices; the completed maps are held by the Public Record Office (PRO). Surveyors' field books, also in the PRO, were compiled between 1911 and c. 1914 on the basis of questionnaire returns and site visits. They include the same information as the 'Domesday Books' together with descriptions of the nature of the tenancy, rent payable, dates and values of recent purchases, charges on property, responsibility for repairs, insurance and maintenance, and details of both the exterior and interior of buildings. When cross-referenced with surviving building applications and contemporary trade directories, these documents allow an unparalleled insight into the nature of the urban property market.

The empirical data for this study have been drawn from three towns of comparable size, with contrasting industrial, occupational and demographic profiles in North-west England, which the census tables of 1911 suggested had very different forms of retail provision.[14] Lancaster (population in 1911: 41,410; 1724 shops per 100,000) was a long-established market town with a substantial professional and service middle class, which had been transformed from the 1870s by the expansion of large-scale oilcloth and linoleum manufacturing under the control of two local companies.[15] Accrington (population in 1911: 45,029; 2227 shops per 100,000), a cotton town in North-east Lancashire, had experienced rapid growth from the mid-nineteenth century as a consequence of the revolution in power loom weaving.[16] Neither town was characterized by employer housing. Barrow, in present day Cumbria (population in 1911: 63,770; 1548 shops per 100,000), had developed from a small village in the 1860s into a shipbuilding and heavy industrial town dominated by a few large firms. These companies not only employed the majority of the adult male population, but were also initially responsible for erecting accommodation for the waves of migrant workers who were attracted to the town.[17]

Basic information on every building identified as a retail property (shop, shop and house, warerooms, stores etc) in each of these towns was extracted from the 'Domesday Books'. This provided the necessary hereditament numbers to trace properties in the field books. The data was then cross-referenced with trade directories to compile a picture of the commercial infrastructure of each town. Stalls in market halls have been omitted from the statistical analysis because only in Lancaster were they separately identified and valued. Shops in which owners and occupiers shared the same surname have been classified as tenanted if the field books indicated that a rent was paid; otherwise they have been considered to be owner-occupied.[18] Because the main concern here is with property, the results relate to separate hereditaments rather than to businesses.

II

The valuation survey confirms what the census implied; the characteristics of the retail structures in these three towns were very different and broadly reflected their industrial and social profiles (Figure 1).

Accrington, in common with other textile towns, had a preponderance of small premises.[19] Only 20 per cent of retail outlets had rateable values in excess of £30; over 50 per cent were rated at less than £20. Most of the cheaper properties doubled as residences. Lancaster's more diverse customer base, and its role as service centre for an extensive rural hinterland, supported a larger number of substantial shops. Forty per cent were rated over £30, but a similar proportion was still less than £20. Barrow had fewer shops per head of

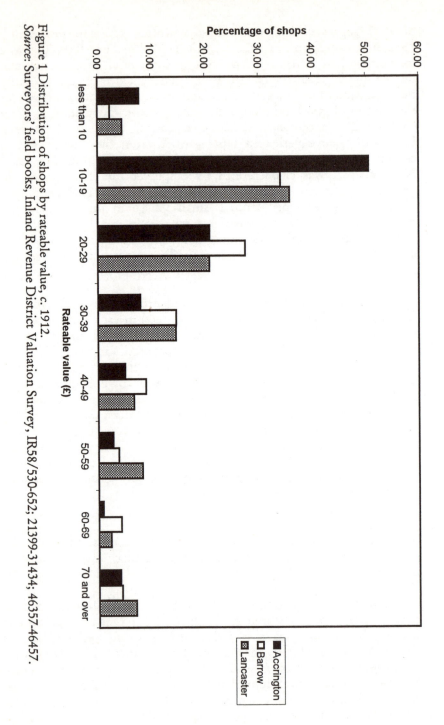

Figure 1 Distribution of shops by rateable value, c. 1912.
Source: Surveyors' field books, Inland Revenue District Valuation Survey, IR58/530-652; 21399-31434; 46357-46457.

the population but a higher proportion of these were rated at between
£20 and £30. Although the data strictly relate to hereditaments and not
to retail outlets, this does not invalidate the conclusion that the
majority of businesses were small, since *most* shopkeepers occupied
just one property. Multiple occupation of hereditaments was more
likely to be associated with larger businesses in the town centre, or
with the co-operative movement, which was prominent in all of these
towns.

The significance of larger traders in the retail infrastructure is
increased if aggregate rateable values for each band of property are
calculated (Figure 2). Properties rated above £70 per annum accounted
for only 4 to 7 per cent of the retail premises in each town, but for
between 17 and 25 per cent of their total rateable value. Nevertheless,
smaller properties valued at less than £30 still accounted for just over
30 per cent of the value of retail premises in Lancaster, nearly 40 per
cent of those in Barrow and 50 per cent in Accrington.

Even more significant is the fact that only 20 to 24 per cent of all
properties can be clearly identified as being owner-occupied[20] (Figure
3). The proportion of owner-occupiers correlated positively with
rateable value, but the relationship was not particularly strong. Indeed,
in Accrington, there was no discernible increase in the incidence of
owner-occupiers in properties with a rateable value above £20. In
Barrow and Lancaster the proportion only increased significantly
above £50. Although the *proportion* of property-owning occupiers was
higher in the more valuable properties, *numerically* the majority of
owner-occupiers had premises rated at less than £30, so
owner-occupiers accounted for only between 25 and 30 per cent of the
value of retail properties.

Owner-occupiers did not comprise a cohesive social or economic
group. The largest owner-occupiers were local co-operative societies
that had expanded dramatically during the last quarter of the
nineteenth century to become the largest single owners of retail
property in each of these towns.[21] In Barrow the co-operative owned
nine of the 20 most valuable, owner-occupied retail properties.
Although the society's premises amounted to only 5 per cent of
owner-occupied outlets, these contributed 22 per cent of their value. In
Lancaster the co-operative movement owned just under 10 per cent of
owner-occupied properties, but the higher proportion of substantial
shopkeepers in the town kept its share of their value down to 13 per
cent. The co-operatives' dominance was most marked in Accrington,
where the combined valuations of the two local societies' shops
amounted to 35 per cent of the estimated market value of all
owner-occupied retail outlets in the town.

The co-operatives' policy of acquiring freehold sites enabled them to

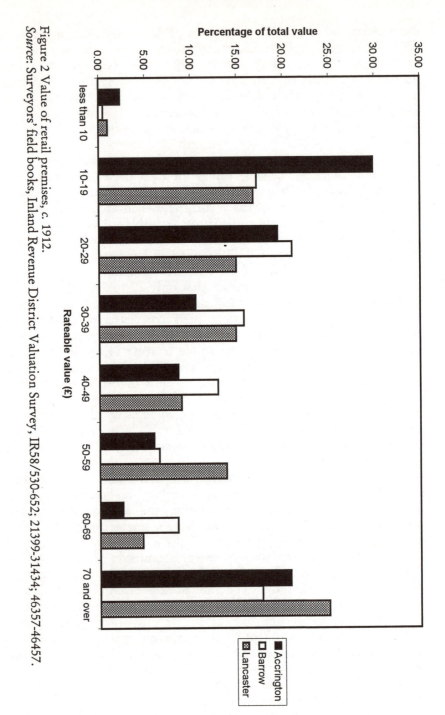

Figure 2 Value of retail premises, c. 1912.
Source: Surveyors' field books, Inland Revenue District Valuation Survey, IR58/530-652; 21399-31434; 46357-46457.

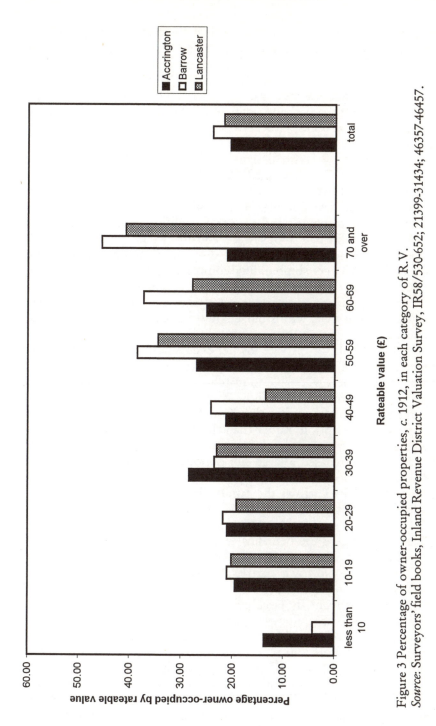

Figure 3 Percentage of owner-occupied properties, c. 1912, in each category of R.V.
Source: Surveyors' field books, Inland Revenue District Valuation Survey, IR58/530-652; 21399-31434; 46357-46457.

invest heavily in modern premises. All of them erected purpose-built department stores on central sites, which they accumulated over several decades by piecemeal purchases of contiguous plots. These central stores were visible manifestations of the movement's success and of confidence in its future.[22] Barrow Co-operative Society's emporium boasted ladies' and gents' outfitting and tailoring, drapery and mantle showrooms, grocery stores, a boot and shoe shop, a furnishing department and large dining rooms. Lancaster's store was rebuilt in 1902 to a lavish design by the renowned local architects, Austin and Paley. Even the small Accrington Provident Co-operative Society's central stores contained grocery, boot and drapery departments, and was considered the epitome of modernity with its elegant stone frontage and electric lighting throughout. The co-operatives' suburban shops were equally well-appointed. Barrow co-operative's purpose-built block of shops in Vickerstown, an estate developed by Vickers shipbuilding company to house its workers in the early 1900s, was described as 'up to date and in good order'. During the 1900s the Lancaster society erected elaborate new branches in a distinctive house style, with stone-engraved beehive symbols above the entrances.[23]

The low levels of private owner-occupancy and the numerical preponderance of relatively small properties meant that few substantial private shopkeepers were able to match the co-operatives' building and modernization programmes. Those who did invest invariably attracted positive media comment, but this should not blind us to the fact that they were the exception, rather than the rule. In Accrington the most prominent private retail developer was J. W. Bridge, an ironmonger who in 1889 purchased a large site opposite the market hall, and in 1891 erected a modern three-storey block, which he partially sublet to other traders.[24] In Barrow, the family firm of Pass and Co., general wholesale merchants, was singled out by the surveyor for upgrading their premises to render them 'new and modern in every way'.[25] Only in Lancaster, where the demands of a fashion-conscious middle class were difficult to accommodate in the cramped and often unsanitary conditions of the old town centre, and where there was also a higher proportion of long-established family businesses, is there evidence of substantial investment by large private retailers. William Atkinson, a gunsmith and sports equipment manufacturer, for example, diversified into car, motorcycle and bicycle production in 1903 by erecting new showrooms and workrooms at a cost of over £10,000.[26] Reddrop's, a family drapery business on Cheapside, increasingly projected itself as a department store after several piecemeal expansions behind and above its street frontage in the 1890s.[27] Mansergh's, occupying a prime site on Market Square, also extended its premises through to Church Street to

TABLE 1 *Tenure in Barrow and Lancaster, c. 1912*

Barrow tenure	Properties	Total RV £	Average RV £	Percentage of properties	Percentage of RV
Week	341	6647	19.5	45	32
Month	59	1704	28.9	8	8
Quarter	59	2130	36.1	8	10
Half	6	229	38.2	1	1
Year	65	2766	42.6	9	13
Lease	71	3612	50.9	9	17
Not specified	128	3434	26.8	17	16
Other	21	453	21.6	3	2
Total	750	20975	28.0	100	100

Lancaster tenure	Properties	Total RV £	Average RV £	Percentage of properties	Percentage of RV
Week	114	1659	14.6	20	10
Month	20	344	17.2	3	2
Quarter	66	1592	24.1	11	9
Half	9	265	29.4	2	2
Year	187	6142	32.8	32	35
Lease	92	4689	51.0	16	27
Not specified	82	2488	30.3	14	14
Other	10	269	26.9	2	2
Total	580	17448	30.1	100	100

Source: Surveyors' field books, Inland Revenue District Valuation Survey, IR58/530-652; 21399-31434; 46357-46457. At the time of publication, the analysis of Accrington was incomplete.

its rear, and claimed a similar department store status.[28] Even in Lancaster, however, most premises on the main shopping thoroughfares were occupied by tenants, not by their owners.

The surveyors' field books strongly suggest that the length and type of tenure, as well as tenants' responsibility for paying rates, were positively correlated with rateable values. Smaller tenants possessed, for whatever reason, little or no long-term security of tenure, a feature underlined by the high turnover among small shops during the period. Many were let on weekly, monthly or quarterly tenancies inclusive of rates. Leases extending beyond one year were restricted to larger properties in town centres. Agreements were rarely for more than seven years; the majority were for considerably fewer, particularly in

Barrow.

The short-term nature of most tenancies had both advantages and drawbacks for retailers. On the one hand, tenants were free to quit if trade was poor, or to relocate if a more attractive site became available; they were not, like owner-occupiers, committed to a particular location. They could also renegotiate rents if trade was depressed. On the other hand, tenants had to ensure that their turnovers were sufficient to meet regular rental payments, which could amount to as much as 50 to 70 per cent of net profit.[29] If trade improved, tenants were vulnerable to increases in rent. They also had little or no incentive to improve their properties, unless their landlords guaranteed compensation for improvements when they quitted. The apparent absence of written agreements, however, would suggest that this could not be relied on.

Within this general picture of short-term tenancies there were clearly differences between the towns. Barrow had a much higher proportion of shops let on weekly tenancies, while annual tenancies were the mode in Lancaster. The latter also had a significantly higher proportion of properties let on long leases. These differences probably reflected Barrow's more transient population and working-class market and Lancaster's more varied customer base and established role as a market town. The majority of the emerging multiples obtained new branches by entering into leases, usually between 7 and 21 years in length. The major exceptions to this policy were a few boot and shoe manufacturers and clothiers who owned freehold properties, meat companies that had a higher proportion of smaller outlets in the suburbs (taken as short tenancies of up to one year), and Singer's sewing machine company, whose tenancies ranged from one to three years.

It is not clear whether multiples were unable or unwilling to commit themselves to the expense of purchasing town centre sites. They may have preferred long leases because they stabilized rents, by preventing landlords from imposing substantial increases if business in the district improved. A lease of 7, 14 or 21 years, especially one that offered a sitting tenant first option of renewal on expiry, also provided the necessary security and opportunity to undertake substantial improvements to premises. In some cases, 'improving leases' specifically anticipated that a lessee would invest in a property by fixing a reduced rent for a restricted number of years. In 1897 Freeman, Hardy Willis, for example, took out a lease for 21 years on a prime site in Lancaster on these conditions, and undertook substantial improvements to the street frontage and layout of rooms upstairs (to facilitate subletting as offices).[30]

TABLE 2 *Leases in Lancaster, Barrow and Accrington, c. 1912*

Length of lease (years)	Number of properties		
	Accrington*	Barrow	Lancaster
2	1	1	2
3	2	7	3
4	0	0	2
5	5	29	19
7	15**	12	19
10	11	6	13
14	3	5	10
15	1	1	2
20	0	0	1
21	6	5	11
Not specified	0	5	9
By agreement	0	0	1
Total	29*	71	92

* Based on incomplete data.
** One of these is for eight years.
Source: Surveyors' field books, Inland Revenue District Valuation Survey, IR58/530-652; 21399-31434; 46357-46457.

III

If most shopkeepers were tenants then, who were their landlords? Few appear to have been exclusively or even primarily rentiers; even fewer specialized in commercial property. Most owned no more than a handful of shops. Their motivations were as diverse as their backgrounds. Aristocratic landlords and the churches did not own significant amounts of retail property in these towns. During his initial involvement in the development of Barrow, the Duke of Devonshire had financed blocks of residential flats that contained some lock-up shops, but otherwise no members of the landed class played any role in these towns' property sectors.[31] Nor did the established church own any retail property. The Unitarians and Society of Friends both owned shops in Lancaster, but only the Centenary Congregational Church speculated with investment in lock-up premises, which they incorporated into the street frontage of their new meeting hall in the 1890s.[32]

Corporate finance also displayed little interest in retail premises. Joint stock banks often incorporated office 'chambers' above their banking halls, and added small rows of shops to their street frontages, but they did not otherwise speculate in retail property. Large-scale property development and insurance companies were also

TABLE 3 *Multiples' tenancies: Lancaster, Barrow and Accrington, c. 1912*

Firm	Lancaster	Barrow	Accrington
Butchers			
Argenta Meat Co.	Quarterly		2 shops: 10 yr/n. k.
Eastmans	3 shops: 14 yr/year/week	3 shops: 21 yr/2 quarterly	year
James Nelson	year (tenancy lapsed c. 1912)	8 shops: 2 year/4 quarter/2 n. k.	year (tenancy lapsed c. 1914)
London Meat Co.	21 yr		
River Plate Meat Co.		4 shops: year/half year/ week/n. k.	
Clothing			
Donegal Tweed Co.			14 yr
Fleming Reid	Lease	Freehold	
Hepworths	21 yr	n. k.	21yr
Stewarts Clothiers	5 yr	month	21 yr
Bradley Brothers		Freehold	10 yr
Cash Clothing Co.	Freehold	5 yr	year
Grocery			
Home & Colonial	Lease	7 yr	
Hunters		21 yr	
India & China Tea Co.		Lease	
Jacksons		10 yr	
Liptons	n. k.	7 yr	21 yr
Maypole	21 yr		10 yr
National Tea Co.	year		
Footwear			
Freeman, Hardy Willis	21 yr	14 yr	7 yr
H. P. Tyler	Freehold	5 yr	
Stead & Simpson		14 yr	
V.H. Symons		5 yr	
Miscellaneous			
Boots	n. k.		21 yr
Marks & Spencer			21 yr
Singers	year	3 yr	year
Thomas Cook		7 yr	
W. H. Smith	21 yr		

Source: Surveyors' field books, Inland Revenue District Valuation Survey, IR58/530-652; 21399-31434; 46357-46457.[33]

unrepresented. The degree to which major manufacturing employers invested in retail property merely reflected the extent to which they were responsible for housing provision in a town. Employers in Lancaster and Accrington owned virtually no houses or shops. Tied housing was more evident in Barrow, where the Furness Railway Company, the Barrow Haematite Steel Company and the shipbuilding firm of Vickers, Sons and Maxim built multi-storey blocks of flats and a housing estate for the waves of migrant workers attracted to the town. In comparison to working-class streets elsewhere in the town, which were developed by smaller private builders, these employers' developments contained relatively few retail premises. The flats were serviced by small, ground floor, lock-up shops situated at either end of the block. Retail provision in Vickerstown, home to over 6000 people by 1912, consisted of just 14 private shops and the co-operative society's stores.[34] These shops displayed characteristics more commonly associated with inter-war suburban and council estates. All were purpose-built and located centrally. Stricter regulations on property use meant that there were no shops dispersed throughout the estate, as was the case in working-class developments financed by smaller speculative builders.

Railway companies owned retail outlets adjacent to stations in Accrington and Barrow, although there is little to suggest that they sought to capitalize on these central locations. Amphitheatre Buildings and 1–7 Cavendish Square, owned by the Furness Railway Company, were described by the surveyor as 'one of the most valuable blocks of property in Barrow', despite being simple 'one storey buildings of fair construction, being partly brick and wooden erections'. The railway company let the properties on a seven-year lease to a local solicitor, John Lowden, who sublet to various tenants.[35] The Lancashire and Yorkshire Railway's properties in Accrington were also small, single-storey, lock-up outlets alongside the railway viaduct that spanned Blackburn Road. These had been erected about 1894. The company's legal agent justified their poor specifications on the grounds that they would only have to stand for seven to fifteen years. The fact that they were adjacent to railway land and what were euphemistically referred to as 'open stretches of country' was advanced as a legitimate reason for dispensing with 'the usual outside facilities'.[36]

Entrepreneurs involved in other aspects of the service economy sometimes sought to increase returns on investment by incorporating retail outlets into new premises.[37] When the new indoor skating rink was built on Church Street, Lancaster, in 1907, two lock-up shops were incorporated into its street frontage. Lock-up shops were also situated beneath billiard halls. The most ambitious scheme was undertaken in Lancaster in 1897, when two brothers, John and

Christopher Fell, transformed ten back-to-back cottages into five shops, converted the theatre above them into a billiard hall, and erected additional retail premises on the adjacent corner plot, which they let to Liptons and Boots.[38]

Brewers were major investors in retail outlets. Their interests in property dated back only to the defensive scramble for licensed premises during the 1890s, and were prompted by fears about declining alcohol sales.[39] By the end of Edwardian era, virtually all the pubs and beerhouses in the three towns under consideration were tied houses controlled by big brewers, a feature totally obscured in contemporary trade directories, where they were listed under the names of the tenants, who confusingly continued to be referred to as 'landlords'. Brewers also purchased retail off-licences, which frequently functioned as general shops, 'grocers', confectioners, tobacconists and chemists. Whether their acquisition of such properties made them 'owner-occupiers' is a moot point. The majority of their licensed premises were tenanted, but tenants were not free to stock competitors' products. In some respects, therefore, they were franchisees, their shops effectively acting as retail branches for the sale of a particular manufacturer's products.

The brewing trade's involvement in each of these towns reflected the broader characteristics of the local community and its economic base. In Lancaster, local men, William Mitchell and Yates and Jackson, owned most of the tied houses. Accrington was dominated by regional brewers based in the textile districts of South-east Lancashire, with Blackburn and to a lesser extent Manchester and Burnley firms to the fore. In more cosmopolitan Barrow, three substantial local businesses – Case and Co., James Thompson and Co., and G. S. Heath – were challenged by Burton brewers – Allsops, Ind Coope, Truman, Hanbury and Buxton, and Worthington – and by firms from as far afield as Liverpool and Dumfries.[40]

Local brewers, and to a lesser extent publicans, also purchased other retail properties. William Mitchell, for example, owned the shops that flanked his Central Brewery between Church Street and Market Street, two of Lancaster's main shopping thoroughfares. In the 1890s, when he redeveloped the Wheatsheaf Inn on Penny Street, another main thoroughfare, he incorporated two lock-up shops on the street frontage, which by 1912 had been let to the London Central Meat Company and Maypole. W. H. Smith occupied the street frontage to the Royal King's Arms, the town's leading hotel. In Barrow, G. S. Heath owned a block of five premises on Dalton Road, the premier shopping street, as did the proprietor of the Derby Hotel. Blackburn and Burnley brewers and Accrington publicans owned retail outlets that were occupied by traders as diverse as butchers, cabinetmakers, drapers, fish and fruit dealers, fried fish dealers, milliners, tailors, a piano dealer, an undertaker, a hairdresser, a tobacconist, a saddler and a tripe dealer.[41]

The municipal authority was the largest single owner of retail property in each of these towns, and was rivalled only by the local co-operative society. Although councils remained reluctant to get involved in the development and ownership of residential property, they showed less scruples about intervening in the commercial sector. Their primary involvement came about through the construction and ownership of covered market halls, which were erected in almost every northern industrial town in the mid-to-late Victorian period.[42] Like the co-operatives' central stores, these were both ornamental and functional, and they incorporated the latest building technologies. Above all, they occupied prime central locations that reflected their commercial importance within the towns, and acted as magnets for other retailers. Accrington's market hall epitomized all these features. When it opened in 1869 it was hailed by one newspaper, somewhat extravagantly, as a 'living treasure of art'.[43] It could accommodate 83 stalls on two floors and provided basement storage space for a significant minority of the stallholders. By the 1900s it was the hub of the corporation's tramway system. Based on estimated takings, the surveyor valued the site and buildings at £64,000.[44] Barrow's market hall, adjacent to the Town Hall and also in 'a good position in the centre of town', was originally designed by the Lancaster firm of Paley and Austin, and had been purchased from the railway company in 1874. It, too, had 'plenty of stall accommodation' and was 'fitted with lock-up stall shops'.[45] In Lancaster the corporation substantially extended the market hall in 1879–80 to accommodate 33 shops and 65 stalls.[46] Permanent market stallholders accounted for approximately 10 per cent of retail outlets identified in the surveys of these towns, and councils also rented open air sites to temporary stall holders.

Local government's influence on retail development, however, extended beyond the provision of market halls. 'Improvement' programmes, especially street widening schemes, although often officially justified in terms of benefits to public health or convenience, were widely recognized as catalysts for major retail restructuring.[47] Compulsory purchase and the demolition of property facilitated the redrawing of site boundaries on major thoroughfares, making them more attractive to potential developers and ambitious retailers.[48] As chapter 8 in this collection shows, department store owners did not always support such schemes at the outset, at least in public. However, they were more likely to benefit from the outcome than smaller owners and tenants, in much the same way that larger landowners had gained from parliamentary agricultural enclosure a century earlier.

David Lewis, for example, was able to erect purpose-built stores in Birmingham and Leeds in the wake of redevelopment initiatives.[49] Manchester Corporation's widening of Deansgate in 1871 facilitated the construction of the enormously successful Barton Arcade. Thirty years later the Leeds Estate Company's elaborate shopping arcades were 'made possible by the Council's involvement in land assembly, and the initial proposal for the modernization of that area of the city was made by the city engineer'.[50] On a smaller scale, street-widening schemes undertaken by Lancaster Corporation in the 1890s necessitated the construction of new shops in three central thoroughfares: St Nicholas Street, China Street and Moorgate.[51]

Councils envisaged that private capital would be responsible for the redevelopment and subsequent ownership of the premises erected on these vacant sites, but it was not unknown for the council to retain possession of some central locations. In 1912 Hepworth's, Piper's Bazaar and Studholmes (drapers) were all tenants of Lancaster Corporation.[52] When schemes faltered, however, the council became a reluctant landlord. The collapse of business confidence and the rise of ratepayer resistance to municipal expenditure after 1904 halted an ambitious scheme to widen Blackburn Road in Accrington, and left the local authority in possession of 19 retail properties. Unable to dispose of them, but lacking the finance and incentive to redevelop them, the council was obliged to let the premises on short tenancies and failed to attract major retailers.

Prior to 1904, however, the council had successfully disposed of some properties to local builders and companies. Small-scale 'builders' were often specialists such as joiners, slaters and masons, who acquired the responsibilities and status of 'builder' by subcontracting work or collaborating with other tradesmen.[53] Such men were usually speculative developers who borrowed short term to finance construction with the intention of selling on completion rather than acquiring a portfolio of properties for letting.[54] It is likely that some of the properties that they owned at the time of the Inland Revenue's survey reflected the difficulty they experienced in disposing of recently completed properties in the straitened circumstances of the 1900s. The partnership of a local builder, joiner and mason who purchased some of the sites on Blackburn Road, adopted a variant of builders' usual strategy by initially letting the properties before gradually disposing of their shares in them to other parties. The Blackburn Road Building Company acted more like a property company, retaining ownership and letting the premises on 21-year leases to substantial retailers, many of them incoming multiples. Dugdale Estate Company, which refurbished another block of shops on the other side of the road, initially let them on seven-year leases from 1907, but had sold all of them to sitting tenants before the First World War.[55]

IV

Co-operative societies, municipal authorities, the drink trade, property developers and a variety of entrepreneurs primarily concerned with other sectors of the economy, all increased their share of the retail property market from the late nineteenth century onwards. The majority of premises, however, were owned by individuals.

The professional classes were not particularly prominent among these. More surprisingly, perhaps, solicitors, architects, house agents and accountants, whose livelihoods relied on fees obtained from servicing property development and transactions, also owned relatively few retail properties in these towns other than those in which they lived or worked. Most would appear to have preferred the less risky alternative of managing other landlords' estates and properties.

Far more landlords were drawn from the ranks of retailers, although it should be emphasized that these constituted a small minority of the total shopkeeping population. How and why these retailers came to own other shops is far from clear. Some owned properties contiguous to their own premises. The purchase of these possibly reflected a conscious attempt to control or benefit from adjacent developments, but more likely it was a consequence of the fact that properties were often sold, and therefore acquired, as blocks. A few suburban shops were owned by town-centre wholesale-retailers, and were presumably intended as outlets for their products. Only rarely is there any evidence that retailers were active property developers or substantial rentiers. An Accrington fishmonger, Edmund Riley, developed Post Office Arcade, a covered walkway consisting of 17 premises, but it was not a commercial success and the shops proved difficult to let. J. W. Bridge was more successful: the two substantial shops he incorporated into his new premises were let to the Argenta Meat Company and a local piano dealer. [56] In Lancaster and Barrow, a family of butchers, the Blands, erected a three-storey block of shops on Penny Street in the mid-1890s, occupying one and letting the rest.[57] In Barrow the Happolds, a German family of pork butchers, acquired a portfolio of 15 properties over a period of 40 years from the 1870s. Only one retailer, George Thompson, a pawnbroker, owned properties in more than one town.

Nearly half of all rented properties in Barrow and Lancaster and over a third of those in Accrington were owned by people for whom no occupation was recorded in the local directories. Those living in the more salubrious quarters of towns tended to be listed simply as Mr, Mrs or Miss, but others resident elsewhere in the town were often not recorded at all, implying that they were of more modest social standing. Yet others lived outside the district. The social background and motivations of these people are consequently difficult to reconstruct. The fact that a significant number shared the same surnames as their tenants, however, suggests that some were relatives of shopkeepers. Retail property provided a conduit through which family members could extract income from the business, younger members possibly inheriting businesses on condition that they paid rent to an older generation or to other dependants.

Absentees' addresses also provide significant clues to their backgrounds and ages, and broadly mirror the different social structures of the sample towns. Lancaster's property market was essentially local. Most landlords lived in the town or its immediate hinterland, especially the villages to the north and east. The only significant clusters further afield were to be found in London and Liverpool. Accrington's absentees either lived elsewhere in the textile districts, particularly the neighbouring weaving towns, or in the Fylde coast seaside resorts of Blackpool, St Annes and Lytham, which were closely associated with, and dependent on, East Lancashire for their prosperity. Absentee landlords in Barrow owned approximately twice as many properties as private individuals who were resident in the town. They were much more geographically dispersed. Many lived in South Cumbria, particularly the market town of Ulverston. Others reflected Barrow's maritime connections, and were to be found in settlements along the Irish Sea coast from Holyhead in the south to Kirkcudbright in the north: Liverpool, the Wirral peninsula, Preston, the retirement resorts of Southport and the Fylde, Lancaster and Morecambe, and the West Cumberland coast. Yet others were further afield still: the West Midlands, the south coast resorts of Brighton and Bournemouth, London suburbs, especially Putney, Clapham and Ealing, where females were in a distinct majority, Scotland and overseas. These patterns suggest that absentee landlords were individuals who had personal connections with the towns in which they owned property. Some may have been connected to earlier migrants to the town, who had inherited their relatives' property. The popularity of residential seaside resorts and London also suggests that many were elderly people who had retired away from their place of business. A substantial minority were women, who often owned properties occupied by businesses not usually associated with female proprietors. Some were spinsters, some were married or, more likely, widows of shopkeepers.

Definitive proof of the status and age of such landlords must await the release of the 1911 census enumerators' returns, but it is still possible from sources currently available to substantiate the potential validity of these claims. Mrs Eliza Swann, for example, 63 years old and resident in Liscard on the Wirral in 1912, owned the butcher's shop at 233 Dalton Road, Barrow. The 1881 census reveals that she had been married to William Swann, butcher, who traded from and resided in the premises. Mrs Klyne of Elstree, Hertfordshire, owner of 109 Dalton Road, was the widow of Henry Klyne, previously hatter of that address. Matthew Armer, a retired cordwainer who had returned to his home area of Cartmel (Cumbria), leased his old shop to Tylers', Leicester bootmakers. The empty butcher's shop at 42 Cavendish Street was owned by Walter Evans of Builth Wells, a relative of Edwin Evans, butcher, who had lived there in 1881. F. A. Palmer of Newbarns, near Barrow, the landlord of a joint-stock bank on Dalton Road, was a Swiss immigrant who had run a jeweller's business on the premises. Isaac Grisedale was a retired confectioner who leased his property to a local draper. [58] Few of the private landlords who have been positively identified were under 50 years of age at the time of the survey. Most were over 60; a significant proportion were in their 70s. In Lancaster in particular, the surveyors' field books frequently list 'executors' or 'trustees' of personal estates as the 'owners' of properties. Over the course of his or her life, therefore, a shopkeeper might expect to make the move from tenant to owner-occupier and then to landlord. Ownership was not necessarily coterminous with running a business; nor were landlords a separate rentier class.

V

These case studies confirm much of the accepted picture of urban property as the domain of a commercial petite bourgeoisie, wedded to 'localism, family and property'.[59] As in the housing sector, many retail properties were also held, as Offer found, 'in small parcels by a multitude of small and medium-sized owners'.[60] Most owners lived locally or, if they were absentee landlords, could probably claim a connection with the area through family or previous residence. In inherited family businesses the payment of rent for a property provided an accepted conduit for generational inter-dependency, by providing income for older or female family members.

In other respects, however, the picture is more complicated. Most shopkeepers were not part of this propertied petite bourgeoisie. The majority of shopkeepers in the industrial towns rented their premises on short-term tenancies from a variety of small-scale landlords, although this is not to imply that they did not aspire to the ranks of property owners, however slim their chances of achieving this might be, or that they did not share their values. Nor were the petite bourgeoisie alone in owning property. Although traditional aristocratic landowners and the church were largely unrepresented in the property market, other large-scale organizations were increasingly involved. For railway companies, employers and local authorities, ownership of retail premises was incidental to the pursuit of other goals. In the case of the co-operatives societies and the drink trade, it was central to their business strategy.

This study has sought to open up new avenues for research into retail history. More comparative studies, such as those that have been undertaken on late-Victorian housing, would ascertain the degree to which retail property ownership in other towns reflected their broader social and economic structures.[61] They would also uncover the extent to which local authorities deliberately sought to engineer wholesale changes in the retail infrastructure. The involvement of multiples in the property sector, the potential importance of leasehold as a form of tenure, and the implications of fluctuations in financial markets for investment in retail property, all merit further investigation. Did different trades and forms of business organisation adopt different strategies towards property? What are the implications of property ownership for our understanding of gender relations? Longitudinal studies that focused on the property market rather than on types of shops – multiples, department stores, co-operatives, private traders – would add a new dimension to our understanding of retail change and shed new light on the values, lifestyles and importance of this 'nation of shopkeepers'.

Acknowledgements
This paper represents an amalgamation and extension of working papers presented at the 'New Directions in the History of Retailing and Distribution' and 'Petty Traders and Captains of Commerce. Retailing and Distribution, 1500–2000' conferences, held at the University of Wolverhampton on 10 September 1999 and on 13–14 September 2000. The research has been supported by a small grant from the British Academy. I would also like to acknowledge the assistance of Debbie Hodson in the collection of the data.

Notes

[1] James B. Jefferys, *Retail Trading in Britain, 1850–1950* (Cambridge University Press, Cambridge, 1954); David Alexander, *Retailing in England During the Industrial Revolution* (Athlone Press, London, 1970); Hoh-Cheung Mui and Lorna H. Mui, *Shops and Shopkeeping in Eighteenth Century England* (Routledge, London, 1989); Martin Phillips, 'The evolution of markets and shops in Britain', in J. Benson and G. Shaw (eds), *The Evolution of Retail Systems c. 1800–1914* (Leicester University Press, Leicester, 1992), pp. 64–73; Michael Winstanley, 'Temples of commerce: revolutions in shopping and banking', in P. Waller (ed.), *The English Urban Landscape* (Oxford University Press, Oxford, 2000), pp. 151–74.

[2] Peter Scott, *The Property Masters: A History of the British Commercial Property Sector* (Spon, London, 1996).

[3] Avner Offer, *Property and Politics, 1870–1911: Landownership, Law, Ideology and Urban Development in England* (Cambridge University Press, Cambridge, 1981), p. 119. See also David Englander, *Landlord and Tenant in Urban Britain, 1838–1914* (Clarendon Press, Oxford, 1983), pp. 51–2; R. J. Morris, 'The middle class and British towns and cities in the industrial revolution', and Geoffrey Crossick, 'Urban society and the petty bourgeoisie in nineteenth-century Britain', both in D. Fraser and A. Sutcliffe (eds), *The Pursuit of Urban History* (Arnold, London, 1983), pp. 295, 319. Rack-rent is usually interpreted as the maximum rent possible under existing market conditions.

[4] Geoffrey Crossick and Heinz-Gerhard Haupt, *The Petite Bourgeoisie in Europe 1780–1914* (Routledge, London, 1995), pp. 123–6 and chapters 6 and 9.

[5] Bill Lancaster, *The Department Store: A Social History* (Leicester University Press, Leicester, 1995), chapter 3. The most spectacular and well-documented example was Selfridge's purpose-built store in London's West End. See Reginal Pound, *Selfridge: A Biography* (Heinemann, London, 1960). For the importance of freehold ownership, see Gareth Shaw, 'The evolution and impact of large-scale retailing in Britain', in Benson and Shaw (eds), *The Evolution of Retail Systems*, pp. 139–46, and chapter 8 by Helle Bertramsen in this volume.

[6] Jefferys, *Retail Trading in Britain*.

[7] S. B. Saul, 'Housebuilding in England, 1890–1914', *Economic History Review*, second series 15/1 (1962), pp. 119–37; Brian R. Mitchell and Phyllis Deane, *Abstract of British Historical Statistics* (Cambridge University Press, Cambridge, 1962), p. 239.

[8] Offer, *Property and Politics*, pp. 66, 254.

[9] *Ibid.*, p. 122.

[10] John F. Wilson, 'The finance of municipal capital expenditure in England and Wales, 1870–1914', *Financial History Review* 4/1 (1997), pp. 31–50.

[11] H. V. Emy, 'The land campaign: Lloyd George as a social reformer', in A. J. P. Taylor (ed.), *Lloyd George: Twelve Essays* (Hamilton, London, 1971), pp. 35–9; Roy Douglas, 'God gave the land to the people', in A. Morris (ed.), *Edwardian Radicalism, 1900–1914: Some Aspects of British Radicalism* (Routledge, London, 1974), pp. 148–61.

[12] Bruce K. Murray, *The People's Budget 1909/10: Lloyd George and Liberal Politics* (Clarendon Press, Oxford, 1980).

[13] For a brief guide to the source, see Public Record Office (PRO), 'Domestic records information sheet, 46: valuation office records: the Finance (1909–10) Act'. For a meticulous explanation, see Brian Short, *Land and Society in Edwardian England* (Cambridge University Press, Cambridge, 1997). Short deals exhaustively with problems generic to the survey as a whole, but there are some that are specific to the retail sector. The surveyors' field visits were undertaken over a period of three to five years, and the details in their field books updated beyond that, so cross-referencing with other sources such as trade directories can be problematic. Some shops listed in directories were classified as houses for rateable purposes; some rated 'shops and houses' were

described in the field books as houses and could not be traced in directories. This lack of consistency suggests that much small-scale retailing was both transient in nature and required no specialist accommodation. Direct comparisons between the value of residential and lock-up shops is complicated by the fact that shops within residential buildings were not separately distinguished in the valuation. Aggregate valuations of these dual function buildings, therefore, exaggerate the economic value of the shops themselves. In some cases, buildings in multiple occupancy were valued and returned as one unit; in others, each tenant was returned as occupying a separate hereditament. The field books also reveal that some shops within houses or other buildings, even small suburban premises, were sublet or let separately. Occupiers listed in the valuation books, therefore, could be tenants of the houses, rather than the traders who occupied the shops listed in trade directories. The field books further undermine any straightforward attempt to correlate 'shop and house' listed in rate books with 'residential shop' since they show that rooms above and to the rear of shops previously intended for, and presumably once used as, accommodation were frequently used as storerooms, workshops or even offices. Valuers' recording practices varied within and between districts. In some towns retail premises were variously described as warerooms, warehouses, showrooms, rooms, studios, stalls and stores. The term 'stores' was doubly ambiguous, since it was also used to describe warehouses or outhouses. Tenants of market stalls were not consistently listed. Other premises, like bakehouses and dining rooms, defy easy categorization.

[14] 'Census report for England and Wales 1911', Table 1: Classification of Buildings ... distinguishing for 1911 the various kinds of buildings and the population enumerated therein, and also buildings not used as dwellings.

[15] Guy Christie, *Storeys of Lancaster, 1848–1964* (Collins, London, 1964); Michael Winstanley, 'The town transformed, 1815–1914', in Andrew White (ed.), *A History of Lancaster, 1193–1993* (Ryburn Publishing, Keele, 1993), pp. 145–98; Philip J. Gooderson, *Lord Linoleum: Lord Ashton, Lancaster and the Rise of the British Oilcloth and Linoleum Industry* (Keele University Press, Keele, 1996).

[16] Susan Halstead and Catherine Duckworth (eds), *Aspects of Accrington: Discovering Local History* (Wharncliffe Books, Barnsley, 2000).

[17] Sidney Pollard, 'Town planning in the nineteenth century: the beginnings of modern Barrow-in-Furness', *Transactions of the Lancashire and Cheshire Antiquarian Society* 63 (1952–3), pp. 110–11; John D. Marshall, *Furness and the Industrial Revolution: An Economic History of Furness, 1711–1900, and the Town of Barrow, 1757–1897* (Barrow-in-Furness Library and Museums Committee, Barrow-in-Furness, 1958); Bryn Trescatheric, *How Barrow was Built* (Hougenai Press, Barrow-in-Furness, 1985).

[18] This distinction was obscured in cases where the owner of a business traded under a different name and/or owned a company that paid rent to him/her.

[19] 'What the consumer wants', *Planning*, 18 July 1933, p. 9; S. Martin Gaskell, 'A landscape of small houses: the failure of the workers' flat in Lancashire and Yorkshire in the nineteenth century', in A. Sutcliffe (ed.),

Multi-Storey Living: The British Working-Class Experience (Croom Helm, London, 1974), pp. 88–121.

[20] The figure would be much lower if market stalls, permanent and temporary, were taken into account in these figures.

[21] James Haslam, *Accrington and Church Industrial Co-operative Society Ltd: History of Fifty Years' Progress* (Co-operative Newspaper Society, Manchester, 1910); Co-operative Congress, *Lancaster: A Souvenir of the Forty-Eighth Co-operative Congress, 1916* (Co-operative Wholesale Society, Manchester, 1916).

[22] Peter Gurney, *Co-operative Culture and the Politics of Consumption in England, 1870–1930* (Manchester University Press, Manchester, 1996).

[23] Surveyors' field books, Inland Revenue District Valuation Survey, IR58/531/176; 533/308; 577/4712; 31391/9767-8; 46381/2596-2602; 46385/2962-4; PRO, London; James Price, *Sharpe, Paley and Austin: A Lancaster Architectural Practice, 1836–1942* (Centre for North-West Regional Studies, Lancaster University, Lancaster, 1998).

[24] Accrington Corporation building plans, 1516 (1889), Lancashire Record Office (LRO), Lancaster.

[25] Surveyors' field books, Inland Revenue District Valuation Survey, IR58/31368/7365, PRO.

[26] '"Messrs W. Atkinson and Sons" new motor car and electric bicycle works, North Road, Lancaster', *Cross Fleury's Journal*, June 1904, p. 19.

[27] Lancaster Corporation building plans, 1450 (1896), 2180 (1903), LRO; Surveyors' field books, Inland Revenue District Valuation Survey, IR58/49393/3605-7, PRO.

[28] Surveyors' field books, Inland Revenue District Valuation Survey, IR58/46382/2594-5; 46385/2893, PRO.

[29] Offer, *Property and Politics*, p. 122.

[30] Surveyors' field books, Inland Revenue District Valuation Survey, IR58/2894/2922, PRO; Lancaster Corporation building plans, 2911 (1912), LRO.

[31] Sidney Pollard, 'Barrow-in-Furness and the seventh duke of Devonshire', *Economic History Review*, second series 8/2 (1955), pp. 213–21.

[32] Surveyors' field books, Inland Revenue District Valuation Survey, IR58/46379/2200-5, PRO.

[33] Figures in years refer to length of lease. Blanks indicate no presence in town.

[34] Bryn Trescatheric, *Vickerstown: A Marine Garden City* (Hougenai, Barrow-in-Furness, 1983).

[35] Surveyors' field books, Inland Revenue District Valuation Survey, IR58/31302/367-77, PRO.

[36] Application and letter from R. and R. H. Radcliffe, Victoria St, Liverpool, solicitors, Accrington Corporation building plans, 1873 (1893), LRO.

[37] These were most evident in central Blackpool, where major hotels such as the Royal Hotel Company and Palatine Hotel Company, as well as Blackpool Tower Company, Blackpool Winter Gardens and Spiers and Pond, all incorporated shop premises into the ground floors of their buildings. Preliminary survey of Blackpool 'Domesday Books', LRO.

[38] Surveyors' field books, Inland Revenue District Valuation Survey, IR58/46392/3532-40; 46393/3614-5, PRO; Lancaster Corporation building plans, 1603 (1897), LRO.

[39] David W. Gutzke, *Protecting the Pub: Brewers and Publicans Against Temperance* (Boydell Press, Woodbridge, 1989), pp. 11–29; Terence R. Gourvish and Richard G. Wilson, *The British Brewing Industry, 1830–1980* (Cambridge University Press, Cambridge, 1994). Gutzke argues that the policy of property purchases in the provinces had an earlier origin than the 1890s, but the evidence from the field books suggests otherwise.

[40] Data from Surveyors' field books, Inland Revenue District Valuation Survey, IR58, PRO. William Mitchell owned a total of 34 retail or related premises in Lancaster, in addition to pubs and beerhouses.

[41] Data from Surveyors' field books, Inland Revenue District Valuation Survey, IR58, PRO.

[42] Deborah Hodson, '"The municipal store": adaptation and development in the retail markets of nineteenth century urban Lancashire', *Business History*, 'Special issue on the emergence of modern retailing, 1750–1950' 40/4 (1998), pp. 94–114; James Schmiechen and Kenneth Carls, *The British Market Hall: A Social and Architectural History* (Yale University Press, New Haven, 1999).

[43] Quoted in Schmiechen and Carls, *The British Market Hall*, p. 286.

[44] Surveyors' field books, Inland Revenue District Valuation Survey, IR58/530/2, PRO.

[45] Surveyors' field books, Inland Revenue District Valuation Survey, IR58/31358/5093, PRO.

[46] Jon Catt, *A History of Lancaster's Markets* (Lancaster City Museums, Lancaster, 1988).

[47] Alan Mayne, *The Imagined Slum: Newspaper Representation in Three Cities, 1870–1914* (Leicester University Press, Leicester, 1993), pp. 57–97.

[48] See chapter 8 by Helle Bertramsen in this volume.

[49] Asa Briggs, *Friends of the People: The Centenary History of Lewis's* (Batsford, London, 1956), pp. 80–9; 156–7.

[50] Margaret MacKeith, *The History and Conservation of Shopping Arcades* (Mansell, London, 1986), p. 66.

[51] Winstanley, 'The town transformed, 1815–1914', p. 210.

[52] Surveyors' field books, Inland Revenue District Valuation Survey, IR58/46392/3608-9; 46401/4497, PRO.

[53] Christopher G. Powell, *An Economic History of the British Building Industry, 1815–1979* (Methuen, London, 1982), pp. 71–4; J. W. R. Whitehand, 'The makers of British towns; architects, builders and property owners, c. 1850–1939', *Journal of Historical Geography* 18/4 (1992), pp. 417–38.

[54] For the strategies adopted by one small builder, see Andrew White and Michael Winstanley, *Victorian Terraced Houses in Lancaster* (Centre for North-West Regional Studies, Lancaster University, Lancaster, 1996), pp. 31–4.

[55] Surveyors' field books, Inland Revenue District Valuation Survey, IR58/558/2618-2624; 578/4838-4844, PRO.

[56] *Ibid.*, IR58/555/2549-63; 2574-9.

[57] *Ibid.*, IR58/46399/4246-50.

[58] These examples have been compiled by cross-referencing names of owners in the Inland Revenue survey with 1881 census enumerators' schedules, which have been converted to electronic form by the Church of the Latter Day Saints.

[59] Crossick and Haupt, *The Petite Bourgeoisie*, p. 222.

[60] Offer, *Property and Politics*, p. 119.

[61] Caroline Bedale, 'Property relations and housing policy: Oldham in the late nineteenth and early twentieth centuries', in J. Melling (ed.), *Housing, Social Policy and the State* (Croom Helm, London, 1980), especially pp. 50–1; Martin J. Daunton, *House and Home in the Victorian City: Working-Class Housing 1850–1914* (Arnold, London, 1983), pp. 108ff.

CHAPTER 8
REMOULDING COMMERCIAL SPACE: MUNICIPAL IMPROVEMENTS AND THE DEPARTMENT STORE IN LATE-VICTORIAN MANCHESTER
Helle B. Bertramsen

Within the larger history of retailing, many cultural and social historians have been interested in the department store not only as a physical space, but also as a social and cultural space.[1] Only a few historians and geographers, however, have focused on locational space as a way of explaining how the department store developed and how it was linked to the wider process of 'urban improvement'.[2] Social historians seeking to summarize the changes in the geography of nineteenth-century urban retailing have commonly noted: 'In the larger towns, retailing and commercial interests replaced residential buildings in the final third of the century with office blocks and department stores.'[3] However, this general statement somewhat obscures the processes involved in the development of department stores and of their neighbourhoods. In particular, it does not explain how department store owners obtained the financial resources necessary for expansion and rebuilding.

This chapter will illustrate how the expansion of one Manchester department store, Kendal, Milne and Faulkner (hereafter Kendal Milne), was the result of a 'public' conflict. During the 1870s and 1880s, the Manchester Corporation decided to widen one of the city's medieval thoroughfares. Yet, contrary to what one might expect, some retailers, including the owners of Kendal Milne, opposed the proposed improvements. As a result, the Corporation faced a long legal struggle, which ended in the House of Lords. The ultimate result of the case was not only that the Corporation received permission to continue its redevelopment plans, but also that Kendal Milne was transformed in ways neither party to the suit had anticipated. This chapter will show how the owners of Manchester's first department store rebuilt and enlarged their premises as the result of a legal controversy.

Like Victorian London and Paris, Manchester was eager to emerge as a physical symbol of capitalist progress. Such aspirations involved the introduction of extensive city improvement schemes, which, as Alan Mayne observes, 'meant remodelling and renewal of inherited city forms, and an obliteration of the old and obsolete'.[4] The City Corporation had much the same goal. At the end of the nineteenth century, it declared: 'It was not until the first quarter of the nineteenth century that any serious attempt was made to alter the plan of the town.' At that time Manchester still retained its medieval outline: 'The central parts of the town were narrow, inconvenient, and totally inadequate to the strain of the great traffic that then began to flow through the streets.'[5] Just as Baron Hausmann and Napoleon III changed the topography of Paris by opening up the city's centre and widening its narrow and crooked streets, the Manchester City Corporation also changed the shape of its city.[6] Aside from the sheer practical advantage of facilitating traffic, any city that embraced a new, more open street plan and adopted new technologies (such as elaborate water systems), was seen as representing the 'modern'. As Nigel Thrift observes, the modern city was understood as a city of spatial transformations.[7]

A number of existing studies of urban improvement schemes have linked these developments to the evolution of department stores. For instance, in her work on Paris, Vanessa Schwartz shows how closely the rebuilding of the city was linked to the emergence of the new Parisian department stores. 'The department store interiors mimicked not only the architectural style of the rebuilt Paris, but also the "boulevards of the *grand magasin* interior were so many extensions of the *grands boulevards* that stretched from the Madeleine to the Bastille".'[8] Likewise, Gareth Shaw employs a useful approach to changes in the scale of retailing in Birmingham by focusing on linkages with urban improvement schemes. 'The growth of large stores in Birmingham', he explains, 'was also greatly influenced by the newly built Corporation Street which was the centre of Joseph Chamberlain's improvement scheme.'[9]

Yet well before the City Corporation in Birmingham initiated its well-known improvement schemes in 1875, the Corporation in Manchester had received permission to exercise powers of compulsory purchase in order to start street developments. As Asa Briggs noted in *Victorian Cities*, Birmingham actually generally lagged behind other cities in not making civic improvements until the 1870s.[10] By this time, Manchester's grand street scheme was well underway. The change was part of a deliberate policy of widening streets, beginning in Market Street and King Street with the Street Improvement Act of 1821, and continuing for much of the century.[11] As it rapidly grew in the course of the nineteenth century, Manchester sought to recreate its centre as a visible and concrete symbol of its metropolitan status, and to present itself as a major player in the wider process leading to the establishment of a capitalist modernity.[12] By focusing on the city's first department store, Kendal Milne, this chapter will show that its emergence was not the result of an initiative from within the store, but from without. Manchester's first department store was part of the broader transformation of the urban landscape, a transformation that had a political dimension – as well as winners and losers.

The necessity of widening one of Manchester's oldest thoroughfares, Deansgate, had long engaged the attention of the City Corporation. Map 1, representing the Deansgate area in the early part of the nineteenth century, clearly shows the need for a major street connecting the north and south of Manchester. Deansgate was a likely candidate for becoming such a thoroughfare, both because it was nearly straight, and because it already ran unimpeded from north to south for a longer distance than any other street. Deansgate had previously linked 'Roman Mamucium to medieval Manchester',[13] but, according to *The Manchester City News*, the growth of the populous suburbs beyond the city had transformed this main ancient artery into what the paper called 'an inconveniently crowded and perilous channel'.[14]

Deansgate had already been broadened in 1836, but by mid-century the Corporation had decided to widen it even further, from 8 to 20 yards, and to carry out the street improvements section by section. In 1853, an act of parliament had been obtained, according to which 'a line had been laid down to which all buildings were required to conform'. In 1873, however, *The Manchester City News* stated that 'the act obtained for that purpose was so slow in its operation that another century would probably not have seen the completion of work that was dependent upon partially voluntary and exasperatingly tedious efforts.'[15] The City Corporation had tried to carry out the improvement by acquiring land sold voluntarily, but it had only managed to buy five lots in the course of a decade.[16] In 1868, after 'a long and anxious discussion', the City Council sanctioned compulsory purchase.[17] The Manchester Corporation Waterworks and Improvement Act, which was passed by parliament in 1869, had many purposes. It prohibited the keeping of swine, regulated the abattoirs in the area and improved sanitation.[18] However, its major purpose was to use profits from the gasworks to fund the widening of Deansgate from Victoria Bridge to John Dalton Street.[19] Funds were made available to purchase property and to pay the owners compensation,[20] although the Corporation was only required to give eight weeks' notice before evicting the 'labouring classes' who rented property in the area.[21]

The widening of Deansgate was initiated in the early 1870s, shortly after the act of parliament was obtained in 1869. One contemporary observer described the street's transformation in these glowing terms: 'Deansgate, the most ancient of all our public thoroughfares ... was only a narrow and inconveniently-crowded thoroughfare. By the spirit of modern enterprise it has become transformed into one of the most spacious as well as one of the handsomest Streets in the Kingdom.'[22] The transformation was not as dramatic or as sweeping as it had been in Paris, where whole areas had been ripped out and replaced by new residential and shopping districts. Nor were Manchester improvements driven by private enterprise, as had been the case in the Bayswater area of London, which had developed from a residential neighbourhood to gradually becoming a prosperous commercial area with cafés, restaurants, hotels and theatres.[23] In all these cases, however, as Alan Mayne observes, 'the rampant commercialism of these cities' was within nineteenth-century discourse translated in terms of 'metropolitan vigour'.[24]

Before the street improvements were undertaken Deansgate had been a mixed residential, manufacturing, and commercial area. In 1822 it was reported that businesses in Deansgate included, among others, a watchmaker, tallow chandlers, soap boilers, philosophical instrument makers, a surgeon and a hat manufacturer.[25] Here goods were both manufactured and sold, and nearby were slaughterhouses and a large produce market. Customers could purchase everyday necessities from the provision shops as well as luxury goods from specialist retailers.[26] It was within this marketplace that, in the early years of the nineteenth century, John Watts decided to locate his shopping 'Bazaar', an establishment that Alison Adburgham argued 'had a great deal of similarity with the modern department store, and which did in fact develop into the famous store of Kendal Milne'.[27] However, if Deansgate was characterised by mixed land use when Kendal Milne took over the business from John Watts' sons in 1836, this was no longer so by the 1870s.[28]

Even before mid-century, the Corporation had been intent on improving the traffic flow. Perhaps the most dramatic of the early changes was the establishment of an entirely new thoroughfare, John Dalton Street, constructed parallel to King Street (Figure 1). The general outcome of the early alterations was an opening up of space. The streets and side streets became more linear, this being achieved by demolishing some buildings and keeping their replacements in line with the width of the new street. The streets also became more symmetrical once the junction of Deansgate and St Anne's Street had been rounded off, and the projections of some buildings into the street had been removed.

As these improvements were made, more fashionable shops opened on Deansgate, and gradually the Corporation determined that the street should become one of Manchester's two main shopping streets. Market Street was already an important shopping area, and Deansgate was designated for a similar role. Figure 1 shows the location of Kendal, Milne and Faulkner in the central area around St Anne's Street, a location that accidentally benefited from changes over which the store proprietors had no control. When the Corporation decided to push King Street through to Deansgate in the 1840s, for example, the result was that even more traffic passed by the store. Next to the store, however, due to an old 'right of passage' law, the Corporation had to keep open Hatter's Lane, which connected Deansgate to Police Street, and as a result leaving a small parcel of land (and part of Kendal Milne) isolated from the rest of the block. Thus some of the old medieval streets survived even the improvements of the 1870s. It would take the rest of the century for Kendal Milne to close this passageway and add the land to their holdings, achieving a 'modern' use of space, albeit as a slow, piecemeal process.[29]

In the midst of these topographical alterations, the store of Kendal, Milne and Faulkner was slow to develop. For a decade after the three owners took over from John Watts, no major alterations occurred, perhaps in part due to the economic depression of the late 1830s.[30] However, between 1845 and 1847 the store absorbed two adjacent shops, Sarah Bowker's eating house and Elizabeth Hodson's hosiery business. On a trade card of 1847 Kendal, Milne and Faulkner were now listed as occupying numbers 93–97, and had added upholstery, furniture and carpets to their range of drapery merchandise. Soon complete mourning outfits were on offer as well. As the variety of merchandise for sale increased, it obviously seemed necessary to expand the store. According to Bradshaw's guidebook of 1856, Kendal, Milne and Faulkner had by then built a considerable extension to the original 'Bazaar' structure. The guidebook explained that this was one of the most extensive establishments in Manchester: 'The recent addition at the angle of St. Ann's Street and Police Street [a side street to King Street] has been erected from an elegant design in the Italian style ... This part is appropriated to cabinet furniture and general upholstery ... The entire block of buildings comprises an area of nearly two thousand square yards.'[31] While the owners had clearly already made an elegant addition to the store, further expansion was gradual. It took some years before Kendal, Milne and Faulkner gained control of the entire city block.

During the early 1870s, when many changes occurred in the physical appearance of the street, the store also underwent a

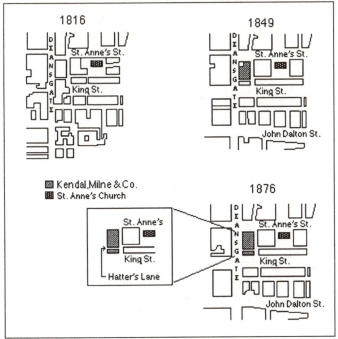

Figure 1 Deansgate in 1816, 1849 and 1876.
Source: *Pigot and Deans' Manchester Directory*, 1817; Ordnance Survey map, 1849; *Manchester City* (J. E. Cornish, Manchester, 1876).

fundamental transformation. Fittingly, its rebuilding in 1872 was marked by a change of name, from Kendal, Milne and Faulkner to Kendal, Milne and Co.[32] The new, larger building symbolized the rejection of tradition in favour of the 'modernity' of a new city centre.[33] A map of the improvements reprinted as a lithograph in *The Manchester City News* of 1873 showed what properties had already passed into the hands of the City Corporation, and marked where the new edge of the street would be (Figure 2). Only a few buildings on the opposite side of Deansgate to Kendal Milne were to be demolished. However, on the store's side, 'the whole of the property will be swept away, that lying between John Dalton-Street and St. Mary's-Gate ... [and] all the property extending from St. Mary's-Gate to the Victoria Bridge end of Deansgate ... will have to come down.'[34] In effect, the Kendal Milne building was to disappear.

Deansgate need not have been widened in the way eventually chosen by Manchester's Corporation. In 1869 a London architect had, for example, suggested in *The Builder* that rather than tear down entire shops, the ground floors alone could be set back 10 ft on each side of the street. Colonnades would hold up the upper floors. If this scheme

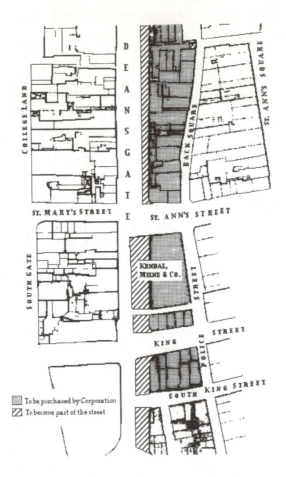

Figure 2 Deansgate in 1873.
Source: Enhanced version of street improvement map, supplement to *The Manchester City News*, 1 March 1873.
Courtesy of Manchester City Library, Local Studies Unit.

had been adopted in Manchester, only a small portion of any building would have had to be purchased; yet 20 ft would have been added to the roadway. However, this proposal was not widely adopted, and the custom of outright purchase remained common.[35] When the City Corporation had first embarked on its improvement scheme, it had done so without the aid of compulsory purchasing powers. But as we have seen, many owners were unwilling to sell, and this method of street improvement was generally acknowledged as too slow. Therefore, compulsory purchase was mandated by the Manchester

Corporation Waterworks and Improvement Act of 1869.[36] The process was not, however, a straightforward one, and the Corporation's attempt to acquire compulsory purchasing powers met with stiff local opposition, eventually leading to an appeal in the House of Lords.

The Corporation argued that 'In their experience, if they only set the line of the street back and removed part of the properties, it often took long before any suitable frontages to the street would be put up.' Therefore, the City Corporation wished to acquire not only enough property to establish the new line of the street, but also all the sites lying immediately behind. They claimed that they needed 'a much freer hand to determine the improvements they wanted'.[37] Full ownership would give them more control over the frontages, and a more uniform, coherent street. During the House of Lords hearing, the Town Clerk from Liverpool testified that his city had for years followed the same procedures that Manchester wished to adopt. Indeed, Liverpool

> was in the habit of acquiring more land than was absolutely required for the purpose of widening the streets. When a corporation widened a street they ought to have the opportunity of securing good property in the improved street, for the purpose of repaying the outlay through an increased rate.[38]

Manchester's plans for extensive purchase of private property for resale after streets were widened was apparently becoming common practice in the 1860s. The City Corporation itself had learnt by trial and error that compulsory purchase was preferable to other improvement methods.[39] The land wanted for the improvements was stated to be 5000 square yards, yet the actual land 'sought for and obtained, with the view to the purchase ... was 27,000 yards'.[40] The reason for acquiring extra land was to 'lessen the cost of the general improvement'.[41] The darkly shaded blocks on Figure 2 indicate the properties that would pass into the hands of the City Corporation after 1869. Most of these sites were located on Kendal Milne's side of Deansgate. As the Town Clerk, Joseph Heron, explained, the Corporation could not afford the double expenditure of improving both sides of the street. Although property owners may have felt victimized by being on the 'wrong' side of the road, the City Corporation was convinced that once the widening of the street had taken place, 'The parties [would] find that it is worth their while to rebuild, and to put up satisfactory "constructions" and whereupon they do rebuild they must under the powers of the our Act submit the plan to us.'[42]

Despite the Corporation's optimistic tone, however, it was by no means a foregone conclusion that they would be able to have their way on the issue of compulsory purchase. Precedents had not all been in their favour. The Corporation had, for example, once proposed to remove a number of deteriorating old buildings and instead establish a large wholesale market in Queens Street. However, as the Town Clerk explained, 'the owners of the property obtained a clause giving them a right of pre–emption over all the land.' In other words, the owners had managed to have a clause written into the bill that apparently had made it difficult – indeed, impossible – to carry out the proposed improvement. As a result, the Corporation had abandoned all plans of improving that particular district.[43] Therefore, the Deansgate improvement scheme should be understood not as an isolated case, but rather as part of a larger, ongoing struggle between commercial interests and property owners on the one hand, and the City Corporation on the other. Evidently, with respect to the Deansgate improvements, the omens for the Corporation were not positive. As *The City News* revealed, 'Few private measures have ever had combined against them such a formidable array of legal ability.'[44]

Those who went to law to argue their case did not oppose the Deansgate street improvements as such.[45] They contended 'that the Corporation should only be allowed to take so much land as would be required for the new line of street'. One of the property owners objected to the City Corporation acting as what he called 'land jobbers'.[46] The principal plaintiffs among the Deansgate landowners included Sir Edmund Buckley, the MP for Newcastle-on-Lyme; John Hope Barton, who owned the Barton's Buildings; William Cunliffe Brooks, an MP; Mr Hoare, head of a large banking firm in Fleet Street, London, and Thomas Kendal. James Milne did not own land, and so was not a party to the suit. Mr S. Pope, Queen's Counsel, representing Thomas Kendal, claimed that his client's firm did not wish to stop public improvements. They felt, however, that they had a fair right to complain when they found the Corporation sweeping away the whole of their business, after it had taken half a century to build it up. The Corporation, he continued, ought not to be allowed to take all of the land and tear down the store completely.[47]

Kendal Milne was by no means the largest property affected by the improvement scheme: John Hope Barton's 'Buildings', for example, covered 1800 square yards, 355 more than Kendal Milne. According to *The Manchester Guardian*, however, Kendal and Milne's 'Bazaar was a special case'.[48] Their situation was unusual because William Cunliffe Brooks, who had no part in the business, owned 635 square yards of the land under the building, running from Deansgate to Police Street.[49] Thomas Kendal owned the remainder, 810 square yards. The two owners had the freehold of a property that constituted an area of 1445 square yards, but the entire area was occupied as one 'Bazaar' owned by Thomas Kendal.[50]

During the House of Lords hearing, Joseph Heron sought to reassure the Corporation's opponents, including Thomas Kendal. He acknowledged that the 'Bazaar' had been in Deansgate for decades, and had become a very large as well as a profitable concern, organized as one large 'haberdashery warehouse'. 'In fact, you may buy almost everything there', Heron added.[51] He concluded that together with the peculiar nature of the ownership of the 'Bazaar', this provided Kendal Milne with 'distinct grounds for compensation ... I have no doubt that Messrs. Kendal if such a case is to be decided [in favour of the City Corporation] will get a very large compensation for their business quite irrespective of the price' obtained for the property.[52] No primary source reveals the amount of the 'large compensation', but it was clearly more than sufficient to construct the new, larger store.[53] As for the other property owners and petitioners, Heron sought to disarm the opposition by emphasizing that the City Corporation would pay a very 'high percentage for its compulsory sale'.[54] In other words, the other owners would – apart from receiving money for their property – also receive a high price for the land on which their property was located. Some were paid in kind. For instance, John Hope Barton, who owned much property in and around Manchester, received in exchange land on the other side of Deansgate.[55]

When in 1869 the House of Lords ruled in the Corporation's favour, the City could finally execute its ambitious improvement scheme. The Corporation's success had largely been due to the impressive performance of the Town Clerk, a man described by Asa Briggs as one of Britain's 'outstanding local officials' and 'a dominating personality'.[56] As the principal spokesman for the City, 'Mr Heron's defence and conduct of the bill was admitted to be one of the greatest of his parliamentary triumphs.' It was perhaps no coincidence that in the same year he was granted a knighthood. *The Manchester City News* enthusiastically claimed that the Deansgate undertaking would prove to be 'one of the most striking and successful enterprises ever entered upon by the City Council'.[57]

The Corporation anticipated that widening the street (to 20 yards) would at the same time increase the value of land in Deansgate. Indeed, property owners had already been warned during a meeting of the City Council in 1869 of the correlation between a narrow street and the loss of value of the property: 'the owners in Deansgate ought to remember that the value of property in Deansgate was gradually deteriorating, because of the inconvenient narrowness of the thoroughfare.'[58] This, however, did not mean that all shops prospered equally after the improvement scheme had been implemented. The draper Andrew Gibb, for example, who was located at nos 59, 61, 65, and 68 on the same side of Deansgate as Kendal Milne, and who seemed to sell the same range of merchandise, disappeared in 1870. When Andrew Gibb died, his executors advertised an 'immense clearance sale'. They announced that 'they have sold their premises to the Corporation, and as the building will shortly be required for pulling down, they propose winding up the business.'[59] Thus one of Kendal Milne's larger competitors disappeared. A different case was that of Samuel Smith and Sons, another drapery store located close to Kendal Milne. Based around the same location, no. 54, since 1821, they sold the same goods as Kendal Milne, perhaps with the exception of furniture.[60] They too by the 1870s had expanded, and at the time of the street improvement occupied nos 46–54. As they were located on the opposite side of the street to Kendal Milne, Samuel Smith and Sons were not forced to redevelop. This ought to have given them at the least a temporary advantage, but, ironically, it appears that given the lack of impetus to rebuild, they never grew larger. It is significant that when another large Deansgate drapery business, namely Shellard and Hodgson's, ceased trading, it was Kendal Milne who took over their warehouse site, rather than Smith and Sons. By 1879, Kendal Milne had established there a cabinet-making workshop.[61] Thus, although street improvements created opportunities for some firms, others stagnated or vanished.

Of the other wealthy property owners, John Hope Barton seems to have made the most of the opportunities presented by the street improvements. Barton had resisted the alterations on the same grounds as all the other landowners, yet he soon completed a deal with the Corporation and agreed to build a 'satisfactory' structure. Built of iron and concrete at a cost of £45,000, Barton's Arcade was favourably reviewed in *The Builder*, which accorded it a full-page illustration.[62] *The Free Lance* called it 'a natural and most acceptable retreat, and a fashionable – the fashionable – business promenade'.[63] The arcade, containing extensive shopping and office space, was a new feature of the Victorian high street. It was 'an excellent means of utilizing small strips of land'.[64] It seems, therefore, that with the reconstruction of Deansgate, an entirely new shopping space had also emerged, a space that Susan Buck-Morss has called the 'hallmark of a "modern" metropolis' and of the 'first international style of "modern" architecture'.[65]

Not only had Kendal Milne made common cause with John Hope Barton in taking their case to the House of Lords, but once defeated, they also used their compensation to create a new architectural space. However, while the new store was being built, the owners had to convince their customers not to stay away, although both the site and the store would be in disarray.[66] They therefore inserted a large advertisement in the local paper, emphasizing that they 'acknowledged the importance of the improvement', and announcing with regret that 'the partial demolition and reconstruction necessitate the unreserved sale at a great sacrifice of their valuable stock'. The decision was based on the 'inevitable loss and damage which had occurred due to dust and other causes'.[67] Besides, the time allowed by the City Corporation was brief, and the circumstances demanded a 'speedy clearance'. The sale was designed to attract a large crowd, and the owners claimed in their advertisement that it was 'the most important which has ever occurred in the North of England'.[68]

As the store was being rebuilt, the owners orchestrated a series of sales, rearrangements of departments, and refurbishments. They never closed entirely. In January 1873, for example, they announced that while the main portion of the premises was being reconstructed, their furniture had been 'appropriated by several departments of the general drapery'. Besides, they also reduced prices considerably in order to dispose of the 'principal part of the stock'.[69] The following month they had to rearrange all their drapery goods to where the furniture had previously been, removing the latter to other showrooms elsewhere in the neighbourhood.[70] These dislocations, which no doubt involved considerable extra work for the employees, occurred over a period of less than two months, during which time the store must have been chaotic and dusty. At the same time, however, the well-publicized rearrangements of goods and large sales would have served to keep Kendal Milne in the public eye.

A new construction emerged gradually in the course of just over a year.[71] The new premises were larger than the original, no longer looking like a shop to which other shops had been added. *The Manchester Guardian* noted that the new structure was four storeys high, with 128 ft of frontage on Deansgate. 'The general style of architecture' it characterized as 'a mixture of Roman and Italian, and the elevation entirely of polished stone, introducing columns of Doric order between the windows on the first floor.'[72] The exterior resembled that of many other Victorian commercial 'palazzos': insurance buildings, banks, warehouses and larger stores.[73] The 1846 extension to the 'Bazaar' had also been built in the 'Italian style', and looked somewhat similar to the London Royal Exchange, completed two years before.[74] The new store, however, designed by local architects Southern and Son of Salford, was more eclectic, blending Italian and classical elements, as was common with contemporary architects.[75] Compared to the enormous and imposing Watt's Warehouse, built in 1858 by the founder of the 'Bazaar', the 1873 building had fewer ornaments and larger windows on all floors.[76]

Blending into the red brick commercial cityscape, the new premises moved tentatively toward a more functional style. As one of the most expensive stores in Manchester, it was built to emphasize the goods in the windows, not to call attention to its architectural details.

As a whole, the new construction was what Henry-Russell Hitchcock has called a 'monumental expression of commercial prestige',[77] albeit, to some extent at least, an 'accidental' one. The owners of Kendal Milne found themselves, against their own wishes, with a purpose-built emporium long before Selfridge's flagship London store was opened in 1909. Previously, the store had been split into what Heron called a 'second-class department' and a 'first-class department', the former facing Deansgate, and the latter Police Street.[78] Heron called the Police Street side the 'ladies' side of the shop'. 'Deansgate is so narrow and confined', he explained, that although 'Police Street as everybody knows is a back street in the Town', it was nonetheless apparently better suited for some vehicles: 'ladies carriages are all drawn up in that street rather than Deansgate which is the front.'[79] Together, the widening of Deansgate and the rebuilding of the store meant the re-establishment of Kendal Milne as an integrated and harmonious whole.

The new store expanded the range of services available to customers, including a new 'trying-on-department'.[80] But perhaps the most important change was a new sense of an abundance of goods. As a journalist remarked, the store offered 'almost all that the divine sex require, and a good many things that they don't'.[81] The new premises were planned as conducive to the convenience and comfort of employees, as well as customers. There was 'an absence of closeness', with ventilation improved by the expansion of space generally. The 'working rooms' for the 'young ladies' employed in 'sedentary occupation[s]' were large enough to prevent the disorders that 'close and ill-ventilated rooms and long hours' often contributed to. The lighting in the store was improved by the 'quadrangular aperture in the roofs of each storey of the building'. The temperature was also more even on all the floors.[82]

The new store was not as large as some of the London houses, but was one of the most complete in its 'construction and its appointments'. *The Free Lance* magazine compared the new Kendal Milne to the 'well-known' Meeking and Co. in Holborn, London.[83] Charles Meeking had commenced business in 1826, and from mid-century onwards had expanded into a considerable store.[84] Likewise, during the House of Lords' hearing, Kendal Milne had been compared with Shoolbred's,[85] a middle- to upper-class emporium selling much the same range of merchandise.[86] Thus contemporaries saw Kendal Milne as comparable in size, quality, and selection to the best London 'houses', as well as judging it 'one of the most complete' in Britain. The store may have been perceived by some as something 'new' and so 'unfamiliar' that it seemed 'bewildering', yet it was clearly viewed as pleasing in its 'artistic effects'[87] – a clear indication of contemporary appreciation of what has been called a new 'commercial aesthetic'.[88]

***

Nineteenth-century Manchester aspired to the status of a 'progressive' city, and the widening of Deansgate was only one of many municipal improvements introduced to this end. Given its contradictory reputation as both the polluted 'shock city' of the 1840s and as the harbinger of a new technological and industrial age, by reshaping its civic spaces the Corporation sought to emphasize the latter identity.[89] According to *The British Architect*, the Manchester of 1873 was 'second to no city in the United Kingdom as regards the cultivation of the Æsthetic and Constructive Arts'. *The British Architect* praised municipal monuments such as the new Police and Assize Courts, the Free Trade Hall and the new Town Hall, then in the process of construction.[90] The improvement of Deansgate was part of this larger aspiration: more than merely inner-city renewal, it was part of Manchester's embrace of the 'new'.

Although the Deansgate of the early 1890s was described as 'the Regent Street of Manchester',[91] the analogy with London, while meant as praise, obscured the fact that Manchester was in the process of creating a distinctive public space. Deansgate had not only been widened (the Corporation's original intention), but the use of space had also changed. Barton's Arcade as well as Kendal Milne exemplify this change. Both were taller than the previous structures, and drew a larger number of people into the area. A reporter from *The Manchester Guardian* stressed that such structures provided the blueprint for what 'the Deansgate of the future' would look like.[92] As the new buildings appeared, the street achieved a very different look, while the smaller, lower structures of the early Victorian period disappeared. The transformation of Deansgate should, however, primarily be understood as a transformation of its land use. The old, narrow Deansgate had been only one of many streets, providing both living and working space for its residents, and including a mix of retailing and manufacturing activities. By the end of the nineteenth century, it had gradually become a street primarily of offices and shops.[93] Indeed, by the 1890s it had become *the* shopping street of Manchester, its only near rival being Market Street.

The owners of Kendal Milne had been part of these urban transformations, and their store's history was, in miniature, almost 'a social history of their neighbourhood'.[94] If, as Alan Mayne has suggested, the 'modern' and 'modernity' are expressed by the transformation of 'inherited city forms' and 'the obliteration of the old and obsolete', then, indeed, the new Deansgate was part of the process of creating the 'modern': monumental structures such as Barton's Arcade and the new Kendal Milne had by the 1890s become 'hallmarks' of a modern metropolis.[95]

The nineteenth-century development of cities such as Paris and London had followed different patterns. The new shopping areas in Paris emerged largely as a by-product of the forced reconstruction of the capital, dictated by the national government. 'The new *grands magasins* did not ... open on the older boulevards but rather sprang up on many of Haussmann's new streets.'[96] In contrast, the new shopping area of Bayswater had sprung into existence not due to any government planning, but because of what Roy Porter calls the 'mysteries of the market; population growth, change in transport technology, and profitable building speculation'.[97]

Manchester and its Deansgate improvement scheme fell somewhere between French government planning and London's private enterprise. On the one hand, the Corporation had to gain the assent of central government. On the other, its project also required discussions and compromises with local businesses and landowners. The Corporation forcibly purchased land, transformed the street and negotiated with buyers who could afford to build 'satisfactory' street frontages. The new structures built on Deansgate were not for residential or manufacturing use, but were intended to house impressive shops and services. The people who during the House of Lords hearing had been described as belonging to the 'poorer classes', had been evicted from the street. Hence, while 're-making' Deansgate, the City Corporation took decisions not only concerning the dimensions of the street, but also the architecture, the inhabitants and the social character of the neighbourhood. 'Modernity' was forced upon the town by the local government, with the reluctant assistance of business interests.

Kendal Milne was involved in this larger process. The store underwent a physical and spatial change that the owners had not planned, or initially welcomed. The City Corporation won the right to widen the street, but the store, after resisting change, made good use of its large compensation and improved its location. By contrast to the gradual emergence of Kendal Milne, and its initial resistance to change, in Birmingham it was the major street improvements of the mid-1870s that induced the Liverpool-based Lewis's to open a store in the city, taking a prime location.[98]

In Birmingham, the development of a new shopping space may have been the outcome of a harmonious co-operation between local authorities and retailers, but as the Manchester case shows, at least one British form of 'modernity' emerged out of conflict, as businesses fought city planners over the control of their property. In contrast to the uniform vistas of Paris commanded into existence by Napoleon III, the creation of a new Deansgate and a new Manchester was a piecemeal affair and an ongoing project.[99] It was not a planned vista, but a dynamic process, in which the Manchester City Corporation acted, if not as the architect of the new commercial district, at least as the catalyst that made the owners rethink their store space.

Acknowledgements

I wish to thank Dr Michael J. Winstanley for his encouragement and advice in completing this chapter. For their comments on earlier drafts, I also want to thank Debbie Hodson, Harry Hendrick and the editors of this volume.

Notes

[1] Michael J. Winstanley, *The Shopkeeper's World 1830–1914* (Manchester University Press, Manchester, 1983), especially chapter 3; Judith R. Walkowitz, *City of Dreadful Delight: Narratives of Sexual Danger in Late-Victorian London* (University of Chicago Press, Chicago, 1992), pp. 46–50; and Erika D. Rappaport, *Shopping for Pleasure: Women in the Making of London's West End* (Princeton University Press, New Jersey, 2000).

[2] See, for instance, Asa Briggs, *Friends of the People: The Centenary History of Lewis's* (Batsford, London, 1956); Gareth Shaw, 'The evolution and impact of large-scale retailing in Britain', in J. Benson and G. Shaw (eds), *The Evolution of Retail Systems c. 1800–1914* (Leicester University Press, Leicester, 1992), pp. 135–65; Jon Stobart, 'Patterns of urban retailing: suburbanisation, centralisation, and hierarchies in the Potteries Conurbation, 1872–1932', *Journal of Regional and Local Studies* 18/1 (1998), pp. 11–26.

[3] Robert J. Morris and Richard Rodger, 'An introduction to British urban history 1820–1914', in R. J. Morris and R. Roger (eds), *The Victorian City: A Reader in British Urban History, 1820–1914* (Longman, London, 1993), p. 21.

[4] Alan Mayne, *The Imagined Slum: Newspaper Representation in Three Cities 1870–1914* (Leicester University Press, Leicester, 1993), p. 21.

[5] *Corporation of Manchester: A Historical Record* (Henry Blacklock, Manchester, 1894), p. 180.

[6] Vanessa R. Schwartz, *Spectacular Realities: Early Mass Culture in Fin-De-Siècle Paris* (University of California Press, Berkeley, 1998), p. 17.

[7] Nigel Thrift, *Spatial Formations* (Sage Publications, London, 1996), pp. 257–8. See also pp. 264–5.

[8] Schwartz, *Spectacular Realities*, p. 21.

[9] Shaw, 'The evolution and impact of large-scale retailing in Britain', p. 145.

[10] Asa Briggs, *Victorian Cities* (Penguin Books, London, 1990, first published 1963), p. 185.

[11] Briggs, *Victorian Cities*, p. 1. See also The Manchester Corporation Waterworks and Improvement Act, 1 & 2 Geo4, c 136 (1821).

[12] Mayne, *The Imagined Slum*, p. 17.

[13] Alan Kidd, *Manchester* (Keele University Press, Keele, 1996, first published 1993), p. 11.

[14] *The Manchester City News*, 1 March 1873.

[15] *Ibid.*

[16] *Ibid.*

[17] *Ibid.*

[18] The Manchester Corporation Waterworks and Improvement Act, 32 & 33 Vict, c 117 (1869), sections 28, 30, 31, 32 and 36, pp. 9–11.

[19] *Ibid.*, p. 1.

[20] The City Corporation did not treat all landowners equally. Section 25 of the Act excluded the property of John Hope Barton from expropriation beyond the amount needed to widen Deansgate. Barton was one of the wealthiest property owners in the city. In contrast, Kendal, Milne and Co.'s property was not specifically referred to in the Act. The Manchester Corporation Waterworks and Improvement Act, pp. 7–8.

[21] *Ibid.*, section 26, pp. 8–9.

[22] Alfred Brothers, *Old Manchester* (J. E. Cornish, Manchester, 1875), p. 1.

[23] Roy Porter, *London: A Social History* (Harvard University Press, Cambridge MA, 1995), pp. 237–8.

[24] Mayne, *The Imagined Slum*, p. 18.

[25] R. A. Varley, 'Land-use analysis in the city centre: with special reference to Manchester', unpublished MA thesis, University of Wales, Aberystwyth (1968), p. 87.

[26] This evidence is extracted from trade directories, especially *Slater's Manchester City Directory*, 1845, 1849 and 1852, John Rylands Library, Manchester.

[27] In 1796 John Watts had opened a small draper's shop on the Salford side of Deansgate, but had soon relocated on the opposite side of the road. Alison Adburgham, *Shops and Shopping 1800–1914: Where, and in what Manner the Well-Dressed English Woman Bought her Clothes* (Barrie and Jenkins, London, 1989, first published 1964), p. 18.

[28] Varley, 'Land-use analysis in the city centre', p. 9.

[29] H. Baker, 'On the growth of Manchester population, extension of the commercial centre of the city, and provision for habitation: census period, 1871–82', *Manchester Statistical Society: Transactions* (1882), pp. 8–9.

[30] This evidence is extracted from trade directories, especially *Slater's Manchester City Directory*, 1845, 1849 and 1852.

[31] *Bradshaw's Descriptive Guide to Manchester* (W. J. Adams, London, 1856), p. 57.

[32] Adam Faulkner had died in 1862. However, Alison Adburgham observes that customers continued to call it affectionately 'the Bazaar' until its demolition in 1872. Adburgham, *Shops and Shopping*, p. 21.

[33] Susan Buck-Morss, *The Dialectics of Seeing: Walter Benjamin and the Arcades Project* (MIT Press, Cambridge MA, 1995, first published 1989), p. 39. See also Henry-Russell Hitchcock, 'Victorian monuments of commerce', *Architectural*

Review 105/2 (1949), pp. 61–74.

[34] *The Manchester City News*, 1 March 1873.

[35] *The Builder*, 4 December 1869.

[36] The Manchester Corporation Waterworks and Improvement Act, pp. 6–7.

[37] *The Manchester City News*, 1 March 1873.

[38] *The Manchester Guardian*, 30 June 1869.

[39] *Corporation of Manchester*, p. 180; Minutes of evidence taken before the Select Committee of the House of Lords on the Manchester Corporation Waterworks and Improvement Bill, 29 June 1869, vol. 8, pp. 30–1, House of Lords Record Office, London. I thank staff at the House of Lords Record Office for allowing me access to these documents.

[40] *The Manchester City News*, 1 March 1873.

[41] *The Manchester Guardian*, 30 June 1869.

[42] Minutes of evidence taken before the Select Committee of the House of Lords, p. 69.

[43] *The Manchester Guardian*, 3 June 1869.

[44] *The Manchester City News*, 1 March 1873.

[45] *The Manchester Guardian*, 3 June 1869.

[46] *Ibid.*, 30 June 1869.

[47] *Ibid.*

[48] *Ibid.*

[49] Minutes of evidence taken before the Select Committee of the House of Lords, p. 2.

[50] Thomas Kendal had bought the Bazaar from John Watts, while James Milne had a part interest in the business, a distinct entity from the building. At the House of Lords' hearing, Milne and the late Adam Faulkner were not listed as owners. Both had been apprenticed in the textile trade, and, presumably in 1835 both had brought some capital, along with their expertise, into the business.

[51] Minutes of evidence taken before the Select Committee of the House of Lords, p. 7.

[52] *The Manchester Guardian*, 30 June 1869; Minutes of evidence taken before the Select Committee of the House of Lords, pp. 9–10.

[53] *The Manchester Guardian*, 30 June 1869.

[54] Minutes of evidence taken before the Select Committee of the House of Lords, p. 17.

[55] *The Free Lance*, 29 May 1874.

[56] Briggs, *Victorian Cities*, pp. 238–9.

[57] *The Manchester City News*, 1 March 1873.

[58] *The Manchester Guardian*, 3 June 1869.

[59] *Ibid.*, 15 April 1870.

[60] Samuel Smith and Sons were listed as wholesale and retail linen drapers, silk mercers, hosiers, haberdashers, shawlmen and mourning warehousemen. Unlike Kendal Milne, they did not sell furniture. *Directory of Lancashire*, 1864, p. 1469, John Rylands Library.

[61] *Slater's Manchester City Directory*, 1879, p. 77, John Rylands Library.

[62] *The Builder*, 12 August 1871.

[63] *The Free Lance*, 29 May 1874.

[64] Margaret MacKeith, *Shopping Arcades: A Gazetteer of Extant British Arcades* (Mansell, London, 1985), p. vii.

[65] Buck-Morss, *The Dialectics of Seeing*, p. 38.

[66] If the owners had won their case, they would have had to tear down only part of the building and build a new frontage to the store.

[67] *The Manchester Guardian*, 14 June 1872.

[68] *Ibid.*

[69] *Ibid.*, 14 January 1873.

[70] *Ibid.*, 1 March 1873.

[71] The estimate of one year is based on two sources. The first is an article in *The Manchester Guardian*, which explained that the partial demolition of Kendal Milne had commenced in June 1872. The other is a piece in *The Manchester City News*, which explained that 'The rebuilding of property to the front of Deansgate commenced soon after the destruction of it, and ... the Deansgate bazaar for Messrs. Kendal, Milne and Co. is being reconstructed.' Hence, after ten months, the new store had still not been completed. *The Manchester Guardian*, 14 June 1872; *The Manchester City News*, 1 March 1873.

[72] *The Manchester Guardian*, 1 March 1873.

[73] Hitchcock, 'Victorian monuments of commerce', p. 62.

[74] For an image of the London Exchange and a discussion of monumental warehouses in Manchester, see Nikolaus Pevsner, *A History of Building Types* (Thames & Hudson, London, 1976), pp. 214–15.

[75] Roger Dixon and Stefan Muthesius, *Victorian Architecture* (Thames & Hudson, London, 1978), pp. 23–4.

[76] Kidd, *Manchester*, p. 106.

[77] Hitchcock, 'Victorian monuments of commerce', p. 61.

[78] Minutes of evidence taken before the Select Committee of the House of Lords, p. 103.

[79] *Ibid.*, p. 14.

[80] *The Free Lance*, 29 May 1874.

[81] *Ibid.*

[82] *Ibid.*

[83] *Ibid.*

[84] Adburgham, *Shops and Shopping*, p. 142.

[85] Minutes of evidence taken before the Select Committee of the House of Lords, p. 51.

[86] Adburgham, *Shops and Shopping*, p. 142.

[87] *The Free Lance*, 29 May 1874.

[88] William Leach, *Land of Desire: Merchants, Power, and the Rise of a New American Culture* (Pantheon Books, New York, 1993), p. 9.

[89] Briggs, *Victorian Cities*, pp. 111, 135.

[90] *The British Architect*, 8 January 1873.

[91] *Manchester, Faces and Places* (J. G. Hammond & Co., Birmingham, 1891), p. 181.

[92] *The Manchester Guardian*, 1 March 1873.

[93] This evidence is extracted from trade directories, especially *Slater's Manchester City Directory*, 1845, 1849, 1852, 1864, 1879, John Rylands Library.

[94] Adburgham, *Shops and Shopping*, p. xii.
[95] Mayne, *The Imagined Slum*, p. 21.
[96] Schwartz, *Spectacular Realities*, p. 21.
[97] Porter, *London*, pp. 237–8.
[98] Briggs, *Friends of the People*, pp. 80, 84. See also Miles Ogborn, *Spaces of Modernity: London's Geographies, 1680–1780* (The Guilford Press, London, 1998), p. 28.
[99] Corporation Street in Birmingham was also completed piecemeal. See Briggs, *Victorian Cities*, pp. 228–9.

CHAPTER 9
AGENCY MAIL ORDER IN BRITAIN c. 1900–2000: SPARE-TIME AGENTS AND THEIR CUSTOMERS
Richard Coopey and Dilwyn Porter

By the early years of the twentieth century, the sale of goods to the general public via mail order was an established feature of retailing in Britain. The General Post Office was delivering around 130 million parcels annually by 1913, a significant proportion of these for mail order retailers of one kind or another. Of the 145 million postal orders issued, with an aggregate value of £57 million, the one pound (20 shilling) denomination was the most widely used, 'a fact evidently due to the mail order business'. Many of these postal transactions represented mail order in its simplest form, as customers responded to advertisements placed in newspapers and magazines. 'Women in the provinces', it was noted, 'like to get their finery from London'; on a more prosaic level, it was reported that 'one very big mail order business in East Anglia is in potatoes.' Some transactions were generated by specialist retailers or by department stores. 'Mail order trading pays', observed the director of a fashionable Kensington shoe shop, 'because the mail order advertiser is able to supply the needs of people in provincial towns and country districts with things which they could not obtain at the local shops.'[1] A growing proportion of this traffic in parcels, however, was generated by the activities of a cluster of retailers specializing in mail order and offering what later would be called 'home shopping' facilities to their customers. Fattorini and Sons of Bradford were pioneers in this line of business, along with Kay & Co. of Worcester, J. G. Graves of Sheffield, Freemans and John Myers of London. Their catalogues offered a wide variety of goods for sale on weekly terms, including watches and jewellery, clothing and footwear, and items of household furniture. The sales pitch for Fattorini's 'working man's eight-day alarm clock', priced at 25 shillings, was fairly typical. 'Send five shillings today and the clock will be despatched to you tomorrow.'[2]

What made these firms different from other warehouse-based retailers of the late nineteenth century was the extensive range of goods on offer and the facility for customers to pay in modest weekly instalments. The Royal Welsh Warehouse at Newtown, which established 'an extensive system of shopping by post' around 1860, had some claim to being Britain's first major mail order retailer, but the range of goods it sold in the late nineteenth century was narrow, consisting mainly of wool, woollen cloth and articles of clothing. Moreover, its customers, characterized in its promotional literature as 'the Ladies of England', were not offered the opportunity to pay by instalment.[3]

The emerging cluster of general mail order retailers at the end of the nineteenth century had also begun by selling a limited range of goods. Fattorini and Sons, Graves, Kays and John Myers could each trace their origins to the manufacture and sale of watches. In order to generate sales of what was an expensive purchase for working-class customers, firms encouraged the development of the 'watch club', with members making small fixed payments weekly, sufficient in total to pay for a single timepiece. Lots would be drawn each week to decide who would take the watch home. It was a simple and effective way of boosting the purchasing power of individual customers, many of whom would have been unable to make such a purchase outright. For the firms, it had the advantage over more conventional instalment payment systems of allowing customers to cover immediately the full price of each item sold. At the same time, profitable connections were being established with self-regulating groups of consumers who were already linked through family, neighbourhood, pub or workplace.[4]

The club system proved a solid platform from which to launch general mail order retailing. Once an initial round of purchases had been completed and weekly payment had become a habit, it was relatively easy to persuade club members to make additional purchases. 'As the third Club has now expired, having given every satisfaction, it is the wish of several of the old members to commence a Fourth One', explained a handbill issued in connection with a Fattorini Watch Club in Carleton, West Yorkshire, in 1875.[5] Significantly, watches were not the only items mentioned in connection with this initiative; it was clear that 'clocks of all kinds', 'sewing machines of any make', various items of cutlery and even writing desks could be supplied to order. Kays was especially keen to promote the idea that it was some kind of universal provider, listing multifarious 'departments', arranged alphabetically in its 1899 catalogue. The list began with 'Axminster, Tapestry and Other Carpets' and ended, rather prosaically, with

'Workmen's Clothing', taking in 'Bassinettes and Mail Carts', 'Gladstone and Other Bags', 'Opera and Field Glasses' and 'Umbrellas and Walking Sticks' along the way. Its clubs were known as 'Kay's Universal Clubs'; they provided the structure on which the firm's extensive mail order business came to rest. And for Kays it was big business, with around 500,000 customers served annually by 1919; 'we often receive A THOUSAND LETTERS, and despatch TWELVE HUNDRED PARCELS a day.'[6] By this time the simple watch club 'turn' had been supplemented or replaced by extended credit arrangements enabling customers, on payment of the first instalment, to receive goods chosen from the catalogue with the balance paid off over twenty weeks. For many working-class families, accustomed to setting aside a fixed amount each week for food, rent and other essentials, it was no doubt helpful to be able to buy relatively expensive items, like clothes and shoes, in the same way.

The corporate landscape that characterized agency mail order retailing in the second half of the twentieth century was in place by the end of the 1930s. Of the first wave of companies, J. G. Graves had shifted into direct mail order before 1914, but the other major players which had emerged towards the end of the nineteenth century survived. Fattorini and Sons had grown into Empire Stores and also into Grattan Warehouses, both still based in Bradford, the latter having been established in 1912 when John Enrico Fattorini left the parent company after a disagreement. Meanwhile Freemans and the much smaller John Myers continued to trade from London. The inter-war period saw the arrival of a second wave of firms, notably Great Universal Stores (GUS) and Littlewoods. Though the origins of GUS are traceable to 1900, when the Rose family began trading in Manchester, it was not until the 1920s that Universal Stores, as the company was then known, became mainly concerned with mail order. After 1931, as GUS, it grew under the direction of Isaac Wolfson to be the major power in this sector of retailing, swallowing Kays, thereafter its principal agency mail order brand, in 1937. The second wave also brought the Liverpool-based Littlewoods Mail Order Stores into contention. Founded by John Moores in 1932, it successfully marketed the club system to customers who already had sufficient disposable income to play Littlewoods football pools each week, many of whom had already organized themselves into family, neighbourhood, pub or workplace syndicates. Stanley Cooke, who joined Littlewoods in 1937, recalled that the firm 'had ready access through their pools mailing lists to the names of people who did business by post, and in the right strata too'. This was, he observed, 'a gift from the gods'.[7] Vernons, its Merseyside football-pools rival, followed Littlewoods into mail order in 1936.

Thus both waves of entrants into this sector, in the late nineteenth century and in the inter-war period, comprised firms utilizing clubs organized by spare-time agents to exploit pre-existing networks of working-class consumers. But, though this form of retailing was becoming more popular in the 1930s, the sale of goods by mail order remained a very small proportion of total retail sales, probably less than 1 per cent in 1938.[8] After 1950, having survived the trials of war and post-war austerity, Britain's 'Big Five' catalogue houses (GUS, Littlewoods, Freemans, Grattan and Empire Stores) were well positioned to divide the expanding UK home shopping market between them when consumer spending accelerated from the early 1950s. Thereafter, the proportion of total retail sales attributed to mail order houses rose from an estimated 0.9 per cent in 1950 to 5 per cent in 1978 before falling away in the 1980s. Mail order was especially important in terms of non-food sales, its market share peaking at 8.7 per cent of the total in 1978.[9]

The importance of spare-time agency

Though the origins of general mail order retailing on a large scale are conventionally traced to the United States at the end of the nineteenth century, it would be a mistake to characterize Britain's major catalogue houses simply as pale imitations of Montgomery Ward and Sears Roebuck. 'Differences between the mass markets in the two countries', as Alfred Chandler has observed, 'led to noteworthy differences between the institutions created to serve them.'[10] One of the major differences was the extensive employment by British retailers of neighbourhood-based spare-time agents to supply the essential link between the company and the customer, a strategy that their Chicago counterparts bypassed in favour of a more direct approach to sales.

Surveying the sector in 1960, the *Economist* noted that Britain's mail order specialists could not rely on 'the steady month-in month-out business from isolated country dwellings that make it worthwhile for Sears Roebuck to send its expensive catalogues directly to American customers'. Instead, 'the bulk of the business' was conducted through agents who carried the catalogue for the company, making it available to their immediate social circle and sometimes a little beyond. For a commission, usually 10 per cent in cash or 12.5 per cent in goods, agents accepted orders from customers and passed them on to the retailer. They also received goods sent from the warehouse, often delivering them personally to their final destination. Agents were also responsible for collecting weekly payments from customers and passing these on to the company. This system had taken root, as the companies themselves recognized, because it encompassed a tradition of neighbourhood co-operation deeply embedded in British working-class culture. 'The companies say that they believe the spirit of co-operation is at its strongest in Britain, making club buying possible.'[11] 'Agency mail order', so-called in current trade literature in order to distinguish it from retailing via catalogues sent direct to individual customers, was essentially a British phenomenon, predominating to an extent unparalleled elsewhere. It was reported in 1980 that whereas 80 per cent of mail order sales in Britain were via agency, the comparable figures for West Germany and France were 40 and 15 per cent respectively.[12]

Christmas clubs, burial clubs, crockery, stocking and other savings clubs were a part of everyday experience for working-class people in the nineteenth century. Those who organized them, both men and women, generally sought no more than to make their own lives just a little more comfortable by supplying a service that was entirely compatible with the modest aspirations of those who lived in the same street. Clubs established for such purposes reflected the rhythms and imperatives of working-class life. They were easily adapted to the purposes of the retailer seeking to sell mass-produced watches or jewellery at a distance, and the organizers of such clubs might be regarded as prototypes of twentieth-century mail order agents. The pools syndicates of the 1930s and those who collected the weekly stake money performed a similar strategic function for Littlewoods Mail Order Stores.[13] Agency was the key that allowed British catalogue retailers to gain access to millions of homes and to utilize by proxy the pre-existing social networks to which the spare-time agents themselves belonged. The commercial potential was enormous. Research commissioned by the Post Office in 1976, when the number of agencies was estimated at 4.2 million, underlined the point. 'Nobody knows how many agents "show" two or more catalogues – estimates range from a third to a half – but it is calculated that if each agent services five customers, then 72 per cent of households in the UK will be seeing a mail order catalogue.'[14]

This helps to explain why British mail order retailers have been so heavily committed to sales via agency, and why they were so well-placed to service the widening material aspirations of their mainly working-class customers as they crossed the threshold of post-war affluence in the late 1950s. James Mann, surveying the mail order sector in 1967 for the *British Journal of Marketing*, reported that the 'acquisition of new agents was regarded as being the major objective of the marketing strategy of all the firms in the industry – although some firms differed from others in the stress they appeared to lay upon quantity rather than quality'.[15] One indication of the strength of the sector's commitment to this strategy was supplied by a National Opinion Poll survey in 1980, which suggested that 46 per cent of all women over the age of 16 either were currently or at some time had been agents. As late as 1995, when agency mail order was in decline, the Mail Order Traders Association (MOTA) claimed a total of between 5.5 and 6 million part-time mail order agents in Britain, around one in ten of the total adult population.[16] Spare-time mail order agency remained a significant feature of the social landscape at the end of the twentieth century, as well as an important phenomenon in the history of British retailing.

The extent of agency mail order and its principal characteristics

Estimates of the number of mail order agents active at any particular time have to be treated with some caution. A certain amount of double counting is inevitable, because many agents carry catalogues for more than one company. There is the additional problem of the frequency with which names are added to or deleted from company lists. Moreover, a simple head count fails to differentiate between different types of agent. There are important distinctions to be drawn between agents seeking to build up an extensive business in their neighbourhood or workplace, the lineal descendants of nineteenth-century 'penny capitalists', and agents using the catalogue to sell to a small circle comprising immediate family and friends. In addition, there were agent-customers, attracted by the convenience of catalogue shopping, who bought largely for themselves while claiming the agent's commission on their purchases – an increasingly important phenomenon in the 1980s and 1990s. The conflation of these types under the single heading of 'agents' tends to exaggerate the upward trend in estimated numbers persisting across the second half of the twentieth century. It also disguises, to some extent, the recent decline of agency mail order in its more traditional form and the inexorable rise of the customer-agent or personal shopper.[17]

After a period of rapid expansion in the 1950s, when agency mail order experienced a rate of growth faster than any other form of retailing, the *Economist* estimated a total of around 500,000 active agents in 1960. As the sector continued to expand in the 1960s and 1970s, the number of agents grew rapidly. Mann offered a 'tentative suggestion' that there were at least 2.5 million agents active in 1967.[18] Four years later, the Crowther Committee on consumer credit was equally circumspect, suggesting only that 'the numbers probably run into three or four million'.[19] The Monopolies and Mergers Commission (MMC), reporting just after mail order sales had peaked as a proportion of total retail sales in the late 1970s, made use of figures supplied by the companies, estimating that approximately 4.8 million active agents had received one or more catalogues in 1981.[20] With the rapid growth of direct mail order sales in the 1990s retailers seemed more inclined to make a distinction between the 'traditional agent', placing orders for customers outside their immediate household, and the agent who used the catalogue to buy only for themselves and/or their immediate household. In 1997, on the basis of information supplied by the major companies, the MMC arrived at an estimate of 7.4 million agents in the United Kingdom, after deflating by a quarter to allow for those carrying more than one catalogue. It went on to give a 'best estimate' of 2.5 million agents (34 per cent) operating in a traditional fashion while classifying the remaining 4.9 million (66 per cent) as personal shoppers.[21]

According to the same source, agents were 'overwhelmingly women', but it had not always been this way. Before 1939 the vast majority of mail order agents were men. The testimonials published in an early Kays catalogue underline the point. All were attributed to men and many made male-specific references to the world of work. Writing from the railway station at Bath, one club organizer observed: 'Your Watches are especially suitable to Railway men, being such reliable timekeepers.' Another, from the Manchester Ship Canal (Section 7), claimed that 'the watches you sent me are well appreciated by all the men here.' Moreover, it is clear from William Kilbourne Kay's advice to his travellers that he expected them to recruit only men: 'I want you to distinctly bear in mind that no agent is to be appointed whom you have not seen at *his* home.'[22] Oral testimony from Alf Yeo, a Freemans traveller in the 1930s, indicated that until just before the Second World War, he was 'not allowed to appoint women'.[23]

Given what is known, however, about working-class wives in the early twentieth century and the strategies they devised for managing the household budget, it seems likely that many agencies registered in the name of the husband may actually have been conducted by the wife.[24] This impression is reinforced by the increasing amount of catalogue space devoted to women's and children's clothing in the inter-war years. The reluctance of mail order retailers to recruit female agents appears to have been prompted by the uncertain state of the law regarding the liability of a husband for debts incurred by his wife. Once this had been clarified by the Law Reform (Married Women and Tortfeasers) Act of 1935, those companies offering credit facilities could change their approach and appeal directly to housewives. Significantly, Alf Yeo recalled that 'women were allowed to be agents just previous to the war.'[25] The radical gender shift in mail order agency appears to have occurred in the post-war years, coinciding with the rapid expansion of the sector in the 1950s. By the 1960s around 85 per cent of agents were said to be women, and promotional literature was routinely written with them in mind. Thirty years later MOTA described agents for the 'Big Five' as 'in the main women ... housewives, women working in offices, shops and factories'. Thus it is hardly surprising to find that guidance issued by Kays to its telephone call centre staff in the 1990s contrasted sharply with the advice given by the firm's founder in the early years of the century. 'What does the caller want from you?', 'Why is *she* calling?', and 'What does *she* expect to gain from the call?'.[26]

When John Moores held a reception for Littlewoods club organizers in 1934, those attending included a council labourer and his wife, a baker's wife, a solicitor's wife and a clergyman's housekeeper.[27] It would be misleading, however, to draw firm conclusions from such anecdotal evidence. In the second half of the twentieth century, female mail order agents keeping house for their working-class husbands, especially those who could be classified as skilled or semi-skilled, have outnumbered those performing the same function for middle-class managers and professionals. Available statistics for 1979 lend support to this view. Although agents were spread across all social groups, those identified as C2 (skilled working-class) predominated, comprising 45 per cent of the total. With a further 20 per cent of agents located in categories D (semiskilled and unskilled workers) and E (casual workers, pensioners and people dependent on state benefits), it is clear that mail order agency was not only a predominantly female, but also a predominantly working-class activity. Lower middle-class C1s, at 25 per cent, outnumbered Ds and Es combined, but only 10 per cent of all agents were identified as AB, either upper middle or middle class.[28]

More recent figures, dating from 1996, indicate some significant recent shifts. The proportion of C2 agents has fallen to 30 per cent of the total; at the same time the proportion of Ds and Es has risen to 32 per cent. Thus the proportion of agents identified as C2, D or E has remained about the same as in 1979, but weighted more heavily towards the lower end of the classification. Over the period 1979–96 the percentages for C1 and AB agents remained virtually unchanged.[29] It seems likely that more ABs were buying goods, especially clothes, by mail order over this period, but they were purchasing direct from upmarket niche catalogues such as those issued by Laura Ashley, Racing Green or Beauty World Direct. When Boden launched its mail order clothes catalogue in 1991, it was said to have become 'cult reading among the (London) SW10 classes'.[30] This, however, was a world apart from what remained of traditional agency mail order, where about two-thirds of all agents were married women between the ages of 30 and 50, classified as C2, D or E.

On average, the number of customers serviced by each individual spare-time agent was much larger at the start of the twentieth century than it was at its close. The watch club origins of many mail order companies would suggest that agencies often comprised twenty people or more. Littlewoods Clubs, operating their own variation on the turn system after 1932, tended to be based on groups of ten or twenty customers. The rapid expansion of mail order retailing in the 1950s and 1960s was underpinned by a massive increase in the number of agencies, but relatively few grew to be as large as the average nineteenth-century watch club. Most agents of this period were content to order for their own family or, perhaps, for some members of their family plus a few neighbours or workmates. There were some large agencies incorporating several different groups of customers; these might include the agent's in-laws, contacts made through social clubs or simply 'friends of friends'. A few were large enough to have developed an informal structure of sub-agencies, when it had become difficult for agents to maintain contact with all their customers.[31]

Nevertheless, an agency such as that operated for Littlewoods by Mrs Giles, a London housewife married to an airport fire officer (C2), was more typical of this period. Mrs Giles explained, perhaps somewhat disingenuously, that she had 'never gone looking for customers'; 'they are all my friends and relations who happen to see the catalogue when they pop in for coffee or tea.' Orders taken from her eight customers generated payments amounting in total to £3 10s (£3.50) weekly.[32] The agency operated by Mrs Giles would have been well above average in size by the 1980s. This reflected to some extent the erosion of working-class neighbourliness as old communities were fragmented or dispersed, a process accentuated by de-industrialization in regions like the North-east of England, where mail order customers were most likely to be found. It remained company policy across the sector to accept 'as many agents as it found to be consistent with commercial prudence', but the average number of customers attached to each agency was falling, a trend that continued through to the end of the century. 'A typical agent', according to a 1979 report, was 'a young married woman with two children and four or five customers, two of them consisting of herself and a member of her family, the others being near neighbours'.[33] Evidence presented by Littlewoods to the MMC in 1997 was especially striking. Whereas the average Littlewoods agent had purchased for 16 people in 1960 'the average agent today purchased for only 2.8 people ... of which two (including the agent) were within the agent's household.' Freemans reported that the number of customers per agent had fallen from 4.6 in 1989 to 3.6 in 1995.[34]

The function of agency: what agents did and why
'They sell through agents, mostly women, who each handle between five and fifteen customers, and who take round the catalogue, collect

orders, deliver goods, and collect weekly payments.'[35] This description dating from 1965 indicates the basic tasks associated with mail order agency in what is now referred to as its 'traditional' form. It should not be inferred from this, however, that the tasks undertaken by the agent were necessarily simple or mechanical. Arguably, even a simple form of agency, such as that operated by Mrs Giles, required neighbourhood knowledge and well-developed social skills, not to mention a degree of confidence in handling cash and routine paperwork. A handbook issued by Kays to new agents in the 1960s is instructive here.[36] Agents were advised that they should not be discouraged if at first they could recruit only a few customers. 'From small beginnings', it explained helpfully, 'large and profitable agencies have been built by constant and enterprising effort'. It continued:

> So spend a little time making out a list of reliable people from whom you think you may be able to obtain orders. Call on them and show the catalogue. There is bound to be something they will see and want for themselves, their home or children. It only needs *you*, as the agent, to show the wide variety of goods available, to obtain orders.

Embodied in this advice was the expectation that an agent would possess or develop the presentational skills necessary to alert customers to the catalogue and its contents, the social confidence required to call on them in their homes and, in addition, the knowledge required to form a judgement as to whom might be regarded as 'reliable'. Neither should the relative complexity of agency mail order clerical tasks be underestimated:

> WHAT YOU SEND TO US
> At the end of four weeks when you have filled the four divisions on the first sheet of your Ledger, tear this out and send it to us with your Weekly Statement No. 4. Please also send to us the top copy of your list of Customers from the right hand side of your Ledger. Thereafter every four weeks you send us the top copy of your Ledger Sheet and every week you just send your Weekly Statement.
> ... Please enter on the BACK of the Monthly Ledger Sheet the name, address and account number of any NEW Customer since your last Ledger Sheet. We should also be notified of any changes of address in this manner.

And this was not all. The Weekly Statement required six separate arithmetical calculations including, in the example given, working out commission at two shillings in the pound on £2 13s 9d. Though, to some extent, this burden was lifted with the introduction of telephone ordering in the 1970s, any agency that was not conducted simply on a personal shopper basis required attention to detail and careful record keeping.

Promotional literature issued by the catalogue houses, especially when agency was largely a male preserve in the first half of the twentieth century, tended to stress its potential as a profitable part-time business. A circular letter to new agents, drafted by William Kilbourne Kay in 1913, typifies the genre:

> We understand you are an energetic, industrious man, anxious to 'get on', and possessing common sense and discretion; also that you come into contact with a considerable number of steady working people, which provides you with an excellent opportunity of making *extra* money, and – what is really more valuable – of widening your commercial and business experience.[37]

This approach would probably have struck a chord with a proportion of potential agents across the twentieth century, especially those later identified by Mann as being primarily 'commission-orientated'.[38] The link between mail order agency and self-improvement remained a persistent theme. One young married couple from Haworth, West Yorkshire, running 'a small but fast growing Grattan agency' in an enterprising fashion, were featured in company publicity in 1970, having just enjoyed a holiday in Spain thanks to their earnings from commission. The moral was clear: 'Service with a smile paid off with a place in the sun for the Whitakers.'[39] For some agents, even a relatively modest amount of commission could make a significant difference to their standard of living. 'When I draw this commission I will have earned enough money to pay for having my home laid on with electric light', was one testimonial that impressed John Moores of Littlewoods in the 1930s. 'During 1934', one Kays agent later recalled, 'we earned £13 commission, a wonderfully acceptable sum in those days, and I remember that we went on a fortnight's holiday – the first and last that we had for some time.'[40]

However, though the motivation supplied by the prospect of commission and what it would buy should not be dismissed lightly, it was probably not of paramount importance for most agents in the post-war period. In 1967, Mann described 'commission-orientated' agents as 'a small but vociferous minority' who ran complex agencies and were quick to inform the company if a customer complained. Such communications were, more often than not, articulated 'in terms of the effect on commission and inconvenience to the agent, rather than in terms of inconvenience to the customer'. It has been suggested that they comprised only about 6 per cent of the total number of agents active at that time, and that they were predominantly male.[41] As only around 10 per cent of all mail order agents were men, this is a statistic of some importance. Moreover, in the late twentieth century, with so many 'agents' using the catalogue for personal shopping, attitudes to commission were changing. As sales per agent had declined, noted the *Observer* in 1996, mail order companies had embarked on recruitment drives. Fewer and fewer of those recruited, however, behaved like traditional agents. 'They buy for their families, and treat the commission as a discount.'[42]

In British mail order retailing, and for women agents in particular, the sociability factor has always been important. This was so even in the years when mail order agency was a predominantly male activity. Watch Clubs 'were social gatherings in pubs, where inevitably much of the conversation turned to the Fattorinis' products'.[43] Though the temptation to represent such gatherings of northern working-class men as ale-fuelled Tupperware parties should be resisted, it seems likely that a degree of conviviality would have done no harm to sales. Women, often tied to the house by family commitments, seemed especially attracted by the prospect of weekly club meetings and a widening social circle. When Littlewoods entered the market in the 1930s, John Moores quickly came to appreciate the importance of this aspect of agency, adopting the slogan 'Organise a Littlewoods Club and Make Friends', while actively targeting the wives of his pools clients through company publicity. 'Right from the start', it has been noted, 'the emphasis was on *women* organisers.'[44] The wisdom of this strategy was reinforced in the 1950s, when a vast expansion in the number of women agents underpinned sector growth. Market research confirmed that, for the new recruit, 'the social contacts she makes attract her as much as the money'; perhaps more so, as estimated earnings from commission averaged only about £20 a year, a sum which would not by then have stretched as far as in pre-war days.[45]

'Socially-motivated' agents, to adopt the term used by Mann, were not necessarily indifferent to commission, but they were more strongly attracted by the social relationships that might be reinforced or developed through agency. On a very basic level, as most people enjoyed receiving parcels, there was some satisfaction to be derived from delivering goods personally to a customer. Such agencies, if well-conducted, tended to be more stable and, over the long run, more profitable for the companies, than those operated by commission-orientated agents. The vast majority of agents in the late 1960s, 82 per cent, were identified as being essentially socially-motivated and this impacted on the size of agencies in two quite different ways. For some, agency supplied an opportunity 'to have a role in the local community and to meet people'. For most, however, the time and effort involved in running a large agency detracted from the sociability of the experience and they made a decision, consciously or unconsciously, to restrict themselves to a few customers whose company they enjoyed.[46]

There was also, it seems, some satisfaction to be derived from the relationship with the company. Until the 1970s, agents were recruited by travellers employed solely for that purpose. For Kay, and for other mail order pioneers, the quality of the agency force was as important as its size, and travellers were urged to visit a man's home and make relevant inquiries. They were required to ask 'whether he belongs to a Sick Club, such as Oddfellows – Foresters etc., and in chatting with him you must of course use your wits to discover his habits.'[47] Such attention might in some instances have been resented as unduly intrusive. It was just as likely, however, to have been regarded as flattering, especially if it appeared to validate a potential agent's view of himself as a respectable, hard-working sort of chap with a nice home who had organized his own finances prudently. Once they had been signed up, companies went to great lengths to cultivate an agent's loyalty. Recalling work at J. E. Fattorini's in the 1920s (the name Grattan Road Warehouses Ltd was not adopted until 1930), one long-serving employee observed that 'more than the average courtesy had to be transmitted through the medium of letters (to agents).' Each agent was assigned a personal contact at the company's Bradford headquarters; agents of long-standing often came to regard these contacts as 'pen friends'.[48] Letters selected for publication in promotional literature often referred to the good relationship between the company and its agents. 'I should like to take this opportunity of thanking your staff, for all the help which they have given me from time to time.' Thus ran a fairly typical example, used in a recruitment pamphlet issued by Kays in 1953.[49]

There were other ways in which an agent could be made to feel important. Alf Yeo, travelling in a new company car for Freemans in the late 1930s, proved especially adept in this respect:

> It was prestige to have a car. Arriving at a prospective agent's door in it was quite impressive especially as most people didn't have their cars then. When I called on someone I always made sure I knew their name ... I'd go to the house and say: 'Mr or Mrs Jones, your name has been mentioned to me'.

Such techniques, not to mention the prestige attached to a visit from a company representative in his Standard 12, appeared to work wonders for Mr Yeo, 'top traveller' and 'Cock of the North' for Freemans between 1949 and 1953.[50]

Throughout the era of post-war expansion, mail order retailers continued in their efforts to make agents feel important. 'Maybe you never considered yourself a V.I.P.', ran one article in Grattan's in-house magazine *Pennywise* in 1970, 'but as a Grattan agent you are more important to your local community than you ever realised.'[51] Later, as companies turned increasingly to recruitment by newspaper and television advertising, there was a greater emphasis on competitions, prize draws and other devices to attract new agents and to keep existing agents interested and loyal. Significantly, the car, a key signifier of upward social mobility in mid twentieth-century Britain, appears to have been important in this respect. Recalling his work for John Myers in the late 1950s, Stanley Cooke observed that competitions offering cars as prizes 'proved a tremendous boost to the rapid recruitment of agents'.[52]

From the retailer's viewpoint: the advantages of agency

There were good reasons, therefore, to justify the tongue-in-cheek observation of a Kays executive that he was part of 'a professional team of women-wooers'.[53] But why did the major catalogue houses devote so much of their resources to building up and sustaining spare-time agency as a way of doing business? It seems likely that what propelled them along this particular path was the need to compete with more conventional forms of retailing by offering a different kind of service. The catalogue offered customers the advantages of shopping without leaving their homes, and there were circumstances in which this offered a significant convenience. A survey conducted by *Which?* in 1972 indicated that mail order was especially attractive 'if you live a long way from a good shopping area', 'if you are tied to your house or job when the shops are open', or 'if you don't like dragging your children through crowded shops or if you feel hurried by eager shop assistants'.[54] And there were certainly reasons to think that both agents and customers might enjoy a transaction conducted in a congenial social situation where they felt comfortably 'at home'. 'Stout women', for example, 'could try on clothes in privacy, without the insults, real or imaginary, of willowy sales girls.'[55]

The other way in which the catalogue houses offered a service that was different to that available from other retailers was by making credit facilities available to working-class consumers at a time when they would have had difficulty in obtaining them elsewhere. This was especially important in the 1950s and 1960s, when the material aspirations of mail order consumers in social groups C2, D and E were expanding rapidly. Women, especially if they were married, continued to be disadvantaged in obtaining independent access to credit in department stores both before and after the Sex Discrimination Act of 1975, and it seems likely that this would have made the mail order option relatively more attractive.[56] Kays Autumn/Winter catalogue for 1959–60 offered customers 'the golden key' which would 'open the door to more comfortable living':

> Kays 'Continuous Credit' is planned to increase your buying power and give you the chance of obtaining the goods you require, without waiting until you have cash-in-hand. When you have opened an account and made weekly payments, additional goods may be purchased without 'doubling up' on the amount you pay each week.

'Direct orders', it was added, 'cannot be accepted – customers must order through an approved Kays agent.'[57] By 1969 credit sales by the mail order companies accounted for 48 per cent of all instalment credit sales in Britain's retail sector.[58]

It is important to emphasize the various ways in which the spare-time agency system has underpinned the competitive advantages of convenience, congeniality and credit that the retailers sought to exploit. 'Traditionally', as has recently been acknowledged, 'the function of agents has been to promote sales from the company's catalogue by inviting orders from customers (typically family, friends and neighbours) who are not themselves agents and to place these orders with the agency mail order company on their behalf.' Thus agents were largely responsible for maintaining the flow of orders to the company. Once goods had been despatched from the warehouse, a further set of agency functions was activated. 'Agents then take delivery of the goods ... distribute them to their customers, return unwanted items to the agency mail order company, collect payments from their customers, remit payments to the company periodically and maintain the necessary accounts.' Though agents were not required to make a formal assessment of a customer's creditworthiness, or to chase up bad debt, it was anticipated that they would apply their local knowledge in a way that was beneficial both to themselves and to the company. 'Reliance is placed on the agents to form their own view about who among their own customers should be given credit and the amount of credit to be extended.'[59] Payment of spare-time agents on a commission-only basis kept labour costs at a level that helped mail order firms to compete with other retail outlets. In 1966 MOTA estimated the total cost of agency commission and expenses at 2s 2d (11p) in the pound. Even with a further 1s 3d (6p) added for the wages of office and warehouse staff, this meant that sector labour costs were broadly in line with those of department stores.[60]

Though the performance of agents and their value to the retailer varied, some less obvious benefits were to be derived from having an experienced agent at point of sale who was known and trusted by the customer. Mann reported that most customers in the 1960s regarded the agent as *their* agent in dealing with the company; they tended to associate the catalogue with 'my sister', 'Joan from down the street', 'Auntie Kathleen' or 'Mrs Brown', rather than with Freemans or Littlewoods, Empire or Grattan. Whereas the sales assistant in a department store, for example, was seen as the representative of the retailer, the agent remained an aunt or a neighbour, a peer whose opinion could be trusted when trying on clothes. Reassuring comments such as 'That's a good fit' or 'That colour suits you', addressed to the customer hovering at the point of purchase, helped to confirm the intention to buy, reducing the number of expensive 'returns' to the warehouse. With women's shoes and clothing accounting for about a third of all mail order spending, this was a significant advantage of the agency system. Market research dating from the heyday of agency mail order also testified to the ability of an agent to boost sales, either by exerting personal influence or by organizing her agency in such a way that customers experienced peer pressure to place an order. Hugh Crawshaw detected 'a fairly strong element of Normative Compliance in agencies run by agents with strong characters or where a group collectively spends time "going through" the catalogue'.[61]

A further facet of agent behaviour that worked to the retailer's advantage was a reluctance to let the company down. Perhaps the insistent propaganda portraying the company and its agents as part of one large happy family was influential here. It was not unknown for agents to cover payments for customers who were struggling to meet a weekly commitment, thereby informally assigning to themselves what was essentially the company's responsibility. Similarly, some agents were said to be reluctant to return goods ordered 'on approval' because they were 'concerned about their image with the company'.[62] Moreover, circumstances did arise from time to time when the goodwill of agents was especially important. When Grattan's Bradford premises were destroyed by fire in 1933, the firm's spare-time agents 'responded magnificently'; 'unsold goods in their possession were returned with utmost speed to help set us up on our feet again.' Even with a vast army of agents in the post-war era it remained possible to rely on a significant degree of goodwill. During the lengthy postal strike of 1971, Kays was forced to make special arrangements whereby agents were asked to hand in orders and payments at GUS stores. Their response was such that the company 'managed to carry on 70 per cent of their normal business, and collect 80 per cent of the normal amount of cash'.[63]

However, it is in relation to the development of their important role as providers of consumer credit that the agency system has served the companies especially well. The rapid expansion of sales volume from the 1950s through to the late 1970s was fuelled by credit advanced by the companies themselves. The company history of Littlewoods is illustrative here. Though its initial development in the 1930s had been based on the one shilling or two shilling 'turn', Littlewoods moved decisively into credit-based mail order in the 1950s, starting with its Burlington catalogue in 1952, quickly followed by Brian Mills in 1953, Littlewoods Warehouses in 1960, Janet Frazer in 1964 and Peter Craig in 1968. Companies offered 'free credit' in the sense that the cost was bundled into the price of the item sold from the catalogue. There was, inevitably, an element of risk involved in trusting a customer, about whom the company knew very little, to make regular weekly payments, but the agency mail order retailers appear largely to have overcome this problem. According to an informed company source, the amount of bad debt carried by Kays, an early entrant into credit trading, was 'very small', even during years of high unemployment in the 1930s. The Crowther Committee, reporting in 1971, observed that that 'the overall bad debt ratio of the catalogue companies is low'; for most companies it was less than 1 per cent of sales, representing a very advantageous trade-off between risk and return.[64]

Given the pressures on budgets in working-class households, this was a significant achievement. Mail order companies were competing with other demands on often quite limited resources and, in such circumstances, 'the organisation with the weakest credit control system is likely to be last in the queue for payment – it may acquire a reputation for being a soft touch.'[65] Though the growing numbers of personal shoppers from the 1980s began to pose the companies a different set of problems in relation to credit control, there seemed much to be said for the efficacy of the agency system in ensuring that mail order retailers avoided this unhappy fate. Ironically, when defaults did occur, it was likely to be an agent rather than a customer who found themselves in difficulties. While the amount of bad debt generated by agency default was low in relation to turnover, there were sufficient numbers of such cases to prompt the Crowther Committee to observe, in passing, that they comprised a substantial proportion of the small debt litigation dealt with by the County Courts.[66]

Provided that agents were chosen with care, their performance monitored regularly and agency credit limits adjusted as circumstances changed, they had offered significant advantages in ensuring a steady flow of payments back to the retailers. The use of spare-time agents, who knew their neighbours well and were themselves well known to their neighbours, maximized the social pressure on the customer.

There was a far greater incentive to make a scheduled payment when it was collected, not by some remote accounts department, but by a neighbour whom one might run into at any moment. For this reason, as Patrick Beaver has noted, the Empire Stores agent was regarded as 'a highly efficient means of credit control, for it takes a tough customer to bilk her neighbour'.[67] At the same time, the agent's personal judgement relating to the ability of people he or she knew well to keep up payments was an invaluable resource, especially before companies began to utilize more sophisticated means of credit referencing in the 1970s. Agents were as likely as their customers to be motivated by the desire to avoid embarrassing confrontations over missed payments, and this reinforced their value to the company as suppliers of *de facto* credit references for those who were part of their social network. Informal credit referencing may have been a highly subjective process, but it seemed to work, thus enabling mail order retailers to float increased sales on a wave of consumer credit.

Agency mail order at the millennium

Spare-time agency and credit provision, inextricably linked, stand as defining features in the history of British mail order retailing. But before catalogues could be distributed, orders secured and credit repayments guaranteed, the agent had to be securely based within a social network. '*Why*', asked one commentator in 1963, 'does the housewife buy something, often quite a major item in her year's budget, from a picture book, when in nine cases out of ten she could see a similar range of items in a shop or shops not unduly far from her home?'[68] For most British consumers in the second half of the twentieth century, the main reason for choosing to buy goods from an agency mail order catalogue has been 'that they have a friend or relative who is an agent'.[69] Given the closely matching social profile of agents and their customers, it seems clear that the companies derived much benefit from an arrangement that gave them entry to communities of customers that were relatively difficult for outsiders to penetrate, but generally sociable as far as insiders were concerned. For a commission that often generated little more than 'pin money', spare-time agents facilitated privileged access to customers in their own homes. In addition, because they were themselves a part of the family and neighbourhood networks from which agencies were constituted, agents helped retailers to keep their fingers on the pulse of economic and social change. The major mail order houses continued to derive substantial benefits from agency until the 1990s, dovetailing their activities with the everyday imperatives that shaped the lives of most of their customers. 'As recently as the seventies', it has been observed, 'credit was hard to come by, wages were generally paid weekly in cash and it was still rare for women to work outside the home.' Buying from an agency mail order catalogue 'fitted that lifestyle perfectly'.[70] This analysis understates the extent to which women in the 1970s worked outside the home, but encapsulates neatly the conditions in which agency mail order could flourish.

Since the 1980s the conditions that sustained agency mail order as a form of retailing and as a way of shopping have been progressively eroded. Credit facilities have become more readily available than previously, especially to women, of whom more are now in part-time or full-time employment. Alongside the widespread use of credit cards by banks and other financial institutions, many high street stores have begun to offer similar facilities to customers. 'The trick is to get people to shop regularly in your store', it was reported in 1987. 'Store credit cards have been found to help.'[71] At the same time many of the close-knit, urban communities in which this almost peculiarly British retailing form thrived have suffered the ravages of recession and social decay. Neighbourhoods where catalogues might be passed around in a sociable fashion were harder to find. The advantages to be derived from agency and credit provision, the twin pillars that defined British mail order retailing for most of the twentieth century, appeared to be crumbling.

As for the retailers, the historical commitment to agency mail order has come to be regarded as a significant weakness, with at least one City page report on GUS suggesting that the time was fast approaching when it would make sense for the company to abandon it completely.[72] Certainly the balance between agency mail order and direct mail order has changed, and continues to change rapidly. Traditional mail order customers, the *Financial Times* noted in 1999, 'could now more easily get credit cards and were switching to high street and direct sale catalogues'.[73] Traditional mail order retailers were seeking to follow this trend, either by moving into the high street – the acquisition of Argos by GUS is an indicator here – or by developing their own range of direct mail order catalogues. What had emerged by the end of the twentieth century was a bifurcation of the market for mail order goods and services. As Mike Hawker of the Empire Stores Group observed in 1997, 'the traditional business where five very large companies fight for their share of a reasonably static market' was now in a new situation. It was confronted by a series of challenges arising from the emergence of 'a new fast growing market' where customers 'are normally better off and simply want the convenience of shopping from home'.[74] In these market conditions the prospects for agency mail order in its traditional form seemed bleak.

Acknowledgements
The authors wish to acknowledge the generous support of the Leverhulme Trust in funding their work on mail order retailing in

Britain, *c.* 1890–1990. They also wish to acknowledge the significant contribution of Sean O'Connell to this project.

Notes

[1] Thomas Russell, 'The romance of mail-order advertising'; 'A business with 24,354 branches: how local business can be made national', *Advertising*, January 1914, pp. 3–9, 23–5.

[2] Patrick Beaver, *A Pedlar's Legacy: The Origins and History of Empire Stores 1831–1981* (Henry Melland, London, 1981), pp. 45–6.

[3] Unpublished notes on the history of the Royal Welsh Warehouse (n.d.), Kays, Worcester; see also the obituary for Pryce Jones, *Montgomeryshire County Times*, 17 January 1920.

[4] For the origins of these firms, see Richard Coopey, Sean O'Connell and Dilwyn Porter, 'Mail order in the United Kingdom, *c.* 1880–1960: how mail order competed with other forms of retailing', *The International Review of Retailing, Distribution and Consumer Research* 9/3 (1999), pp. 262–4.

[5] For the watch club origins of Empire Stores see Beaver, *A Pedlar's Legacy*, pp. 32–8. See also Keith Farnsworth, *The Graves Inheritance: The Story of the J. G. Graves Charitable Trust 1930–1990* (Graves Charitable Trust, Sheffield, 1990), pp. 9–10; *Kays Journal: Celebrating Two Centuries of Success* (Kays, Worcester, 1994). For John Myers, see Stanley G. (Andy) Cooke, *It Wasn't All Work* (Regency Press, London, 1983), pp. 141–5.

[6] 'Kay's Universal Stores Catalogue' (1899); Kays brochure entitled 'The history of 125 years' (1919), p. 2, BA 5946/1, Kay & Co. deposit, Worcester Record Office (WRO). For a survey of archives relating to the major mail order retailers, see Sean O'Connell and Dilwyn Porter, 'Cataloguing mail order's archives', *Business Archives* 80 (2000), pp. 44–54.

[7] Cooke, *It Wasn't All Work*, p. 52.

[8] See James B. Jefferys, *The Distribution of Consumer Goods: A Factual Study of Methods and Costs in the United Kingdom in 1938* (Cambridge University Press, Cambridge, 1950), pp. 151–2.

[9] Coopey, O'Connell and Porter, 'Mail order in the United Kingdom', p. 268.

[10] Alfred D. Chandler, *Scale and Scope: The Dynamics of Industrial Capitalism* (Harvard University Press, Cambridge MA, 1990), pp. 255–6.

[11] *Economist*, 27 February 1960.

[12] *Economist*, 8 November 1980.

[13] For the way in which Littlewoods grafted the club system onto its existing football pools business, see Barbara Clegg, *The Man Who Made Littlewoods: The Story of John Moores* (Hodder and Stoughton, London, 1993), pp. 52–3.

[14] Edward McFadyen, *The Future for Mail Order in the United Kingdom* (The Post Office, London, 1976), p. 1.

[15] James Mann, 'The pattern of mail order', *British Journal of Marketing* 1 (1967), p. 49.

[16] National Opinion Poll survey data cited in Monopolies and Mergers Commission (MMC), *The Great Universal Stores PLC and Empire Stores (Bradford) PLC: A Report on the Existing and Proposed Mergers*, Parliamentary

Papers (PP), (1983), Cmnd 8777, p. 9. Estimates for 1995 supplied by the Mail Order Traders Association (MOTA), Liverpool.

[17] For the difficulties associated with making an accurate count of agents, see *Consumer Credit: Report of the Committee*, PP, (1970–1), Cmnd 4596, vol. 2, Appendices, p. 97n.

[18] *Economist*, 27 February 1960; Mann, 'The pattern of mail order', p. 42.

[19] *Consumer Credit*, vol. 2, Appendices, p. 443.

[20] MMC, *The Great Universal Stores*, p. 9.

[21] MMC, *The Littlewoods Organisation PLC and Freemans PLC (a Subsidiary of Sears plc): A Report on the Proposed Merger*, PP, (1997–8), Cmnd 3761, pp. 11–14.

[22] 'Catalogue' (1893–4), Kays, Worcester; William Kilbourne Kay's advice to travellers, 27 September 1907, BA 5946/3, Kay & Co. deposit, WRO, authors' italics.

[23] Transcript of an interview with Alf Yeo, 20 June 1985, Freemans, London.

[24] See David Vincent, *Poor Citizens: The State and the Poor in Twentieth Century Britain* (Longman, London, 1991), pp. 5–10. Though Vincent does not specifically mention mail order agency he argues that 'running a small shop' was one of the income-generating activities that a working-class housewife might undertake at home.

[25] Transcript of interview with Alf Yeo, Freemans, London. We owe this point to Sean O'Connell.

[26] *Economist*, 27 February 1960; information from MOTA, 1995; GUS Home Shopping Group, 'Company standards for telephone calls' (1996), Kays, Worcester, authors' italics.

[27] Clegg, *The Man Who Made Littlewoods*, pp. 57–8.

[28] MMC, *The Great Universal Stores*, pp. 8–9, table 2.3.

[29] MMC, *The Littlewoods Organisation*, pp. 14, 73.

[30] *Daily Telegraph*, 3 October 1997. For another example of upmarket mail order, see *Financial Times*, 18–19 July 1998.

[31] Mann, 'The pattern of mail order', pp. 46–7.

[32] For Mrs Giles, see 'The department store on 6,000,000 doorsteps', *Focus*, July 1966, pp. 9–13.

[33] MMC, *The Great Universal Stores*, p. 8; *The Future of Mail Order in Britain* (Economists Advisory Group, London, 1979), p. 25.

[34] MMC, *The Littlewoods Organisation*, pp. 131, 145.

[35] *Economist*, 27 March 1965.

[36] 'How to establish and conduct a successful spare time agency' (c. 1967), Kays, Worcester.

[37] Draft letter to 'Mr Smith', 1 October 1913, BA 4946/2, Kay & Co. deposit, WRO.

[38] Mann, 'The pattern of mail order', pp. 46–7.

[39] 'Agency builds up on smiling service', *Pennywise*, November 1970, p. 7, Grattan plc, Bradford.

[40] Clegg, *The Man Who Made Littlewoods*, pp. 57–8; 'This Walker leads Kays through four reigns', *Moneymaker*, Winter 1964, p. 28, Kays, Worcester.

[41] Mann, 'The pattern of mail order', pp. 46–7; see also Hugh S. Crawshaw, 'Does mail order fit the retail life cycle? An investigation into the mail order

sector and the implications for the future of Empire Stores', unpublished MBA thesis, University of Bradford (1980), pp. 85–6.

[42] *Observer*, 28 July 1996.

[43] William Kay, *The Battle for the High Street* (Piatkus, London, 1987), p. 145.

[44] Robert Brandon, 'The origin and development of mail order in the United Kingdom', *Journal of Advertising History* 8 (1984), p. 10.

[45] *Economist*, 27 February 1960.

[46] Mann, 'The pattern of mail order', pp. 47–9; Crawshaw, 'Does mail order fit?', p. 86.

[47] 'Advice to travellers', 27 September 1907, BA 5496/3, Kay & Co. deposit, WRO.

[48] Anonymous compilation labelled 'The Grattan story' (*c.* 1973–4), pp. 21–3, Grattan plc, Bradford. See also Mann, 'Pattern of mail order', p. 51, who states that 'companies who channel all correspondence with an agent through one particular clerk signing his or her own name will by this personalisation of the relationship tend to make it stronger.'

[49] 'The House of Kays 1794–1953' (1953), Kays, Worcester.

[50] Transcript of interview with Alf Yeo, Freemans, London.

[51] 'How important are you?', *Pennywise*, November 1970, p. 7, Grattan plc, Bradford.

[52] Cooke, *It Wasn't All Work*, p. 160.

[53] Typescript notes on a talk delivered by A. D. Arbuckle, assistant managing director, to the Worcester and District Management Association, 12 October 1972, Kays, Worcester.

[54] 'Mail order', *Which?*, June 1972, pp. 78–9.

[55] 'Picture book shopping', *The Director*, February 1963, p. 260.

[56] See *Equal Credit Opportunities: A Report of a Joint Review of Debenham's Retail Credit Procedures* (Equal Opportunities Commission, Manchester, 1979), p. 3.

[57] 'Kays Autumn/Winter Catalogue 1959–60' (1959), Kays, Worcester. 'Continuous credit', sometimes known as 'rolling credit', offered customers the opportunity to assign outstanding instalment payments to a new 20 or 38 week period whenever new items were ordered from the catalogue.

[58] For the mail order retailer and credit, see Coopey, O'Connell and Porter, 'Mail order in the United Kingdom', pp. 269–70.

[59] MMC, *The Littlewoods Organisation*, pp. 11, 90.

[60] 'The department store on 6,000,000 doorsteps', p. 12.

[61] Mann, 'The pattern of mail order', p. 48; Crawshaw, 'Does mail order fit?', pp. 78–9.

[62] Mann, 'The pattern of mail order', p. 48.

[63] 'The Grattan story', pp. 64–70; Typescript notes on a talk delivered by A. D. Arbuckle.

[64] T. C. Barker, 'The Littlewoods Organisation PLC', in A. Hast (ed.), *The International Directory of Company Histories* (St James Press, Detroit, 1992), vol. v, pp. 117–19; typescript notes on a talk delivered by A. D. Arbuckle; *Consumer Credit*, vol. 2, Appendices, p. 97.

[65] *The Accountant*, 11 February 1982.

[66] *Consumer Credit*, vol. 2, Appendices, p. 97.

[67] Beaver, *A Pedlar's Legacy*, pp. 11–12.
[68] 'Picture book shopping', p. 260.
[69] Crawshaw, 'Does mail order fit?', p. 79.
[70] *Observer*, 28 July 1996.
[71] *Daily Mail*, 21 October 1987. According to this source, the number of store cards in use had grown by 88 per cent between 1984 and 1986.
[72] *Birmingham Post*, 3 December 1999.
[73] *Financial Times*, 3 December 1999.
[74] See his editorial comment in *Talents: L'information du Groupe Redoute*, November 1997, p. 3.

INDEX